DECONSTRUCTING POPULAR CULTURE

Deconstructing Popular Culture

Paul Bowman

Cardiff University

First published 2008 by
PALGRAVE MACMILLAN
Houndmills, Basingstoke, Hampshire RG21 6XS and
175 Fifth Avenue, New York, N.Y. 10010
Companies and representatives throughout the world

PALGRAVE MACMILLAN is the global academic imprint of the Palgrave Macmillan division of St. Martin's Press, LLC and of Palgrave Macmillan Ltd. Macmillan® is a registered trademark in the United States, United Kingdom and other countries. Palgrave is a registered trademark in the European Union and other countries.

ISBN-13: 978–0–230–54535–9 hardback
ISBN-10: 0–230–54535–1 hardback
ISBN-13: 978–0–230–54536–6 paperback
ISBN-10: 0–230–54536–X paperback

This book is printed on paper suitable for recycling and made from fully managed and sustained forest sources. Logging, pulping and manufacturing processes are expected to conform to the environmental regulations of the country of origin.

A catalogue record for this book is available from the British Library.

A catalog record for this book is available from the Library of Congress.

10   9   8   7   6   5   4   3   2   1
17   16   15   14   13   12   11   10   09   08

Printed and bound in China

For Keira, Lilly, Alice – and the future

Contents

    'Deconstructing'**   **147**

    The popular response to the death of the guardian   147
    Popular hate objects, and their hate objects   152
    McDeconstruction, embarrassment and studying
        popular culture   158
    Nerds Я Us   166

8   **Alterdisciplinarity: Deconstructing Popular
    Cultural Studies**   **169**

    The critique of critique   169
    The alterdisciplinary theory of theory   172
    The vanishing intervener   176
    The end of the intervention   178
    Retheorizing political critique   179
    Altering alterdisciplinarity   180
    Altering conclusions   182

    **Afterword: (An Incomplete) Glossary of
    (Impossible) Terms**   **187**

    Notes   204
    References   210
    Index   220

Acknowledgements

With the growth of crass managerialism and the short-sighted anti-intellectual 'professionalization' of the university, more and more academics are finding it nigh on impossible to engage in any serious study, scholarship or writing, or indeed even to engage in regular sustained thinking. However, I have been lucky enough to have been surrounded and supported by wise colleagues and 'line managers' at Roehampton University, who have fought to preserve the time and space necessary for researching, thinking, debating and writing. Anita Biressi and Paul Rixon not only 'managed me' but always actively supported my research and writing; as did my other close colleagues and friends at Roehampton from 2003 to 2008, in particular Heather Nunn, Caroline Bainbridge, John Seed and the rest of the Media and Cultural Studies team. Similarly, the scholarly and collegial ethos engendered and encouraged – in doubtless difficult times – by Lyndie Brimstone, Dean of the School of Arts, was surely a significant factor in my ability to write this book.

Outside Roehampton, other colleagues and friends have provided direct and indirect help, encouragement, support, advice and opportunities. These include, but are not limited to: Alena Alexandrova, Benjamin Arditi, Jon Baldwin, Claire Birchall, Merel Boers, Nick Chare, Mark Devenney, Barbara Engh, Jeremy Gilbert, Greg Hainge, Gary Hall, Kurt Hirtler, Bram Ieven, Véronique Martin, Martin McQuillan, John Mowitt, Michael O'Rourke, Adrian Rifkin, Richard Stamp, Margaret Shaw, Jeremy Valentine, Joanna Zylinska, and – certainly not least – my students. For although almost all students arrive in class each week with an obdurate 'resistance to theory', it has been my delight to expose, every week, their collective Achilles Heel: namely, their shared attachment to all aspects of popular culture. For, even though they don't *want* to start thinking about popular culture, when prodded or provoked they *just can't help doing it*. Without their resistance to theory coupled with their inability to resist thinking about popular culture, I doubt whether it would have occurred to me to write this book, in this way. But nor would I have been able to do any of this were it not, as ever, for Alice.

The author and publishers wish to thank the following for permission to use copyright material: For epigraphs: Stanford University Press for *Resistances of Psychoanalysis* (Derrida 1998b: 45–6); Taylor & Francis for Stuart Hall's 'Notes on Deconstructing "the popular" ' (Hall 1981: 227);

Stanford University Press for *Monolingualism of the Other* (Derrida 1998a: 21); University of Chicago Press for *The Post Card: From Socrates to Freud and Beyond* (Derrida 1987: 24, 88) and for *Margins of Philosophy* (Derrida 1982: 3); Polity Press for *A Taste for the Secret* (Derrida 2003: 12); and Sony/ATV Music Publishing for use of lyrics from 'Wonderwall' by Noel Gallagher.

Every effort has been made to contact all the copyright-holders, but if any have been inadvertently omitted the publishers will be pleased to make the necessary arrangement at the earliest opportunity.

Epigraphs

[I]t has always been impossible in the theoretical field of cultural studies – whether it is conceived of in terms of texts and contexts, of intertextuality, or of the historical formations in which cultural practices are lodged – to get anything like an adequate theoretical account of culture's relations and its effects.

Stuart Hall (1992: 285)

I consider it an act of cultural resistance to pay homage publicly to a difficult form of thought, discourse, or writing, one which does not submit easily to normalization by the media, by academics, or by publishers, one which rebels against the restoration currently underway, against the philosophical or theoretical neo-conformism in general (let us not even mention literature) that flattens and levels everything around us . . .

Jacques Derrida (1998b: 45–6)

User Guide

Use. This book is not simply 'about' popular culture. It is also not 'about' deconstruction. It does not try to *talk about*. It tries to *do*.

Functionality. What this book *does* is carry out a series of readings. What it reads are, first, examples taken from what is often thought of as the 'field' of popular culture, and, second, examples taken from what is often though of as the 'field' which studies popular culture: cultural studies.

Performance. Each example is introduced, examined, opened up or unpicked, using insights provided by (or related to) deconstruction. The aim is not to argue that the examples in question are amazingly important in themselves, even if they are. Rather, it is show both the complex *textuality* of the objects themselves and the network or tissues of 'relations and effects' into which they are stitched. It is also to clarify the value and importance of deconstruction as a method of *reading culture* and *making sense of culture*.

Direction. So, the chapters tend to *read outwards*. That is, starting from a specific text, they unpick it – or rather, an aspect of it (for no reading can be complete or impartial) – and look at the ways it has been stitched together (or constructed), as well as revealing some of the ways that it connects with or relates to other texts and contexts.

Orientation. The book is a series of *readings*. These readings do not purport to speak 'the truth, the whole truth, and nothing but the truth'. Interpretation is always (also) a process of *invention*, of *making* connections and associations, and *drawing* conclusions. Reading is, in fact, always a kind of rewriting. So, instead of looking for 'the truth' (or the 'final signified' – the mythical end-point of interpretation), the focus is on *interpretation*. The readings ask: *how* are we to interpret things, and *why* do we interpret in this or that way? *Can* we interpret differently? *Should* we? What are the implications of the *ways* we interpret?

Nota bene. However, the book does not ask all of these questions all the time or all at the same time. This would be very dull.

Accessibility. The book is designed to be read from beginning to end. However, for those who just want to dip into it, it will be best to start with one or more of the first four chapters first (Part I). This is because, in Part II, half way through the book, the examples, issues and focus turn increasingly to questions, problems and issues to do with *the study of* popular culture. This is because no deconstruction can pretend to focus simply on 'the thing itself'. Deconstruction always asks questions about *what we think the thing itself is* – questions about the *way* we conceptualize 'it'. This aspect of deconstruction comes to the fore in Part II, the second half of the book.

Torque. So, half way through the book, the examples, issues and focus turn increasingly (also) to matters to do with *the study of* popular culture: with *how* to study it, and with the *implications* of different orientations. However, the hope is that, by that stage, you should have gained a sufficient familiarity with the issues to appreciate *why* this 'inversion and displacement' is called for.

Attention. The chapters in the second half assume that you are familiar with the issues introduced in the earlier chapters. Because the book is in a sense all about *reading*, it assumes that the reader is trying to pay attention.

Clarification. Nevertheless, I have tried to be as clear as possible without either (1) compromising too much the complexity of a deconstructive reading, or (2) spending too much time on boring explication. The readings do try to clarify *why* certain argumentative or interpretive 'moves' have been made. But mostly the readings try to draw or 'tease out' the deconstructive insights 'from' the thing that is being read, rather than from, say, other people's arguments – unless what is being read are other people's arguments, as is increasingly the case in Part II.

Further reading. Don't worry: even Part II takes lots of examples from popular culture. The point is merely that any act of *deconstructing* popular culture (or anything) will always have to come to focus on the *way* popular culture (or anything) is studied. For whenever we study something, we shouldn't forget that our act of 'looking' is never neutral. It is actually an act of *constructing* the thing looked at. Or do you see it differently?

Disclaimer

Examples. By the time you read this, some (and in the long run, all) of the examples that this text deals with will seem dated. This is fine. Don't worry. The book is neither about predicting the future nor about trying to cover everything. It is designed to equip you with the critical tools to begin your own deconstructive studies and analyses.

Coverage. This book does not try to cover everything. It is not an encyclopaedia. Rather, it tries to introduce you to deconstructive reading and the importance of questions of bias, orientation, textuality and articulation, in ways that will help you to start to bring them to bear on, well, if you want, everything.

Currency. Sometimes deconstruction is accused of being 'out of date'. The implication is that there are other approaches that are more 'current', more 'up to date'. However, this work argues that deconstruction offers insights and perspectives that are highly unique and constantly important. Deconstruction points out what is political – in other words, what is consequential – in ways and in places that other approaches cannot reach. In the words of Judith Butler, deconstruction looks for 'the constitutive force of exclusion, erasure, violent foreclosure, abjection, and its disruptive return within the very terms of discursive legitimacy' in every 'construction' (1993: 8).

Authenticity. Cultural studies purists may complain that this book does not do popular culture properly, or not like other books on popular culture. On this point, please refer to 'Use' and 'Coverage', above. Similarly, deconstructive purists (as if such a thing could exist) may quibble that this book does not do deconstruction properly, thoroughly or rigorously enough, or provide proper expositions of this or that really important discussion or aspect of deconstruction or popular culture. On this point, again, please refer to 'Use' and 'Coverage', above. I also think I have already covered 'rigour' and 'propriety', which you will have noticed if you have been paying attention (although I will of course come back to these issues again later). But for now, suffice it to recall two things. First, Derrida's observation that

> one never does 'keep to deconstruction'. Deconstruction is never concluded because it is never nihilistic, contrary to what they say in *Newsweek*, but rather affirmative and generative. And it is difficult to imagine seriously, without laughing, what 'keeping to deconstruction' could possibly mean!
> (Derrida 1992a: 211)

Second, Stuart Hall's opening confession, in 'Notes on Deconstructing "the Popular" ':

> I have almost as many problems with 'popular' as I do with 'culture'. When you put the two terms together the difficulties can be pretty horrendous.
> (Hall 1981: 227)

Introduction: Deconstructing 'the Popular'

> I want to tell you about some of the difficulties I have with the term 'popular'.
> I have almost as many problems with 'popular' as I do with 'culture'. When
> you put the two terms together the difficulties can be pretty horrendous.
>
> Stuart Hall, 'Notes on Deconstructing "The Popular"' (1981: 227)

Deconstructing . . .

In mid-January 2007, an international incident flared up. Exactly *when*
it happened is debatable. And exactly *where*. Nevertheless, it provoked
outrage, required the intervention of politicians, solicited many and
varied discussions and reflections from cultural commentators of all
kinds, required responses from official regulatory bodies, preoccupied
the media, precipitated all kinds of complaints, demands, even threats
and public protests, including some that involved the burning of effi-
gies. The precise causes, the exact nature, timescale, status, significance
and effects of the incident remain difficult to assess. Was it trivial or was
it deadly serious? Was it local, private and isolated, or was it national,
international, public and general? As some asked, was it even 'real'? For
almost everything about it remains constantly open to debate, interpretation and reinterpretation. It can be regarded in many different ways,
and each different perspective makes something different out of the
event. Different approaches deem it to be something entirely different.
Moreover, although very many of the interpretations and diagnoses
appeared to contradict each other, they also seemed to remain valid:
contradictory interpretations appeared to dwell together, side by side.
    Perhaps the most that can be said about it all with any degree of cer-
tainty is that at first it looked like mere bickering, arguing, shouting,

1

and the bullying of one person by three others. Those involved were: the Bollywood actress Shilpa Shetty; a former reality TV show winner called Jade Goody; a former pop singer called Jo O'Meara; and a glamour model called Danielle Lloyd. The incident took place (it is not clear whether it came to a conclusion, played itself out, or whether it seemed to begin, flared up, or started) on the reality television show, *Celebrity Big Brother*. But it is quite difficult to put an exact date and time on it, mainly because the 'incident' was not actually 'one' incident: partial incidents led to other, partial incidents. It was instead a series of comments, encounters, exchanges, glances, actions and other events, culminating in a very loud and public argument between Jade Goody and Shilpa Shetty. But it was not *the* culmination. There were others to follow, elsewhere. Perhaps because this was a particularly vociferous argument, in which conflict was obviously apparent, it drew the spotlight of attention to the events of the show. Indeed, because it was so spectacular, this argument was in a sense taken *to be* the event. But was it? Certainly, it was the most filmable, and was replayed on television networks the world over. But it wasn't the *whole* thing, *in itself*. The *thing*, the *event*, the whole conflict or process was not entirely or simply *there*, *in* the argument. It was *more and other and elsewhere* than what was actually argued about, there and then. So, the event was both there and also not really or entirely there. In order for this 'event' to be what it was, it had in a sense to have started happening already, to have been happening already, *before* this spectacular event. And indeed it had: it had been present in snide comments, in nasty little asides and conspiratorial glances for quite some time. You might say, it had been *building up* to this, as if this were another building brick added to a series of building bricks, each one the same but different, different but equivalent; and that if it weren't for these supplements (these other equivalent but different occurrences), the main event would not have been what it was. It may not have been deemed what many deemed it to be – a racist scandal.

It was deemed by many to be the culmination of a growing manifestation of a racially based hostility to Shilpa Shetty. Racism was deemed to be present even though there was very little explicit racism in Goody's certainly aggressive and hostile ranting and raving. On the contrary, the racism itself was regarded as having happened elsewhere: most notably in the ill-informed – possibly tendentious – comments and questions of the young and apparently naïve Danielle Lloyd, and reciprocally in the apparently knowing sniggering and largely tacit approval of Jo O'Meara. For instance, conversations between Goody, Lloyd and O'Meara contained references to how much they disliked Shetty using her hands to pick up and taste food; questions were asked about whether 'they' 'all' ate like that (whether 'that' was India or China); Shetty's accent and mannerisms were parodied; comments were made about Shilpa Shetty not being able 'to speak English properly'; and Lloyd said that she 'wished' Shetty 'would fuck off home'.

Debates flared up about what viewers were witnessing here. To some, it was 'obvious' that it was a reflection of a latent racism. To others the racism was not 'latent', but rather the *apparent* racist overtones were merely the *unintended* results of Lloyd's ignorance of the fact that the sentiments she expressed were historically recognizable forms of racism. Similarly, suggestions were made that the white English girls were merely reacting to the characteristics of *one person* who annoyed them, and that it was unfair to say that therefore they were involved in racism (as anyone who has lived in close confinement with others for any length of time should be able to understand why people may come to find the idiosyncrasies of others intensely irritating). A different inflection – indeed, an inversion and displacement – of this interpretation was the suggestion that this was a clash of *cultural* differences that only looked like (or inevitably took the form of) a clash of *personal* differences. This, too, has several possible interpretations, of course. Either the conflict signified nothing more than that some people could not get along living in close quarters with another person. Or it hinged on the cultural difference. Was it *cultural* difference or just *personal* difference? Were those involved to be taken as representatives or products of different cultures? Did the white English girls grow to dislike the Indian girl *because* she was Indian? In other words, then, because they were English? Are racist responses *likely* in English girls who are forced into close contact with Indian girls? Is that something to do with 'English' culture in its relationship with 'Indian' culture?

But the questions multiply: Is this something to do with *gender*? Is this 'just what girls are like' under certain circumstances? Is this true of all girls? Or, is it, perhaps, just true of 'naïve' or 'ignorant' girls, girls who 'don't know any better' – in this case, young *working-class* girls. Is this about *class*? Is it, in other words, salient to consider that Goody, O'Meara and Lloyd all come from *working-class* backgrounds while Shetty comes from a *wealthy* family? Is this, then, class war (or resentment) playing itself out? A lot of what Goody said in her infamous tirade against Shetty seemed to be less racially or ethnically inflected and more in response to Goody's declared belief that Shetty believed herself to be 'better' than the rest of the occupants of the *Big Brother* house. Is this some kind of class-based resentment? Possibly. But mingled into her diatribes was a lot of evidence that Goody seemed to have a problem with Shetty's *beauty* and *success* too. So was it not also something peculiar to do with Goody's relationship to beauty and celebrity? And is her relationship to beauty and celebrity something that is *personal* (or chance) or something that is more *widespread* ('cultural' or 'ideological')?

Psychologists and psychoanalysts may have a field day with the inversions, displacements and projections at play in such dialogues as those in which the multiple-award-winning Bollywood actress and beauty queen was referred to as a 'dog' and in which Goody apparently suggested that Shetty was famous only for being there on *Celebrity Big Brother*, with her. But even psychological (or psychologistic) interpretations cannot be disentangled from the social and cultural field. For, opinions, judgements, values, relations with and towards others, words and phrases used, expectations, hopes and aspirations, always seem *both* to come from *and* to point outside of and away from the person who expresses them – as if the person who expresses these things is therefore *also an expression of them*. An opinion may come out of someone's mouth, but mustn't it have been 'put there', in some sense? Words and even personal feelings always seem linked to histories and cultural contexts. So the question of *causes* will always be difficult to determine, especially perhaps in an example such as this, in which so many realms and registers appear to be involved: questions of culture, of difference, of ethnicity, of gender, of education, of economic class, of desire and, of course, of the media.

Similarly, the question of what *significance* all of this might have for anything else seems equally difficult to decide. Were these events in *Celebrity Big Brother* 'racist'? Were they evidence of one or another kind of resentment or jealousy? Was Shetty a victim or indeed a scapegoat in some sort of power or popularity contest? Was the drama in the house merely a result of claustrophobia-inducing cramped living conditions, or was it some kind of reflection of the differences between two or more cultures? And would those cultures be 'Indian' versus 'English', or upper class versus working class, or educated versus uneducated? Was the racism or bullying or victimization or ignorance or boredom or whatever an expression of something *latent*? And latent to whom? Latent to some random individuals, or to distinct social groups, or to particular social situations?

When so many factors are all *tangled up* together, when some seem 'obviously' personal and idiosyncratic, but when even the 'obviously' personal factors are *also* in a sense 'obviously' cultural; and when a few small sequences of words and actions on the television touch on so many issues and are disseminated to so many people around the world, how does one decide what is actually *present*, what is actually *happening*, *where* it is happening, what it all *means* and what its ultimate *significance* is? How do we make a decision? How do we decide?

Rather than rushing to a decision about all of this, or busying our-selves with proceeding to a conclusion, a *deconstruction* begins from acknowledging this uncertainty, this complexity, or what might be called this element of *undecidability*. For let's look at some of the things that are complex, uncertain, unclear and undecided in this picture. Firstly, an *event* seems to have happened. But *when* and *where*, exactly? It appears to have been both incremental, dispersed, ongoing and com-plex. It has many dimensions. It didn't take place at exactly one moment. It was spread out, across time and across space, in different conversa-tions, between different people, first those inside and then many outside the house, indeed across the world. In fact, it is unclear *when and where* and indeed *whether* it *arrived* or *happened*: in different contexts it was given a different status; in some contexts it was barely noticed, while in others it led to major outrage. This is as much as to say that 'it' is not the same 'thing' across all of the places where it occurred. Indeed, 'it' was an event, rather than a 'thing'. It still is an event. It is something which 'happens', whenever people experience it, think about it, talk about it – whenever it is *reiterated*. For these reiterations are moments of what was once called 'performative interpretation': what the thing is deemed to be – what we think it is – is always the result of an interpretation, an interpretation that 'produces it' as such.

This is an unusual but important sort of argument. When we ask 'what happened' or 'what that was all about', we are already involved in coming to a decision about it. In other words, we are not necessarily *finding out about*, but (also) *producing an interpretation* of and *coming to a decision* about. The route that our thinking takes can lead to many dif-ferent conclusions. Here, for example, we may decide: it was nothing; it was typical British racism; it was an unusual and isolated instance of a very untypical racism; it wasn't racism at all; it was racially inflected class resentment; it was gender-based beauty resentment; it was based on envy; it was a strange eruption of a kind of bullying normally only seen in schoolyards; it was sadism for the sheer enjoyment of excluding and victimizing someone; it was based on strictly personal differences; it was based on personal differences based on cultural differences; it was a *unique* admixture of all of these factors; it was a *typical* admix-ture of all of these factors; it was pure performance 'for the cameras', etc., etc.

Deconstruction thrives on this uncertainty or undecidability. How we come to decisions, the processes that we follow when coming to deci-sions, working things out, and constructing knowledge, the associations that we make, the steps we take, and so on: this is a primary concern of deconstruction.

... the Popular ...

But why should we share this concern? Why should we care about how decisions are made or how interpretations are reached? What difference does it make? The answer is in the questions: we should care about how decisions are made and interpretations are reached because these relate directly to how differences are made. How things are interpreted can make all the difference in the world. Whether the Jade Goody and Shilpa Shetty affaire was significant or insignificant, racist or not, a scandal or a shambles, and so on, is just one example. For, although it merely made some people laugh or become mildly irritated, it inspired others to protest violently about the protagonists, the show's producers, and even the UK itself.

One of the many things this suggests is that the so-called media 'realm' of certain aspects of popular culture is neither homogenous nor discrete, nor is it part of a unified or predictable 'circuit' of culture. Popular culture is not a realm distinct from other realms. It is, in fact, a complex matter of *articulation*: of texts, productions, interventions and utterances that can become connected with other so-called 'realms'. (A 'realm' is only *relatively* fixed, discrete, or stable: As the *Celebrity Big Brother* 'events' reveal, the putatively trivial 'realm' of reality TV can become involved and entangled with the so-called 'political realm'.) This possibility of articulation means that culture's relations and effects can behave in unpredictable ways, ways which make the very idea of a stable or predictable 'circuit of culture' somewhat doubtful. Ultimately, then, on the one hand, there is no reason why even supposedly trivial texts and moments of popular culture might not become articulated to (connected to, entangled with) (m)any other elements of the human world of culture, politics, society, history and economy, in complex and consequential ways. On the other hand, however, it also means that, no matter how much theorists theorize culture as a 'circuit', this circuit will never run smoothly or behave predictably. Indeed, as Stuart Hall once pointed out:

> [I]t has always been impossible in the theoretical field of cultural studies – whether it is conceived either in terms of texts and contexts, of intertextuality, or of the historical formations in which cultural practices are lodged – to get anything like an adequate theoretical account of culture's relations and its effects. (Hall 1992: 285)

In other words, it is impossible to *know* cultural relations and effects with any certainty, in advance or in general. Every moment or event is an interpretive moment or event, whose status is up for grabs. So, we cannot justifiably *write off* any manifestation of culture as insignificant. The interpretation of events is ethically and politically significant, through and through. (This premise is one of the reasons why cultural studies was among the first academic fields to focus on popular culture in a positive sense.)

... by cultural studies

So, popular culture cannot be written off as trivial or inconsequential. But nor can its consequences be predicted or generalized. Perhaps the most we can do is to study singular examples of 'texts and contexts, of intertextuality, or of the historical formations in which cultural practices are lodged', as Hall puts it. But the question remains, why should we bother?

In an influential essay, 'Cultural Studies and Its Theoretical Legacies', Stuart Hall insists that cultural studies is an intellectual and academic practice that is dominated by a strong 'will to connect' (1992: 278). For Hall, this 'will to connect' means that by definition cultural studies 'tries to make a difference in the institutional world in which it is located' (1992: 285). Accordingly – and despite the embarrassing vagueness of the name 'cultural studies' (a source of embarrassment that we will return to in Chapter 7) – this is a definition which means that cultural studies *cannot* simply be just 'whatever people [choose to] do' (1992: 278). Indeed, says Hall:

> It can't be just any old thing which chooses to march under a particular banner. It is a serious enterprise, or project, and that is inscribed in what is sometimes called the 'political' aspect of cultural studies. Not that there's one politics already inscribed in it. But there is something *at stake* in cultural studies, in a way that I think, and hope, is not exactly true of many other very important intellectual and critical practices. (Hall 1992: 278)

This whole book is informed by this argument. As will be argued in the conclusion (Chapter 8), cultural studies' efforts to 'make a difference' in the world have long hinged on offering reinterpretations and critiques of existing interpretations. Ironically, though, despite Hall's influential characterization of cultural studies as a serious, motivated, politicized, interventional project, its focus on such areas as popular culture has regularly led to it having been (mis)construed and (mis)represented as being precisely the opposite of this: namely, as 'just any old thing', as 'whatever people [choose to] do': as a vague, wishy-washy, 'Mickey Mouse' subject (Young 1999: 5). Doubtless, part of the reason why cultural studies has been given such a bad name is because it had already been given such a bad name. For what could *possibly* sound more vague and unfocused than '*cultural* studies'? How *naff* is *that* for a name? And this name, although merely denoting a perfectly reasonable (albeit potentially limitless) field of study, because of its vagueness, carries connotations that actively help the uninformed to surmise that if cultural studies doesn't have an instantly specifiable or clearly delimitable *object* (as in, definable and delimitable field of study), then it must be that it doesn't have a properly specifiable or delimitable object (as in *point*). But the plurality and openness of 'culture' as a field of study does not mean that *cultural studies* – as a named institutional entity – 'can be simply pluralist', points out Hall:

> Yes, it refuses to be a master discourse or meta-discourse of any kind. Yes, it is a project that is always open to that which it doesn't yet know, to that which it can't yet name. But it does have some will to connect; it does have some stake in the choices it makes. It does matter whether cultural studies is this or that. (Hall 1992: 278)

And *what it necessarily is*, for Hall – constitutively, always already – despite being given a bad name twice over (once, tragically, by its founders and second, farcically, by its critics) – or despite all its wishy-washy connotations – is something of a wolf in sheep's clothing: claiming only to be *studies*, cultural studies sought primarily to *intervene*, ethically and politically, in the discourses of other disciplines and institutions – as a kind of ethico-political 'corrective'. In Hall's account, cultural studies was formed in 'a discursive formation, in Foucault's sense' (Hall, Morley and Chen 1996: 263), emerging within the 'milieu' of the New Left in the UK in the 1960s and 1970s (Rojek 2003: 23). It was a university institution that was explicitly ethically and politically motivated: open to the new and to the other (open to alterity), and it was intent on pushing exclusionary limits, borders, conventions, boundaries, orientations, hierarchies, and so on. In short, as Hall makes clear: cultural studies was intent on *intervening*, on *altering*. It was never 'merely academic', either in the literal or the pejorative sense of this term. Rather, to employ one of Derrida's definitions of deconstruction that will return regularly throughout this book: although it was located within the university institution, cultural studies has always been, by definition, '*an institutional practice for which ... the institution remains a problem*' (Derrida 2002: 53). Thus, for cultural studies as for deconstruction, 'institution' is a central and defining problematic.

For *institutions* are influential. By 'institution' what is meant are both *institutions themselves* and *acts of institution* (the instituting of new sites, practices and, well, institutions). As the title of a book by Sam Weber (1987) puts it clearly, there is a strong, reciprocal relationship between *Institution and Interpretation*. Interpretations influence institutions, and institutions determine interpretations. And these relationships have wider social, cultural and political effects. This is precisely why Chapter 1 of this book focuses exclusively on one 'little' text: the management and self-help book, *Who Moved My Cheese?* For this apparently simple little text is one that has been globally popular for some time now, and popular among all kinds of significant institutions. *Who Moved My Cheese?* has testimonials on its pages from businesses and universities, from television companies and the military, and more. It is reputedly read in many countries, including Japan and America, in family homes, by parents to their children, as a bedtime story. Many major companies have held many major conferences celebrating and exploring the 'usefulness' of *Who Moved My Cheese? So,* although it is only a 'simple', 'little' text, it is arguably a highly significant text of popular culture. Chapter 1, the first of four chapters making up Part I, is, then, a different sort of exploration of the 'usefulness' of a different sort of popular cultural text. Chapter 1 argues – through a close reading of *Who Moved My Cheese?* – that it is primarily an *ideological* text, which seeks to make its readers passive, inert, unthinking, and accepting of their own exploitation. At the same time as this, the chapter works as a clear introduction to deconstructive styles of reading, as it demonstrates that this text clearly says what it does not want us to know that it says: *you are worthless rodents and deserve nothing more than subsistence, if you are lucky.* All that is required in order to be able to see this is an *active* reading process, rather than the 'interpretive passivity' that the book's structure tries to foist upon us.

The theme of *active reading* versus interpretive passivity (or 'interpassivity') is picked up again in Chapter 2. This chapter moves from the theme of *self* (self-help), that dominated Chapter 1, to the (cultural studies) question of a relationship to *you* (to something or someone *other*). The chapter pursues this, first by examining the pop song, 'Writing to Reach You', by the band Travis. This reading serves several purposes. Firstly, of course, it clarifies some key dimensions of deconstruction, and shows the way that ideas and issues that Jacques Derrida developed in his readings of 'complex' philosophical texts can be seen to be at work in the supposedly 'simple' texts of popular culture. Thus, the chapter reveals the complex *intertextuality* of popular cultural texts, cultural productions and cultural practices. At the same time as this, and by way of a reading of this song (and some closely related cultural texts), the chapter explores the significance of the palpable *anxiety* that is present within the lyrics of the song. This anxiety – 'I'm writing to reach you now but I might never reach you' – can easily be related to the contemporary 'postmodern' condition in numerous ways (and particularly to the anxieties that are characteristic – even definitive – of cultural studies).

Chapter 3 turns to the common contemporary theme of *identity*. Because considerations of identity are so current (everyone now 'knows' that 'identity is constructed'), the chapter seeks to suggest some of the myriad potential ways that popular culture *supplements* our identities. It does so, initially, through an opening consideration of one popular cultural example: the song 'JCB Song' by the band Nizlopi. What is particularly pertinent here is the way that this example instantly leads us away to a prior example: the iconic and exemplary figure of Bruce Lee. What is important about Bruce Lee in this context is the way in which Bruce Lee as a source of identification and identity formation opens up onto questions of *cultural* identity. These are terms that we use all the time – we can speak of 'my identity', a culture's 'identity', and so on; but what does it mean? The chapter traces the complex cultural ramifications of the intervention of Bruce Lee, specifically the implications of subjective identification with Bruce Lee. It suggests that popular culture – however 'mediated', 'simulated' or indeed even 'fake' – could be said to deconstruct traditional historical forms and formations of culture *itself*.

So, Chapter 3 suggests that the supposedly fake can deconstruct and reconstruct reality. Chapter 4 clarifies the ways that certain fictions have structured our notions of what is real, but this time in the political 'realm'. This chapter deconstructs popular conceptions of politics and of the political. It examines both popular cultural forms of political action (from popular forms of protest to activities like culture jamming, from direct action to revolutionary theories) and intellectual theorizations of politics (from Marxism to Neoliberalism). The chapter considers several sorts of political events and different forms of political action, and characterizes the dominant notions of *what* cultural and political 'cause and effect' *are*. It does so first in a section which explores what the chapter calls 'street-fetishism'. It argues, through reading 'concrete' notions of street and grass-roots politics, that 'the street' is in fact a *fetish concept* of politics. For in political and politicized discourse, 'the material' is taken to be the 'hard stuff' of 'reality'. So, talking about it seems *real*. But it is merely a *trope* (an image or metaphor that structures one's thinking and orientations).

Using so-called 'concrete examples' from both political action (street protests, first of all) and the arguments of key thinkers of cultural studies, the argument here is that the perceived political need to appear to 'connect' with the 'concrete reality' exemplified by the street is the dominant injunction and fetish concept of politicized intellectual discourse. The chapter argues that 'the street' is the 'royal road' to the traditional political consciousness. This leads into the second section, which deconstructs the hold of the 'metaphysical' image of politics over political discourse: the street appears as (if) 'presence', 'life', activity'. But, the chapter suggests, the street is also to be thought of as an institution of mediation, distance, deferral, absence, etc. So the chapter concludes by (so to speak) crossing to the other side of the street and focusing on the notion of *articulation* – the necessity, inevitability and importance of dis/connection, de/linking, de- and reconstructing. Along the way, the chapter focuses on the status of the historically hugely important political signifier, 'class', and the deconstruction of this category by certain deconstructive political theorists. It concludes with some suggestions for a deconstructed, reconstructed and deconstructive political strategy that could be available to everyone – regardless of class or proximity to the street.

Of course, such suggestions will not be welcomed by all. This is not least because deconstructive approaches to culture and politics have themselves sometimes been deemed by some commentators to be part of the last gasp of the legacy of the radical countercultural movements of the 1950s and 1960s. Part II of *Deconstructing Popular Culture* therefore begins with Chapter 5's examination of the conceptual underpinnings of popular countercultural movements, as well as those of the key criticisms of such movements. The chapter moves into a sustained consideration of the criticisms that the hugely popular cultural theorist Slavoj Žižek makes of 'counterculture' and, reciprocally, of the cultural studies approaches that have championed countercultural movements. So, beginning from a mainstream popular cultural text, the chapter reveals the notion of counterculture to be an unstable one, and goes on to examine the main brands of popular countercultural thinking. It examines the familiar challenge (regularly reiterated by thinkers on both the traditional Left and the Right) that both cultural and countercultural movements can be understood as being the bastard offspring and ideological affiliates of capitalism. This kind of thinking about popular cultural movements is neither new nor unique, but it has, as just mentioned, been given voice most recently by the anti-cultural studies philosopher, Slavoj Žižek, who has developed a sustained critique of many orientations and activities: popular culture, counterculture, deconstruction and cultural studies included. Accordingly, because Žižek is at times the most vociferous contemporary critic of the academic study of popular culture, the remainder of Chapter 5, and Chapter 6, are devoted to elaborating and deconstructing Žižek's critiques of popular culture, counterculture, cultural studies and, indeed, deconstruction.

In other words, Part II begins by deconstructing the arguments of those who would object to the importance and consequentiality of popular culture and, indeed, of deconstructing popular culture. But is that all there is to it? In light of what has been argued about popular culture, deconstruction and cultural studies, the second half of Part II turns to reflect on the popular subjects of deconstruction and cultural studies themselves. For, given their growth and institutionalization, does deconstruction need deconstructing; does cultural studies? What is to be made of their very popularity? How do they relate to popular culture; are they related to popular fashion, or commodification? These latter questions are very regularly posed to both deconstruction and cultural studies. What is more, they are also posed to cultural studies by those associated with deconstruction and to deconstruction by those associated with cultural studies. So, the final chapters engage with and provide a response to these questions. They assess the status and significance of the 'unpopular popularity' of deconstruction and cultural studies.

These two final chapters reiterate why and how Derridean deconstruction and cultural studies have sought to institute responsible intellectual and ethico-political engagement with the popular and the unpopular. They argue that, because of their destabilizing efforts, hostility and resistance to deconstruction and cultural studies was always in a sense *inevitable*, 'pre-programmed', and to be anticipated. Yet, they ask, what is to be made of deconstruction's own institutionalization if, as Derrida put it, deconstruction 'instigates the subversion of every kingdom, which makes it obviously threatening and infallibly dreaded by everything within us that desires a kingdom' (1974: 22)? Is there a kingdom or reign of deconstruction? Might the name and the form of the reign of deconstruction be cultural studies? In a sense, Chapter 8 proposes that this might indeed be the case. Of course, just as Stuart Hall claims to 'have almost as many problems with "popular" as I do with "culture"', and that 'when you put the two terms together the difficulties can be pretty horrendous', so, when you try to put 'cultural studies' and 'deconstruction' together, the difficulties can be equally – if not more – horrendous. Nevertheless, the final chapter offers an analysis, assessment, and series of suggestions for making precisely such a hybrid not only possible but necessary – both for cultural studies and for deconstruction. For popular culture may perhaps be a 'field' that is potentially limitless, unbounded, or immensely difficult to circumscribe and define (although this is not *quite* the case – for reasons that are clarified or reiterated in the Afterword). But our relationship to it should perhaps not be open-ended or aimless. Our relationship to it should, I argue, for ethical and political reasons, be one of deconstructing popular culture.

PART I
Inversion

Help Me If You Can, I'm Feeling Down: Deconstructing Self-Help

1

Let me tell you a story, a story that must (not) be shared

In these brutal, cynically self-serving and often litigious times, wouldn't it be wonderful to come across something that could prove that things are *right*, that it's *right* to subscribe to the 'competition-is-healthy-and-beneficial' story that we are expected to believe, those insistent claims that pursuit of profit is unequivocally good – for the soul and for society? Wouldn't it be wonderful to have a proof that the behaviour demanded of us by capitalism has no bad consequences and only benefits, and is truly altruistic, both individually and collectively improving? Well, one little book, *Who Moved My Cheese?*, by Dr Spencer Johnson, claims to be just such a thing. Part of a growing tide of management self-help books, *Who Moved My Cheese?* claims that whilst it is *also* a management book, its usefulness goes way beyond work, and its 'profound insights' penetrate deep into the heart of the lives of every single one of us. *Who Moved My Cheese?* claims its message can and should be applied to any aspect of our lives we deem needs 'improvement'.

Magnanimously, the book repeatedly tells us that we *must* share the story contained within it, and its profound message: its testimonials and endorsements tell us to, its introduction does, as do its concluding words. So, there is no question about it: I *must* share it with you! The book tells me to. But then come the words: 'Copyright © 1998 Spencer Johnson, M.D. All rights reserved. This book, or parts thereof, may not be reproduced in any form without permission'. These words seem contradictory. They seem to go against the general message about sharing. So, what is to be believed? Are we to follow the example of the book's testimonial-writers, more than one of whom tells us that they regularly share ('reproduce') *Who Moved My Cheese?* One admits to having regular

15

'discussions [about it] with personnel, friends and customers'. Another confides that he 'can picture [himself] reading this wonderful story to [his] children and grandchildren in our family room with a warm fire glowing, and their understanding the lessons in these important pages'. Even the writer of the introduction informs us that he 'tell[s] the Cheese story ... in [his] talks around the world' (14). And the narrator of the book's central cheese-story itself, 'Michael', concludes the book with the words, 'I'm very glad you found the story so useful and I hope that you will have the opportunity to share it soon with others' (94).

We are both urged to 'reproduce' the book *and* forbidden from doing so, in two equally explicit yet utterly contradictory messages. What one message insists upon, the other forbids. Is it *deliberately* duplicitous? Or is it unaware of the impossible position it puts us in? The *double-bind* is that if you try to follow either one of its equally explicit messages, you transgress the other one. In fact, in terms of copyright laws, the *only* straightforward and immediate way to resolve this contradiction is to interpret the word 'share' as meaning 'purchase'. Obviously, this will be one thing the author, as producer of a commodity, will want – although anything like this sort of a cynical profit-driven motivation goes entirely unmentioned within the entire book (in fact, there is very little mention of buying, selling, of money, or indeed of managing within the book, too). But, still, let's believe what the author does actually say. He may well be sincere. It may only be outmoded publishing convention that demands the threatening-sounding legal declaration (and surely we can discount that, if only for being self-contradictory: this assertion of copyright is itself in breach of copyright, for the words it uses have been directly 'reproduced' from other copyright declarations. So this part of the book has been reproduced from others).

A play within a play

So let's put faith in Dr Spencer Johnson's philanthropic intentions, and in his ability to understand what he explicitly says, through his characters and interlocutors. According to his wishes, then, I must share with you the story that takes place at the centre of *Who Moved My Cheese?* – the 'cheese-story', after which the book is named, but which is itself actually only a subplot within a larger drama. The larger drama within which the cheese-story occurs is that of the lives of some fictional characters, former school friends gathered together the day after their school reunion. The entirety of *Who Moved My Cheese?* relates to them. The cheese-story is actually only a 'play within a play', told by one of these characters to the others in a drama about them, told to us. So the tendency to think that the cheese-story itself 'contains the message' is certainly a misreading. But I'll get to this. First, though, who are these secondary but central characters?

They are a group of people who, when introduced, are utterly dejected, totally disheartened with life, and bitter. Except one. He tells them a story that helped him. It's about cheese. Afterwards they discuss it, and manipulate its main analogy (i.e., 'cheese' standing as a metaphor for 'what you want') in ways that help them to come to terms with what they had hitherto understood as the sheer awfulness of their lives. So, the cheese-story enables them to refocus, and come to view what they had previously deemed *terrible* as now being *good*. As the book's dust-jacket, its introduction and every other subsection of the book keep telling us, the book is about how to 'enjoy change'. So, the cheese-story itself is only a play within a play, used, primarily, to 'catch the conscience' of the characters.

The story goes like this. Four characters live in a maze. Two are 'littlepeople' (named Hem and Haw), and two are mice (named Sniff and Scurry). They all eat cheese. In the beginning, the human*esque* characters, Hem and Haw, don't analyse things too much. They don't have to: cheese is just there, and they go to it and eat it. One day, there is no cheese there. There is much consternation. The mice leave. The two littlepeople fret and bicker about what to do. One of them, Hem, decides to stay, believing that he might be able to work out what's going on, and also in the hope that cheese will return again. Haw leaves, and the narrative focus leaves with him: the story does not return to Hem and his (Hamlet-like) dithering and ruminating. We go with Haw, who runs off into the maze and, after a few personal crises of confidence and a lot of writing aphorisms on walls, eventually finds some more cheese. The two mice are already there with the cheese. They have a cheesy party. And that's it. That's the story.

A play within a play within a play

You may ask why I have recounted such a childish (or, at best, childlike) tale as this. Indeed, it is significant that the book goes out of its way to look like a children's storybook: bright colours, large print, not too many words and none of them long or hard, short sentences, furry animals and 'amusing' 'littlepeople', etc., all of which certainly should, I agree, set alarm bells ringing: *A book for adults trying to pass itself off as a kids' book?* (Indeed, everything about its appearance is reminiscent of *The Hitchhiker's Guide To the Galaxy*'s front-cover message, written 'in large friendly letters': 'Don't Panic'. I'll get back to this.) First though, the question is, *why bother with it, why worry about it, why even take it seriously?*

There are two main reasons: the first is that this book is influential. *Who Moved My Cheese?* is 'used' by people and institutions that are definitely influential. Some, you cannot get more 'influential' than (like the US military). And anything that influences the influential is surely important itself. The second reason relates to its 'message', and the 'influence' it might ever be said to have. Now, far be it from me to propose that there is ever a straightforward 'monkey see, monkey do' relationship between any text, any reading of it, and any 'action' undertaken by the reader after or because of that reading. However, institutions do impose *ways* of reading as being *the* 'right' ways. They impose certain meanings as being *the* 'correct' meanings, 'correct' interpretations which imply particular kinds of 'correct' conclusions and 'correct' judgements. And judgements at least 'influence' actions and relationships – or, in other words, *how we live*. And there are many institutions – globally important institutions – all reading *Who Moved My Cheese?* in the *same* way, all 'uncovering' the *same* message and 'deriving' the *same* conclusions about how to live and act, from this childish book. This still might not strike you as a problem or a big deal. However, I will endeavour to suggest just some of the ways in which all of the 'dominant' or 'proper' or 'legitimate' or 'reasonable' interpretations of *Who Moved My Cheese?* are actually delusional, certainly deluding, definitely inane (perhaps even insane), and ultimately socially, culturally, and personally or individually deleterious.

Now this is not to say that there is nothing 'good' 'in it'. Nor is my intention to belittle anyone who has found themselves in a bad, unpleasant, or problematic situation, and found something helpful in the cheese analogy, or in one or another of the book's aphorisms ('What would you do if you weren't afraid?', 'stop smelling bad cheese', etc.). My intention is different. For anyone may well find something helpful, provocative, or insightful in the cheese-story. But my initially pedantic-seeming point is that this is possible *only if you only* 'take bits and pieces', and overlook others. For if you try to read the book as a coherent entity (which it does purport to be), then it becomes apparent that the *way* the book claims it should be read is actually unsustainable, incoherent, and strangely odious, and that the putative 'proper message' of the book falls apart. Furthermore, in order to find any coherence in the book it turns out that you have to read it in ways that are dramatically different than those it itself claims are the 'right' ways to read it. This is my point: *if* you read it attentively it simultaneously reveals how sinister its message is *and* it falls apart, showing that it cannot mean what it wants to mean, nor 'do' what it purports to do. It can, however, be read 'against itself', as containing a radical political and possibly even revolutionary message (entirely different to its intended conservative, depoliticizing, culturally and interpersonally destructive and apathetic message). So, then, bad as it *clearly* is, there is nevertheless something 'good' in it.

If we consider some of the institutions that use this book, and fantasize about the implications of their reading it *properly*, then the prospects become quite exciting. Gushing testimonials from 13 prestigious personages from business, universities, television and the military tell us how moving, thought-provoking, profound and wonderful its message is. We are also informed that the book is used and endorsed by at least 23 massive institutions: Abbott Labs, Bausch & Lomb, Bell South, Bristol Myers Squibb, Citibank, Chase Manhattan, Eastman Kodak, Exxon, Georgia Pacific, General Motors, Goodyear, Greyhound, Lucent Technologies, Marriott, Mead Johnson, Mobil, Oceaneering, Ohio State University, State Farm, Textron, Texaco, Whirlpool, Xerox, countless 'churches and hospitals', unnamed 'government agencies', and the 'United States Military'. In many countries, including Japan and America, *Who Moved My Cheese?* is read widely in family homes, by parents to their children as a bedtime story; and many major UK companies have held major conferences celebrating and 'exploring' the usefulness of *Who Moved My Cheese?* Mention it to just about any marketer or manager in just about any country and they will likely have heard of it, quite probably have read it, and maybe even attended a course or conference extolling it and its 'profound insights'.

Just get the message, right

So what are these profound insights? The title directs our attention exclusively to the cheese-story. It is this parable that we are repeatedly told the message is 'in'. Yet this section – the parable about Hem, Haw, mice, cheese, and faceless forces that move things – covers less than half of its 95 pages. As if to compensate, the parable itself is printed not in large but in *huge* print. It is framed, at the beginning, by sections of smaller-print approbation and instructions about *how* to read it. Its introduction and early scene- and mood-setting sections telegraphically announce and keep repeating *how* to read it. The concluding discussion (of the once dejected but now jubilant friends) reiterates *how you should have read it*. So, the cheese-story itself is indubitably only a subordinate subsection of the book. For *primarily* the book consists of *telling us how to read the cheese-story*.

So, is there profundity in this – in these instructions, if not in the fact that something about the cheese-story seems to demand that *how* it is read be strictly policed and controlled? Why go to such lengths to insist, repeatedly, on *how* to read such a story? The answer can only be: because if you read the story without being told its message, before, after, again and again, then what you risk 'getting out of' this little parable (which allegedly applies to all aspects of the human condition) is something seriously different. This book, avowedly about 'change', wants to shelter itself from the risk of its 'proper meaning' being changed. So what can be 'got out of' the story? To establish that, one has to read it. Yet *reading it* is clearly the very thing this book does not want anyone to do. But it never explicitly says that, so we clearly must do it.

To begin our reading, note this: none of the characters in the cheesy story *ever* has, or ever comes to have, any 'idea where the Cheese came from, or who put it there. They just assumed it would be there' (29). None questions the fact that they are *in a maze* either. Amazingly, being in a maze is just accepted; so much so that Hem and Haw – foolishly, it transpires – come to regard 'the Cheese they found at Cheese Station C as *their* cheese', and 'they eventually moved their homes to be closer to it, and built a social life around it' (29). They do not, however, notice it depleting. When it does run out, it is only the mice, Sniff and Scurry, who 'weren't surprised. Since Sniff and Scurry had noticed that the supply of cheese had been getting smaller every day, [so] they were prepared for the inevitable and knew instinctively what to do' (32). (So, *really*, no one 'moved' the cheese, as such. . . .)

This rodent-like reactivity is celebrated in *Who Moved My Cheese?* (a title which, clearly, from the outset, is inappropriate, as it immediately 'throws us off the scent' or tempts us to bark up the wrong tree or, rather, sniff in the wrong place). In *Who Moved My Cheese?* this *reactivity* is referred to as a propensity to 'change'. From the start, the mice are represented as best, because 'able to change'. More precisely, what is celebrated in particular, is that 'The mice did not overanalyze things. And they were not burdened with many complex beliefs' (32). Hem and Haw, however, are hampered by overactive 'brains', which 'overanalyze', as well as carrying the baggage of burdensome beliefs – 'unproductive' beliefs, such as the expectation of routine, of being able to have a stable home and a social life. But, in *Who Moved My Cheese?*, the deal is exactly as the mice well know: 'To the mice, the problem and the answer were both simple. The situation at Cheese Station C had changed. So, Sniff and Scurry decided to change' (32). 'Change', here and throughout, means only passive responsiveness. It *never* entails resisting anything. Resistance is presented not only as futile, but as ridiculous: when Hem and Haw take badly to having their cheese moved, their consternation is depicted as childish prating: 'as though if [they] shouted loud enough someone would put it back' (33). Hem complains loudest, but unfortunately has no one to complain to other than Haw. The complaint is straightforward, and fair enough: 'It's not fair!' (33). It clearly isn't fair. But such a complaint, the narrative cautions, is to be avoided, as it is 'not very attractive or productive' (34):

> They ranted and raved at the injustice of it all. Haw started to get depressed. What would happen if the Cheese wasn't there tomorrow? He had made future plans based on this Cheese. The littlepeople couldn't believe it. How could this have happened? No one had warned them. It wasn't right. It was not the way things were supposed to be. (35) .... Hem analyzed the situation over and over and eventually his complicated brain with its huge belief system took hold. 'Why did they do this to me?' he demanded. 'What's really going on here?' (37)

Hem becomes bogged down in these questions, obsessed with a grievance that is judged by the narrator as neither 'attractive [n]or pro-ductive'. Accordingly, he is deemed arrogant by the narrative. And we all know what pride comes before. Fool that he is, he believes himself to be too important to be squashed arbitrarily like some hapless insect. The profound and heart-warming message, of course, is that he is noth-ing more than an insect, he is wrong to attach any value to himself or to what he wants or needs (his 'cheese'):

> Hem continued, 'They're just simple mice. They just respond to what hap-pens. We're littlepeople. We're special. We should be able to figure this out. And besides, we deserve better. This should not happen to us, or if it does, we should at least get some benefits'.
> 'Why should we get benefits?' Haw asked.
> 'Because we're entitled', Hem claimed.
> 'Entitled to what?' Haw wanted to know.
> 'We're entitled to our Cheese'.
> 'Why?' Haw asked.
> 'Because, we didn't cause this problem', Hem said. 'Somebody else did this and we should get something out of it'.
> Haw suggested, 'Maybe we should stop analyzing the situation so much and just get going and find some New Cheese'.
> 'Oh no', Hem argued. 'I'm going to get to the bottom of this'. (38)

This is a decisive moment. Hem and Haw differ in opinion: Hem believes they should have rights, support and self-worth. Maybe in this sense he has 'changed'. Something like an embryonic political awareness is dawning. But he hasn't changed 'fundamentally', as he still aims to 'get something out of' the situation, which is a fundamentally parasitic aim. Haw, however, is getting a slightly different message: he's learning that to respond properly to situations now demands plasticity, malleability, 'flexibility'. Of course, he too knows that one should still try to get what one can. But Haw is beginning to learn that now one shouldn't 'expect'. This is the crucial difference. Haw accepts (passively) the 'wonderful' lesson that to survive, one must be like mice, who 'didn't think of anything else but finding New Cheese' (39).

Hem and Haw here embody the two great opposed figures of *Homo Economicus*: on the one hand, the demanding but inefficient Trades Union Man (Hem), and on the other the 'go-getting' entrepreneur (Haw). Just as these were the only intelligible political positions forced on workers during the decisive 'changes' precipitated by Thatcher and Reagan, so they are the only intelligible positions now within the maze: either sit, rooted in the old unproductive ways, or go-get in the newly deracinated economic situation. Either remain, unproductively, or go-get, ceaselessly. Either be a loser or be happy to subsist. The narrative entirely advocates the 'Haw-option' (and 'Haw' has an apt homophone), in which one must actively embrace a life of subsistence, touting it as the enjoyable advantage-taking of new opportunities. One must, in other words, live life as a perpetual-motion masochist.

Unfortunately, though, Haw can't yet quite shake off the baggage of yesterday's outmoded and unproductive 'complex beliefs'. It will take him some time to work them out, to exorcise all those hindering demons, like commitments to one's past, one's environment, one's friends, and so on. Indeed, the rest of the story is about Haw's gradual 'coming to terms' with the need to reject life and adapt to the single-minded pursuit of what you think you can get, but what the book itself decisively represents as an impossible fantasy, namely, 'Getting' the 'Cheese'. (The Explicit Lesson is: it's not yours and you can't 'get' it.) In other words, after rejecting his former life as symbolized by Hem, the rest of Haw's story is about his 'working through', exorcizing, and 'managing' to cope with the trauma of it all, so to speak. It is unsurprising that he oscillates between hysteria and depression: 'Finally, one day Haw began laughing at himself. "Haw, haw, look at me. I keep doing the same things over and over again and wonder why things don't get better. If this wasn't so ridiculous, it would be even funnier"' (43). Henceforth, he oscillates between unprovoked hysterical laughter and fearful depression. But this laughter does enable him to change his relationship with the changed situation – which is what the book is all about. What is uncertain is whether this laughter comes as a defence against cracking up in the face of the horror of his new situation, or whether it is evidence of his having cracked up.

Either way, the solution to the problems of life is portrayed as involving an unavoidable masochistic 'striking at oneself' – denying oneself, 'letting go of oneself': 'As Haw prepared to leave, he started to feel more alive, knowing that he was finally able to laugh at himself, let go and move on' (45). In the maze one must laugh at oneself, and certainly one's former self, and one's unproductive attachments, and 'let go' of any sense of permanence, rights, entitlements, stability of location and social relationships, self-worth, and so on. One must also relinquish thinking, forsake 'excessive' thinking, 'unproductive' thinking (like Lord Haw-Haw): 'Haw smiled. He knew Hem was wondering, "Who moved my Cheese?" but Haw was wondering "Why didn't I get up and move with the Cheese sooner?" ' (47). Hem, of course, is a loser. The very question, 'Who moved my Cheese?' is the loser's question, the wrong question, the question that *Who Moved My Cheese?* actually rejects. 'Who moved my Cheese?' is the very question that the book refuses to answer, refuses even to entertain as a question, and, indeed, cannot answer, without blowing its own cover.

For, ultimately, the only answer that *Who Moved My Cheese?* could possibly allow would have to be 'I moved it myself', which, when stated like this, is embarrassingly problematic (even though, as noted above, Hem and Haw palpably did 'move' it themselves: they ate it). Hence, it remains unspoken, but implied. Why can't it be answered directly? It is because the paradoxical logic of the book is the insistence that everything is your own fault, your problem, and your responsibility to solve, for yourself, by yourself. This is so even though the book does seem to recognize that there are objective problems with the world. It's just that it is real objective problems that this book cannot and will not confront.

So, it is doubly conservative. It speaks doubly – duplicitously – like this: at one and the same time it says, 'So you think there is an objective problem? No, it's all in your mind!', and/or, 'Someone else has moved the cheese you had? Well, revise your cheesy expectations downwards to be in accord with what is now on offer'. In other words, the wonderful message of *Who Moved My Cheese?* is: 'All objective problems notwithstanding, you must only look at yourself and change yourself'. That is to say, the book both acknowledges and denies 'objectivity'. Indeed, even 'cheese' itself has a double and duplicitous status throughout: it operates both as 'actual thing' (as food, sustenance) and as impossible desire (ultimate satisfaction, the end of desire, fruition, plenitude). Needless to say, this duplicity, this shifting and problematically chimerical status is only stabilized and resolved when one realizes that 'cheese' can only equal 'money'. This is perhaps a profound insight, especially if we read the book as allegedly being about 'life'.

What would you do if you weren't afraid?

Throughout his journey, Haw is periodically compelled to write platitudes on walls. One of these reads, 'What Would You Do If You Weren't Afraid?' (48). At the same time, however, Haw himself remains fundamentally terrified, throughout. He thinks he overcomes his fear by setting off running, and by being prepared to keep 'changing', interminably. Indeed, the book proposes fear as a virtue:

> He knew that sometimes fear can be good. When you are afraid things are going to get worse if you don't do something, it can prompt you into action. But it is not good when you are so afraid that it keeps you from doing anything. (49)

This is hardly a warrior-axiom, like 'fear is the friend of exceptional people' (as Cus D'Amato, the former trainer of the exceptionally 'go-getting' and 'competitive' Mike Tyson once put it). This is rather more Chandler's (from *Friends*) 'I'm too afraid [to quit my job]'.

But if we actually answered this question, regarding our own lives, what would we do? Would we keep running? Really? Would we go to work? Would you? The question is a good one – arguably a brilliant one. Posing it could prompt radical, even revolutionary change. Of course, not necessarily for the best. One answer to the question could be 'murder', or even 'suicide', for instance. And, in fact, in a metaphorical way, when Haw daubs this question on the wall, it actually signals the moment of his complete resignation and, more disconcertingly, the unequivocal birth of his state of almost psychotic delusion. For at this point, he thinks he is 'taking control'; he tells himself he is taking control:

> Whenever he started to get discouraged he reminded himself that what he was doing, as uncomfortable as it was at the moment, was in reality much better than staying in the Cheeseless situation. He was taking control, rather than simply letting things happen to him. (50)

But he is, rather, merely becoming resigned to the fact that things will simply happen to him. For, soon, his delusion will palpably deepen. In ruminating about times gone by (itself a dangerous game, in this book – unless one concludes that then was not as good as now), he speculates that 'Mold may even have begun to grow on the Old Cheese' (51). But there never has been, never is, and never will be any mention, anywhere, of this having happened. No one was formerly dissatisfied with the quality of the cheese. Not even the observant if changeable mice. The issue was only that it was 'moved', by ... by ... well, best not dwell on who 'moved' it.

This hallucinatory false-memory, this ambivalent relation to the past, is occasioned because Haw still has to confront the ultimate emptiness of his plight, the absolute nihilism of his situation. He is being forced to acknowledge that you cannot count on cheese 'being there'. You can only count on your having, interminably, to run after cheese. ' "This empty feeling has happened to me too often", he thought .... "What would I do if I weren't afraid?" ' (53). He cannot answer this question. All he can do is be afraid, as the motor for all of his actions. 'What would I do if I weren't afraid?' is not answered. Instead, nihilism, pointlessness, emptiness and repetitiveness are tautologically proposed as being the solution to the problem of nihilism, pointlessness, emptiness and repetitiveness:

> As he started running down the dark corridor he began to smile. Haw didn't realize it yet, but he was discovering what nourished his soul. He was letting go and trusting what lay ahead of him, even though he did not know exactly what it was.
>
> To his surprise, Haw started to enjoy himself more and more. 'Why do I feel so good?' he wondered. 'I don't have any Cheese and I don't know where I am going'.
>
> Before long, he knew why he felt good.
>
> He stopped to write again on the wall:
>
> 'When You Move Beyond Your Fear, You Feel Free'.
>
> Haw realized he had been held captive by his own fear. Moving in a new direction had freed him. (55–7)

Here, 'cheese' is given an entirely 'spiritual' and definitively non-material and non-practical meaning. As noted, 'cheese' has an ambivalent, double status, as representing both need and desire (or, translated, as money: as what you need it for and what you want it for). The writer of the introduction himself claims 'cheese' is an almost infinitely supple metaphor, as *Who Moved My Cheese?* is 'a story about change that takes place in a Maze where four amusing characters look for "Cheese" – cheese being a metaphor for what we want to have in life, whether it is a job, a relationship, money, a big house, freedom, health, recognition, spiritual peace, or even an activity like jogging or golf' (14). But at this point, 'cheese' does not name a 'thing' (like food), it only names a desire, but a desire that produces satisfaction even though the thing desired is not received or attained. In other words, this is about learning to be satisfied with not getting what you want – or, as Adorno and Horkheimer once put it, it is about how to make someone who wants to eat feel satisfied with the menu. This, Adorno and Horkheimer unequivocally associated with masochism (and capitalism).

As with desire, so with fear. At the start of the story, Haw was afraid to start running and searching. His answer to the question of what he would do if he wasn't afraid of running was that he would run. When he was running, he was still afraid. He posed the question again, and the answer came that he would keep running. Eventually, the question became meaningless – not solved or resolved, just meaningless, tired, empty, and irrelevant. Haw now reaches the same condition of existence as that of the mice. In other words, at this moment, Haw is beaten. But this passive, masochistic state denies itself, and comes replete with a warped fantasy or imaginary – hallucinatory – relationship with objective reality. For, note: Haw doesn't have any cheese, and knows that even if he finds any, it won't be permanent. Nevertheless, he tells himself, ' "Imagining Myself Enjoying New Cheese Even Before I Find It, Leads Me To It" ' (58), and ' "The Quicker You Let Go Of Old Cheese, The Sooner You Find New Cheese" ' (60). He even tells himself that he 'was happy when he wasn't being run by his fear. He liked what he was doing now' (61), 'In fact, he sensed he had already found what he was looking for' (62). It is in moments and formulations like these that this kind of ideology tries to pass itself off as almost spiritual – pretending to present a message of not clinging, of going with the flow, of being flexible, of not being attached to worldly things, etc., but in the service of an unending 'clinging', scrabbling after them, in denial. True, this situation does describe a certain 'detachment', but primarily in the sense of being unhinged.

The objective situation unhinges Haw. His semi-spiritual self-abnegation even switches registers, changing from sounding like some bizarre version of worldly and materialistic pseudo-Taoism, or some monstrous abomination of Taoism (don't cling, to cling properly; move with the cheese, to come to terms with never getting the cheese, etc.), into a kind of eminently guilty Catholic discourse. Haw places the blame for all of his troubles onto his own shoulders: 'Haw realized again, as he had once before, that what you are afraid of is never as bad as what you imagine. The fear you let build up in your mind is worse than the situation that actually exists' (63). Even though he still has the ability to acknowledge that objective situations would have seen him perish (70), everything remains squarely refracted through himself, through the individual. Despite the objectivity of the problems, Haw places the blame on himself.

His next graffito is 'Old Beliefs Do Not Lead You To New Cheese' (64). Haw has 'learned' that it's all about 'new beliefs'. And that's all. It's what you believe: 'Haw now realized that his new beliefs were encouraging new behaviors. He was behaving differently than when he kept returning to the same cheeseless situation' (65); 'He knew that when you change what you believe, you change what you do' (65); 'By now, Haw had let go of the past and was adapting to the future' (69). And then he finds some more actual cheese.

> So what was it that made him change? Was it the fear of starving to death? Haw thought, 'Well, that helped'.
> Then he laughed and realized that he had started to change as soon as he had learned to laugh at himself and at what he had been doing wrong. He realized that the fastest way to change is to laugh at your own folly – then you can let go and quickly move on. (70)

So, nothing is worth fighting for? And fear is your invention? (Good: then there can be no war on terror. And no reason for such a war. And no terror.) Be like a feeble-minded rodent. That's all you amount to anyway: 'Sniff and Scurry. They kept life simple. They didn't overanalyze or overcomplicate things' (71). But if you're afflicted with more intelligence than a mouse, you can think, a little: 'Then Haw used his wonderful brain to do what littlepeople do better than mice. He reflected on the mistakes he had made in the past and used them to plan for the future' (71). But planning for the future is the one thing you demonstrably cannot do. Indeed, planning for the future is another duplicitously deployed dimension of *Who Moved My Cheese?* Recall: at the beginning, Haw's outrage at the loss of the cheese he had come to rely on and 'had made future plans based on' (35) is offered as a lesson in the error of 'clinging' and indeed in the silliness of expecting anything at all (38); whilst at the end of the story, 'He reflected on the mistakes he had made in the past and used them to plan for the future' (71). If one is bad and another is good, is there a difference between these two types of planning for the future?

The distinctiveness of this final plan for the future appears to be that it has no content at all, other than the plan to 'keep things simple, be flexible, and move quickly' (71), based on the hilarious 'realization' that 'the biggest inhibitor to change lies within yourself, and that nothing gets better until you change' (71). You must change, and utterly reject the past. The past equals the inferior and even the bad. Any change, no matter how disruptive or even destructive, equals improvement.

He didn't like it at the time, but he knew that the change had turned out to
be a blessing in disguise as it led him to find better Cheese.

He had even found a better part of himself.

As Haw recalled what he had learned, he thought about his friend Hem.
He wondered if Hem had read any of the sayings Haw had written on the
wall at Cheese Station C and throughout the maze. (72)

What's the message again? Beats me

And what about Hem? Forget Hem. He couldn't see the writing on the
wall. *Who Moved My Cheese?* is about helping us to participate willingly
and gratefully in our own exploitation. It is an ideological text that
acknowledges but denies, inverts and warps the problems of global
capitalism, repackaging them and selling them back as problems that
are our own fault. It turns everything upside down and sends it back
out again, back to front; claiming that the causes, the blame and the
solutions for all of life's problems lie with 'individuals'. You and me,
them and us, the message is: So your life has been screwed over by
someone or something else? Well, that's nobody's fault but your own.
You should have known that others can and will cause your life to
collapse, arbitrarily, painfully, violently and traumatically. You have no
right to protection, and no right to redress; no right to objection, and
an obligation to accept. The cultural critic, Slavoj Žižek, speaking of
capitalism and its ideology, puts it like this:

> Here we are at the very nerve center of the liberal ideology: freedom of
> choice, grounded in the notion of the 'psychological' subject endowed with
> propensities he or she strives to realize. This especially holds today, in the
> era of what sociologists like Ulrich Beck call 'risk society', when the ruling
> ideology endeavors to sell us the insecurity caused by the dismantling of
> the Welfare State as the opportunity for new freedoms: you have to change
> jobs every year, relying on short-term contracts instead of a long-term stable
> appointment. Why not see it as the liberation from the constraints of a fixed
> job, as the chance to reinvent yourself again and again, to become aware of
> and realize hidden potentials of your personality? You can no longer rely
> on the standard health insurance and retirement plan, so that you have to
> opt for additional coverage for which you have to pay. Why not perceive it
> as an additional opportunity to choose: either better life now or long-term
> security? And if this predicament causes you anxiety, the postmodern or 'sec-
> ond modernity' ideologist will immediately accuse you of being unable to
> assume full freedom, of the 'escape from freedom', of the immature sticking
> to old stable forms ... Even better, when this is inscribed into the ideology

of the subject as the psychological individual pregnant with natural abilities and tendencies, then I as it were automatically interpret all these changes as the result of my personality, not as the result of me being thrown around by market forces. (Žižek 2001b: 116)

But perhaps it's unfair to expose what is merely a *practical self-help* manual to criticism from a 'theoretical' and unpractical perspective like Žižek's. For, you could say, what *use* is such cleverness as Žižek's? It's *not useful*, whereas *this book is useful*. Such might be the objection. Indeed, all the book claims to be able to do (and I quote, from the dust-jacket) is to 'show you how to anticipate change, adapt to change quickly, enjoy change, be ready to change quickly, again and again'. But the words 'show you how' are misleading, even though this is the entirety of what it claims to do: it claims to be able to *show* you *how*. But, on inspection, teaching '*how*-to' is what it *cannot* do. It is not a 'how-to'. It is rather a 'that-you-must'. There is a difference: the difference being that a how-to would have a specific content. But, this has no particular content, and no particular 'practical' advice at all. It is exclusively a document which dresses up and states in a seductive and beguiling manner the cold hard fact that you are just going to have to handle unpredictable changes, imposed on your life from without.

Simply put, *Who Moved My Cheese?* is basically about coming to terms with having to get another job when you are sacked, or of offering you a way to be able to sleep at nights or look at yourself in the mirror when you have had to sack others. As one character puts it, speaking of when he had to sack huge swathes of his workforce:

> ... practically everyone, those who left and those who stayed, said the Cheese story helped them see things differently and cope better. Those who had to go out and look for a new job said it was hard at first but recalling the story was a great help to them. (91)

Thus, the entire work of the book is that of providing its readers with a 'flexible' metaphor to offer a compensatory pseudo-philosophy – or rather, a *mantra* – of inane platitudes designed to help you soldier on when your business, job, or life goes down the toilet through no fault of your own. When another character confides that she fears she will lose her job very soon, another shouts, 'It's maze time!', about which all present laugh heartily. When she laughs too, she is rewarded with, 'It's good that you can laugh at yourself' (84). Indeed. But good for who, or what?

The book says: this may seem to be no fault of your own, but you shouldn't have stopped running, and certainly if you let it get you down or try to blame anything or anyone other than yourself, you will be crushed. The only way to survive is to keep running. This is the text's explicit message – both literally and in terms of its explicit metaphors: keep running. All the characters in the story, all those unquestioningly stuck in its horrifically banal, in(s)ane and Kafkaesque maze wear jogging clothes and jog everywhere. Keep running. Do it – just or unjust makes no difference: just do it. The very proposition that you should 'enjoy change' demonstrates the sadism of the position from which this book is written, and the masochistic position it would have its readers adopt. One 'human' character, Frank, even says, ' "I think some things shouldn't change. For example, I want to hold on to my basic values. But I realize now that I would be better off if I had moved with the 'Cheese' a lot sooner in my life" ' (86). Sucker! 'Basic values' are so last season! Another 'human' character even diagnoses the epidemic of stress and stress-related illness as being a result of – you guessed it – *personality failings*! She argues:

> 'Some people never change and they pay a price for it. I see people like Hem in my medical practice. They feel entitled to their "Cheese". They feel like victims when it's taken away and blame others. They get sicker than people who let go and move on'. (85)

So who moved the cheese?

Who moved the cheese? You did, yourself, dummy! Well, you might not *actually* have done, but you *might as well have* done, as it can be no one's fault but your own. You think 'they' did it, but you did it. But did you? Don't dwell on it, in case you arrive at a different conclusion. Keep running.

There is much more to say about this book. I have not, by a long shot, exhausted the 'proper' message of the cheese-parable – the 'intended message', the one that's reiterated again and again before and after the parable itself, and that is about 'changing', 'moving', 'running', 'pursuing', about hallucinating yourself into the position of blame, even for your own fears. This message – this proper message – I must admit, disgusts me. But then, people say I'm no 'realist', and they claim that this book *does* practically and pragmatically characterize 'reality': because, well, you've got to run, haven't you? You've got to laugh, haven't you? Well, precisely.

Yet, it's not just me. On inspection, the book itself 'knows' that it is disgusting. Why else would it, at several key moments, try to 'interpret away', interpret out of existence, the antisocial implications of its own message, coming up with more or less convoluted rationalizations to the effect that moving to *new* cheese and *dumping* 'old cheese' does *not* mean running away, severing links, divorcing, rejecting, forgetting, denying? To show how untenable and forced such interpretations are would require a lengthy digression into even more dimensions of the duplicitous status of cheese in the story (for instance, the rhetorical sleight-of-hand by which cheese that has 'been moved' first becomes referred to as 'old', and then as 'stale', and as 'stale' connotes 'bad' this justifies the equation that 'old equals bad', etc.), and a lengthier account of the ways that cheese is set up both as 'real' *and* as an impossible fantasy, like a mirage – or, ultimately, like a carrot dangled in front of a pack-mule's eyes.

As well as the convolutions of the book's own attempts to argue that the moral of the story is *not* that we should have no morality whatsoever, it absolutely glosses over the fact that it demands the immorality that is complete competition. The littlepeople and the mice *smile* at each other and *share* the scarce cheese. *Why? Are they mad?* There is no logic to this, if scarcity demands running and competition. It has to be hard cheese for someone, as a matter of principle. Logically, reasonably, rationally, then, *shouldn't they try to kill each other?* Why would they not if they weren't afraid? Of course, the book is afraid, and *especially* of its two unanswered questions. It is far from an adequate or plausible representation of what its own consequences would be, if anything about it were translatable into 'real life'. The picture painted by this book does seem in(s)ane in the extreme. And yet. . .

Maybe it is all too sane and all too moral in being so simplistic. Maybe indeed we should move with the cheese. *Of course* that's *all* anyone can do. Maybe what we need to understand in no uncertain terms is that our cheese is not ours, not ever. As such, maybe we are morally obliged not to impede anyone else's moving the cheese, even if we think it's ours; that we *must* share it with them. This would mean that if global population movements are merely people dynamically moving with the cheese, and if we must not ask who moved their cheese, then maybe we must just open borders, doors, jobs, institutions, cultures and families to anyone, everyone, including and especially political refugees, asylum seekers and economic migrants, and share 'our' cheese with them. Remember, it's not ours, and they are doing what is advocated in this most capitalist-ideological of books. And if it is the case that, whenever cheese is moved, no one has the right to seek retribution or to attribute blame, then if what seemed most sacred to us is, say, destroyed, demolished, exploded, then there could be no justification for retribution, for waging war. Maybe nothing is worth fighting for. Maybe there is nothing to be afraid of, other than our fear. So, those whose cheese has been moved, those, say, in Africa or the Balkans, should move here, and we should know that what we think we fear is only a silly invention, and that objectively there is nothing wrong with this new cheese. And so on. Move with the cheese . . . . Tenuous? Far-fetched? Unrealistic? Maybe and yes and no, but why, why not?

My most basic point is: every way you read this book you see that the only way that it can make sense, in the way that it tries to and claims to, is if you *don't read it*. This book demands that you don't read it, that you don't interpret it, that you don't think about it. In this sense, too, it is exemplary of the contemporary capitalist/neoliberal condition: not only does it say, be like children, be like rodents, don't think, run, keep your head down, don't resist, don't think you have a real *problem*, if you do think that there is a problem then 'realize' that *you are* the problem, be content with having no rights, be pliable, plastic, malleable, and so on, ultimately what it says is: don't read. By which it means: don't interpret. Don't think. *Reading*, then – properly, thoroughly, rigorously – seems to be the primary and only way to be other than vermin in someone else's laboratory. So, what *would* you do if you weren't afraid?

Can I Help You? Deconstructing(,) Words and Music

My inside is outside

You might want to help, connect, intervene, reach, teach. Such an aim is voiced in 'Writing to Reach You', a pop song by the Scottish guitar-based 'Britpop' band, Travis. To call this song unremarkable would be no criticism. The point is simply that there is not 'obviously' much 'going on' within it. Yet it did, in fact, prove to be very popular, and became a significant international hit in 1999. It is 'unremarkable' only in the sense that the song is musically simple and lyrically uncontroversial. In fact, it would seem to be 'simple' in every sense: mere pop culture. But a closer inspection reveals that the song is simple and unremarkable only if viewed in a limited *technical* way. For, when viewed as a *cultural text*, this pop song can in fact cast important light on what Stuart Hall once called the immense complexity of 'culture's relations and its effects' (Hall 1992: 285). In other words, if we merely evaluate the song on a technical musicological level, then, yes, it certainly is simple. But, if we approach it as a particular textual construction, woven together from other musical and cultural material, in a particular place and period of time, then it becomes apparent that – as the song's lyrics themselves put it – its 'inside is outside': it becomes a complex and eminently remarkable cultural production.

But the important question is: *So what?* This chapter will explore more deeply the matter of how we interpret any text, no matter how supposedly trivial, simple, or straightforward it is supposed to be. The purpose here is to show that the *way* we 'read' (experience and interpret) and relate to objects and practices is highly contextual and at least partially determined by powerful cultural forces. The *apparent* simplicity or 'obvious' straightforwardness of something does not necessarily mean that it *is* simple or straightforward. Rather, as the philosopher G. W. F. Hegel (1977: 35) put it: 'What is "familiarly known" is not properly known, just for the reason that it is "familiar" '. That is, just because something is *familiar* to us, it is a mistake to assume that therefore we *understand* it properly. According to Hegel, such an assumption is 'the commonest form of self-deception' (35). We think we know what is familiar to us. But we should take a second look.

For what do we overlook when we 'read' (listen to, experience) a text like this in standard or unquestioning ways? What *else* is going on – both within this song (or any text) and within our acts of interpretation? If Hegel has a point, then by reading this song attentively we will discover a lot, not only about the song itself, but also about culture's relations and effects, about the work of acts of interpretation, and also about deconstruction and cultural studies – about their *point* and *purpose*, their aims and the reasons for their existence. To do this, all we need do is break into the song.

Writing to read you

Although a song should not be reduced to its lyrics, perhaps the first thing that grabs the listener will be the chorus. We will consider the music itself shortly, but the first sequence of words that are likely to be remembered will be those of the chorus. This is because, after all, a chorus is a *repetition* or *reiteration*, and *reiteration* aids memory. The chorus of 'Writing to Reach You' repeats, again and again:

> I'm writing to reach you now but
> I might never reach you
> Only want to teach you
> About you
> But that's not you

These words, plus the languid guitar-based music – replete with a hint of melancholy in the singer's voice (or is that unintentional?) – would seem to suggest that the song must be 'about love'. But perhaps this is too quick a decision: a snap, reflex decision, made just because the song *sounds like* other songs that are also taken to be 'about love'. Our familiarity with a pool of so many not dissimilar sorts of songs makes it so easy – almost automatic – to assume that every time a singer refers to 'you' they must be addressing some kind of lover. However, a slightly closer examination of the lyrics reveals that this 'about love' interpretation is not at all that certain. (The question of how the *sound* of the music might relate to some 'meaning' is a different matter, that we will touch upon soon.) For although the repeated evocation of 'you' is a familiar convention or cliché in pop music, whose reiteration works to make 'Writing to Reach You' *sound like* a 'love song', in fact, exactly *who* the singer claims to be 'writing to reach' remains unclear. From start to finish, we are never told who 'you' is: we are actually left to work it out for ourselves. However, there is surprisingly little evidence on which to base any decision.

In fact, who this 'you' *is* is actually what Jacques Derrida called *undecidable*. We might *decide* that the 'you' addressed in the song is a particular character. But it is important to realise that, 'within' the song itself, there is little concrete evidence to support *any* decisive interpretation, either way. Any decision we make about the addressee (who this 'you' is) will be an *interpretation*, based on a lot of assumptions that we have brought to our reading of this text. Because of this, it is arguably the case that any interpretative decision we make here will say more about *us* than about the text itself. For, in 'Writing to Reach You', 'you' could be any of a potentially infinite range of addressees: a friend, a relative, a stranger, a past or present girlfriend or boyfriend, an 'ex', an estranged parent, family member, a teacher, a student, an (ex-)employer, a rival, someone the singer knows a terrible secret about, some hapless person the singer is stalking, his next victim, a nemesis or sworn enemy, a figment of his own imagination (an imagination which may or may not be deranged), and so on and so on. All of these and more interpretations are available to us, and any of them is as plausible as any other. *Which* interpretation are we going to choose, and on what grounds? This is a question that deconstruction insists upon. The importance of such a question is not 'merely theoretical'. It is ethical and political, as we will see.

Writing to text you

Before we get to ethics and politics, we should perhaps reiterate what it means to say that this song is a 'text'. It is a text in the sense that we are able to *read* it – to *interpret* it – just like a book. It is also a text in the sense that, like every everything else in culture, it has been constructed, 'stitched together' using material that has been used before. The word 'text' has the same root as the word 'textile', and it clearly has the same sense. So, texts are constructions stitched together using a shared cultural repository of references and allusions that are like threads, that can be stitched together. In this context (again, note that this word 'context' contains the same *textual* reference: 'con-*text*'), *familiar* words, *recognizable* chord progressions, beats and rhythms, etc., are present in the construction of this song. In other words, the song is effectively a recombination or reconstruction of different aspects of other songs. Musically and lyrically, metaphorically and literally, the song is made up of quotations, allusions, echoes, and reiterations of material previously used in other songs. One may not immediately notice this, yet it is a recognizable and fairly common experience to hear a song and to think, 'Isn't this a bit (or a lot) like this or that other song?'

The same goes for any text – which is to say, *anything* that is made and interpreted. This 'textual' character of all construction and interpretation is what led Jacques Derrida to point out that, in a fairly incontestable sense, 'there is nothing outside the text'. This statement has attracted much controversy, because people have taken it to mean that Derrida must be suggesting that 'reality doesn't exist' or that 'nothing is true' or that 'there is no reality, only books'. But Derrida is merely referring us to the way that there is no getting away from the fact that everything in some sense *refers* to other things (everything is *inter-textual*: between and across texts), and second, we have to '*read*' everything (just like a book, a literal text), to make sense of it. The *way* we interpret particular things is strongly cultural. It is decided more by our historical and cultural context than by 'necessity' (or indeed 'free will', if there is such a thing. We will return to this question in subsequent chapters).

As John Mowitt puts it, 'what enables a reading' – of a text, like this song – 'to "make sense"' reaches well into the institutional field of the social' (Mowitt 1992: 217). In other words, both the *way* that songs (or any other texts) are constructed and the *way* we interpret them will always be contextual. Styles of composing and manners of interpretation become 'instituted'. They are 'instituted' or 'institutional' – at least to the extent that 'institution' means 'first of all an established habit or custom . . . like the institution of Christmas or the habit of monogamy' (Connor 2003: 209).[1] So, what determines the way that a text will 'make sense' is 'what is made of it' in its encounter with institutions. As Wlad Godzich puts it, what is meant by institution 'is a social crucible, and it may be something as traditional as a church or as contemporary as a mode of watching television' (Godzich 1987: 156). Or in our case, a mode of listening to music. In other words, because there are familiar ways (institutions) of experiencing texts like this song, therefore interpretations that come to be accepted as standard, normal, acceptable or 'correct' will arise. (For example, the acceptance that 'Writing to Reach You' is a love song.)

Other possible interpretations will be excluded: interpretations that might be equally plausible will come to seem unusual, contrived, shocking, eccentric or just plain silly. (For example, the suggestion that 'Writing to Reach You' is about the sick blood lust of a psychopathic stalker.) What it is important to point out first is that between two such interpretations, there is often very little evidence to either support or refute either of them. The reasons why one reading can 'take hold' while another will be blotted out are, in Freud's term, '*overdetermined*': that is, there are *many reasons why* 'Writing to Reach You' *seems* like a love song, just as there are many historical reasons why Christmas or monogamy are so often taken to be 'wonderful' and not *exploitative* institutions (which they could quite easily be, if represented or interpreted according to different interpretative frameworks). The point is that none – or not all – of the reasons why a text is taken one way and not another are simply 'in' the text itself. As the lyrics of 'Writing to Reach You' themselves say, 'my inside is outside': the reasons we interpret any text in a particular way come from the 'outside', from a *context*. This is what Jacques Derrida calls 'an institution': and an institution, for Derrida, is 'not merely a few walls or some outer structures surrounding, protecting, guaranteeing or restricting the freedom of our work; it is also and already the structure of our interpretation' (Derrida 1992b: 22–3).

However, this does not mean that a text has nothing to it, or nothing going on within it. It is not all contextual. Rather, despite how apparently 'simple' or 'straightforward' any text might appear to be, there is in fact an awful lot going on within it, or running through it, recombined within it. What goes on within and comes out of songs is what might be called *material*. A whole network of traces of cultural references to other texts, genres, styles; a whole set of quotations, questions, concerns, and themes, can be identified within any text. Indeed, texts are so much the product of a cultural context that even the author or producer of a text will not necessarily be aware of even a fraction of the traces, themes and issues that can be discerned within 'their own' texts. So, this raises the question of the extent to which a text can be thought of as the '*property*' of one '*author*'. For, if there is inevitably more going on within it than they *need* be aware of or *can* be in control of, then 'their own' text has a life of its own, quite apart from anything its creator may have intended.

In other words, no matter what an author may say about 'their' text, this *will not* stop it meaning *other* things to *other* people – and, indeed, *even to the author themselves, at other times*. This, surely, is significant. One need only consider the episode of the TV show *Friends* in which Phoebe surprises herself by finding further interpretations for her own excruciatingly silly song, 'Smelly Cat', to see the truth of this, albeit in a comical form. 'My God, that song has *so* many levels!', she concludes with surprise and delight, some considerable time after having written 'Smelly Cat'. These new potential interpretations that she – the song's *author* – keeps discovering, demonstrate that even an author's original *intentions* do not limit, govern or determine what a text can mean, and also that meaning is *produced*, by encounters with a text, in acts of interpretation. So, despite what any author may claim about the 'true meaning' of their text, *their* interpretation does not mean that *other* interpretations are 'wrong' just because they may not conform to what an author claims to have intended. Meanings are *produced* within and out of interpretive encounters, rather than having simply been put into a text by an author.

When it comes to constructing meanings, there are innumerable different potential ways of seeing provided by potentially infinitely different contexts and positions. So it is really only if a reading ignores or overlooks major or salient details or cannot 'make sense' of a text coherently, that it might be said to be 'invalid'. But even then, this remains debatable. For the question of *what* is to be considered a 'major or salient detail' and what is to be deemed not relevant or not significant will always be an interminably debatable or undecidable matter. In fact, even every manner of interpreting can itself also be interpreted: the *way* one interprets things can be taken to suggest a lot about the reader or interpreter, about their position and perspective. When it comes to what guides our own interpretation, *our* 'inside is outside' too: *our* opinions, thought processes, values and judgements are in a sense led, put into us from outside – by our education, our history, our cultural context, and so on.

Contemporary cultural and political studies use the term 'hegemony' to name the dominant institutions that construct, impose and guide the norms, values and commonsense of a particular context. The term 'hegemony' comes from the Greek word '*hegemon*' which means 'leader', 'prince' or 'guide'. So, a 'hegemon' is what guides or leads; and dominant, normal or usual interpretations and values can be called 'hegemonic'. The term 'hegemony' therefore indicates what is in a sense *political* about all culture and all interpretation: namely, that culture and interpretations are *contingent* – changeable, determined by many complex factors, and that ultimately the interpretative decisions made within cultural contexts are therefore fundamentally *politically consequential*. This returns us to the point we arrived at before beginning this section: 'Which interpretation are we going to choose, and on what grounds?'; the question that deconstruction insists upon; the 'theoretical' question that is not 'merely theoretical', but is fundamentally ethical and political.

If the topic of 'interpretation' now seems interminable and unending, this is because – potentially, at least – it is! Interpretation, reading, potentially has no bounds, no start and no endpoint. There is nothing outside the text. Not even an author can fix or legislate about the 'correct' or 'final' interpretation of any text. Thousands of years of often violent and bloody arguments about how to interpret the Bible, for instance, clearly testify to the *interminability* and *changeability* of interpretation. Conflicts over the interpretation of the Bible also reveal the relationship between interpretation and institutional power, as well as between interpretation and potentially the entire structure of society. (The way that the Lutheran reinterpretation of the Bible radically undermined the power of the Catholic Church would be merely one of many potential examples here.) The main point to be emphasized here is something that Derrida (and Barthes) also deconstructed: namely, the belief that an author is supposedly the 'authority' on their own work. For, because a text is something constructed – stitched together – from so many aspects of culture, including untold references that *could* be spotted but that the author or producer was unaware or unconscious of themselves, therefore *texts always say more and other than what their author may have intended*. This is called the deconstruction of 'intentionality'. What texts are held to say is determined more by the *way* they are read. This has everything to do with a context – everything, then, to do with culture.

Reading to rewrite you

We may now appear to have travelled a long way from our supposed love song. But we are only now moving into a position to be able to read it. For to read this song – to *deconstruct* it – it is important first to acknowledge that both the writer (or creator) of a text *and* its 'readers' (this includes listeners, viewers, and anyone who experiences and interprets the text) will inevitably be less than conscious of all of the possible intertextual references that comprise it. In other words, both the writing and the reading of any text – no matter how supposedly simple it is taken to be – are processes that draw from huge numbers of traces of other songs and other cultural material. To try to read a text in the manner of a detective or genealogist, by trying to unearth all of its references and reveal all of the connections, will prove impossible. This is because the question quickly becomes: where do you stop? Where do you draw the line? Which connections is it reasonable to make, and which are unreasonable? And how to we decide where reasonable shades into unreasonable? How do you decide? In other words, once one starts to make connections to other texts, the intertextual traces and allusions spiral off in multiple, unpredictable, potentially boundless directions. It is almost as if – indeed *exactly* as if – the connections we *make* and the things we 'discover in' a text are actually being *produced by* the act of reading itself: as if reading is inevitably a kind of rewriting.

This is another of Jacques Derrida's arguments. Again, it has attracted a lot of controversy, because (again) it seems to state that there is no 'true' reading, and that there is 'no truth'. However, Derrida's point – the *point* of any deconstruction – is quite different: it begins from the observation that *every* interpretation will inevitably be *partial, provisional, incomplete, inventive* and *contingent*. It will support certain values and institutions at the expense of others. There will always be more to say about a text. The more you think about it, the harder you look, the more you 'find'. Every time you re-read it, it becomes like another text. There can be no final word. Something else could always be added, making the text appear different to the way it appeared before.

Derrida came up with a word associated with this process: *différance*. This is a combination of two French words, for to 'differ' and to 'defer'. *Différance* means to *differ* and to *defer*, at the same time (so to speak). And this is what happens when you read anything, when you try to announce the final word on any subject: there will always be more to say. Some *final* interpretation (what Derrida calls the 'transcendental signified') is a myth, it will never arrive: it is permanently deferred. (This is Derrida's first criticism of 'semiotics', or the 'science of signs'. That is, semiotics proposes that there are 'signifiers' (i.e., words, images, sounds, senses, etc.) and 'signifieds' (what these things 'mean'). But Derrida points out that you can never get to the end of the chain: every signifier does not point to a final signified (or meaning). It simply refers us to *another* signifier: there is always more to think and say about something. It never stops. This is what *différance* refers to: the endless slippage and movement of signification. In other words, if one arrived at a 'final signified', everything would cease.) Yet, we seem to reach *relatively* fixed and final interpretations all the time. 'Writing to Reach You' *seems* to be a love song. As Derrida might point out, this is because we have read it in a particular, *limited* way. We have *excluded* other possibilities. But there *are* other possible ways, each of which will 'see' different things 'in' the song (its 'inside is outside'). What else is there to see? What other plausible ways are there to read such an apparently trivial thing as a simple little pop song? And what is the significance of this potential reservoir of different interpretations residing in such a supposedly simple text? This is the question of deconstruction. The hypothesis of deconstruction is that because meanings and relations are *made*, even if they seem eternally fixed, they might possibly be *remade* – differently. This is the aim of deconstruction: not just to interpret the world, but to change it. Deconstruction proposes that it all relates to (re)reading as a kind of (re)writing.

I might never reach you

One way to begin (re)reading 'Writing to Reach You' is to note the abundant textual evidence that the task named in the title and the lyrics – 'writing to reach you' – appears to be fraught with anxiety and uncertainty. The lyrics repeat 'I'm writing to reach you now, *but* I might *never* reach you'. Furthermore, look at the phrase itself: 'I'm writing to reach you now' is actually quite a peculiar expression. It is certainly not a phrase that one would expect to hear in many English-speaking contexts. In the UK it would be much more usual to encounter an expression like 'I'm writing to you'. In the US it would be even shorter: 'I'm writing you'. But here, the title and the repeated expression is 'I'm writing *to reach* you'. The inclusion of '*to reach*' in an expression in which it wouldn't normally even occur creates an unusual emphasis, or indeed *stress*. So the song title and its main repeated refrain *stresses* the desire *to reach* you. This indicates an anxiety (a stress) about whether this is going to happen – whether my writing *is* going to reach you. As we saw in the Introduction, this aim (writing to reach you) and this immediate anxiety (I might *never* reach you) is not just particular to this song: it is indeed characteristic – even definitive – of cultural studies itself. This is because, as we saw in the Introduction, cultural studies seeks not just to *study* but actually to make some kind of a *difference* – to *intervene* in the world of culture that it studies. Like the persona who writes in the song, cultural studies is an agency that sets itself the task of 'writing to reach'. That is its declared intention. So what is the nature of this worry, anxiety or stress? Why is it that 'I might never reach you'?

One possibility is that, like anyone who has ever sent a letter that they have hoped will 'reach' someone else, somewhere else, a worry sometimes arises about the possibility that the letter might *not* arrive at its intended destination. The letter might get lost, and so not arrive at its intended destination. Jacques Derrida took the idea of the possibility of a letter, message, or a meaning 'going astray' as the starting point of the deconstruction of communication, causality and intentionality (Derrida 1987). We will return to this more fully shortly, as it is directly relevant both to understanding this song and to understanding deconstruction as well as culture and cultural studies: a letter 'might never reach' its intended destination.

Derrida uses the idea of a 'letter' possibly not arriving at its destination as one way of linking the themes and problems of 'intention' and 'communication' to 'causality' and to 'power' in general. In other words: what causes what to happen, and what happens if this goes 'awry'? John Mowitt explains that the possibility of any stable and supposedly 'transparent communication' entails a certain saturation of that context in 'disciplinary power': the extent to which communication or meaning is 'clear' and 'immediate' indicates the extent to which interlocutors are subjects of discipline; or, alternatively, the efficiency of a postal (i.e., communication/institutional) system is an indication of the extent to which a society is institutionally stabilized. (See Derrida (1987: 20, 177), Mowitt (1992) and Readings (1996: 182).)

But does the cause of the singer's worries lie in a concern about the reliability of the postal system? It would appear not. For we should notice too that the song obsesses about the likelihood that its addressee ('you') will actually *resist receiving this letter*. Indeed, the song could be said to be literally (lyrically) 'about' *agency*: first, 'my' agency or power (*'I'm* writing to reach you, I only *want to teach you*, about you'); second, the agency of the other ('you') – whoever that is. That is to say, the stress in the lyrical refrains suggests that if I am unable 'to reach you' and unable 'to teach you', this might well have something to do with your *resistance* to being reached and being taught *by me*. At the very least, the lyrics suggest that there are lots of things that could get in the way of smooth access to the other. In this sense, the song can plausibly be read as being 'about' *agency*: first, *my* agency (whoever 'I' am), my ability to 'reach you' and 'teach you, about you'. Second, *your* agency (whoever 'you' are), your distance and independence from me, your ability to resist me or elude me ('I might never reach you ... But that's not you'). And, third, of course, there is the whole range of institutional mechanisms and mediations, social institutions, conventions and cultural relations, that both link us and separate us, and can both enable and frustrate us in 'reaching' each other. So now, although the song may still be 'about love', it would certainly appear to be rather less than innocent, and rather more bound up in questions of *power* and a desire for *control*.

I only want to teach you ... about you

This returns us to the questions faced by cultural studies or any other project or agency that seeks to 'intervene'. For, even (perhaps especially) if it is about 'love', the song is also about 'agency', and accordingly it opens up onto the same sorts of ethical questions as does cultural studies in its loving or concerned aspirations to intervene. For, if someone wants to intervene in your life in some way, you might want to resist that intervention; so all of this opens onto the question of the justification and significance of any intervention in the life of 'the other' at all. Interestingly, both in the case of cultural studies and in the case of

'Writing to Reach You', this relates specifically to *education*. For the song declares: 'I *only* want to teach you'.

However, this is not just any old desire to educate. This is the desire 'to teach you *about you*'. This is the motivated desire to make someone other see something other *about themselves* – an aim which is as common and understandable as it is potentially domineering. Indeed, even if it is quite 'innocent' or 'well-intentioned', it is nevertheless irreducibly problematic: any desire to intervene into and 'change' the other is ethically problematic because it presents itself as 'knowing better' *and as qualified* to intervene. In other words, however well-intentioned, it amounts to a desire to dominate, alter, lead, or indeed to *hegemonize*.

Derrida once put this quite strongly: 'All culture is originally colonial', he proposed (Derrida 1998a: 39). In other words, the desire 'to teach you about you' – or my desire to 'improve' you – can be regarded as a central moment of cultural 'colonizing' or 'hegemonizing'. Not dissimilar to Derrida here, Henry A. Giroux (2000) once argued that *culture itself* could fundamentally be regarded as education. So, given the *contingency* of culture, the non-necessary and the changeable character of cultural beliefs, practices and values, therefore the ethical and political ramifications of this insight are vast. Who has the right to intervene, where, how, when and with what justification?

But that's not you

Of course, some might say that none of this is posed in the song at all – that it is not 'in' the song at all, that we are no longer dealing directly or properly with the song. And it is true, in claiming to draw all of this 'out of' this one song, there is clearly a strong element of 'reading *into* it'. There is a strong element of *adding* and even of *invention*. The deconstructive response to such criticisms is to question when reading might *ever* be free from 'reading into'. From a deconstructive point of view, 'meaning' is never 'found'. Meaning is always *established*. In other words, one lesson of deconstruction is that, even if we want to, we can never simply or directly deal with the 'thing in itself'. As Derrida explains:

> Certain people are always impatient to *access-the-things-themselves-directly-and-reach-right-away-without-waiting-the-true-content-of-the-urgent-and-serious-problems-that-face-us-all-etc.* Thus, they will no doubt judge an analysis that deploys this range of meanings and possible sentences playful, precious, and formal, indeed futile: 'Why be so slow and self-indulgent? Why these linguistic stages? Why not go right to the things themselves?'

Of course, one can share this impatience and nonetheless think, as I do, that not only do we gain nothing by immediately giving in to it, but that this lure has a history, interest, and a sort of *hypocritical* structure, and that one would always be better off to begin by acknowledging it by giving oneself the time for a detour and analysis. (Derrida 2002: 3–4)

In other words, one always relies on a *way* of encountering an object, a *way* of thinking about it and a *way* of approaching it. There are invariably many different possible ways to approach anything, and different approaches produce different 'results'. Therefore it can be argued that the way that we encounter anything is a significant matter, of primary importance. Indeed, according to Derrida, even *what* we 'experience' is determined by the ways in which what passes for reality is constructed as such. This refers to ways of perceiving, discriminating, constituting, identifying, and producing (or 'inventing') objects.

This may sound like a complex idea. Indeed it is. But to start to understand it, one need only consider the familiar complaint of every older generation in the face of every younger generation's new music: *'That's not music*! That's just *noise!'* In my own adolescence, I heard this a lot, first about punk (in the late 1970s) and then about acid house (in the late 1980s). Along the way I also encountered teachers who would solemnly explain that rap music was 'not actually music at all' because it lacked certain 'key' features 'necessarily' associated with 'proper' music, and so on. This points to the *contingency* of the very definition or identification of the musical 'object' as such: when does music shade into 'noise'? When does 'noise' become music? Is the definition in some way 'political'? (Note that punk was associated with anti-establishment 'anarchy' in the UK and rap came from the poor black ghetto 'underclass' in the USA.) This raises interesting questions about the *essence*, and the *borders*, *margins*, and *limits* of music. When does music *start*? With finger tapping? Humming? Talking? Shouting? Or with the use of one or more instruments? But is tapping a table 'playing' a musical instrument? In this case, the reciprocal question appears: where does music *end*? Something so variable, shifting, contingent, social, subjective and fundamentally 'performative' appears not to have an 'essence' at all, just as, at the same time, it could also be deemed to be 'essentially human' – both 'without essence' and 'essentially human' at the same time – an 'essence' indissolubly wedded to the notion of *reiteration*. As Gilbert and Pearson put it: 'Maróthy's notion of rhythm as "the basic principle of reality" seem[s] very close to Derrida's suggestion that iterability (repeatability) and spacing are constitutive elements of all experience' (1999: 60).

There are at least two relevant dimensions here. First, one's *ways* of encountering the world are institutional and conventional. Second, therefore, everything can be 'historicized' – understood in relation to the context within which it emerged. (It gets even more complex when you work out from this that any act of understanding and historicizing is itself inevitably institutional or conventional, and so may itself be historicized or contextualized.) This means that in no sense can my 'choice' of 'Writing to Reach You' have been neutral or arbitrary. Something about cultural studies and deconstruction has made me choose this object and read it in a particular way. In other words, although the very *coincidence* between this popular text and the popular subject of cultural studies may seem striking, arguably this 'coincidence' is not chance at all. It may in fact suggest one or more things about the contemporary context in which both this song and cultural studies co-exist. For, if they 'share' the same sorts of themes, words, problems, and aims, then they may well share the same *cause*. In short, this 'coincidence' may be *overdetermined* because of the historical context, rather than being pure chance. But, once again, there is more than one way to take this possibility.

The right side's on the left side

There are those who could interpret the 'shared' aspects both of a pop song like this and of the study of popular culture itself as evidence that both cultural studies and popular culture are 'symptoms' of the same cause. Such interpretations suspect that cultural studies and popular culture are symptomatic of the much-diagnosed 'postmodern condition'. The postmodern condition is said to be a product of 'the cultural logic of late capitalism', which has been characterized as an increasing *experience of life* as uncertainty, anxiety, confusion, and alienation from power.[2] As we have already seen, this is something that is certainly felt within 'politicized' scholarship like cultural studies. This is because *aspirations to intervene* in culture in effective ways often seem paralysed or warped because it is so unclear *what* our roles, goals, relationships, values, and connections could or should be.[3] This is the problem of postmodern politics (to which we will return in Chapter 4).

For, in the postmodern condition, it is said to be interminably uncertain precisely *what* our responsibilities, aims and orientations, should be. To put this in the terms used by Hardt and Negri in their influential book, *Empire* (2000), this is to suggest that *both* this pop song *and* politicized practices like cultural studies are what they call 'symptoms of passage' (2000: 137–59). Or, 'symptoms' of a confusing culture 'in deconstruction', in constant crisis, uncertainty and the permanent revolution caused by a rapacious and rampaging global capitalism. We will return to this argument much more fully in Chapter 4. But, basically, Hardt and Negri's argument (which is similar to that of many others) is that practices like deconstruction and cultural studies are so prevalent today precisely *because* the dominant 'cultural logic' and the contemporary dominant form of power *itself* is one which 'deconstructs' old, established institutions and states of affairs. In this perspective, both deconstruction and cultural studies *reflect* and *carry out* some of the work of capitalism. It is as if, unsure about how to intervene, the best that cultural studies can do is to 'deconstruct'; which, because deconstruction makes things even *more* undecidable, is like trying to dig your way out of a hole: i.e., counterproductive. (These are accusations which we will consider much more fully in the final chapters of this book.)

Of course, Hardt and Negri are merely reiterating one of Marx and Engels' insightful predictions about capitalism, that increasingly, 'All fixed, fast-frozen relations, with their train of ancient and venerable prejudices and opinions are swept away, all new-formed ones become antiquated before they can ossify. All that is solid melts into air, all that is sacred is profaned' (Marx and Engels 1967: 83). This inevitably leads to *anxiety* – arguably exactly the kind of anxiety dwelt upon both by texts such as 'Writing to Reach You' and those of deconstruction. So Hardt and Negri ultimately reject deconstruction, because it does not seem to get to the heart of the matter. Instead, they, like many others, propose a quick 'anticapitalism', which is at once understandable and yet what Derrida would characterize as 'impatient'. For, to reiterate, the deconstructive position of Derrida is one in which

> one can share this impatience and nonetheless think . . . that not only do we gain nothing by immediately giving in to it, but that this lure has a history, interest, and a sort of *hypocritical* structure, and that one would always be better off to begin by acknowledging it by giving oneself the time for a detour and analysis. (Derrida 2002: 3–4)

So even if we might suspect that there is something in this diagnosis of cultural studies, deconstruction and 'Writing to Reach You' as 'symptomatic' of capitalism, it remains important to remember that this merely returns us to the *fundamental* problem of *interpretation*. For how do we reach *any* reliable conclusion from an observation? In other words, we are back at the eternally returning, 'universal' question, *of interpretation itself*: or, *how to make sense of anything at all*; indeed, *how to work out how to interpret*. This is the problem of establishing the place and meaning of *any* object, no matter how supposedly 'trivial' (at least *potentially*) it is supposed to be.

Meaning(,) what?

As we have seen by looking into and out of 'Writing to Reach You': to determine meanings is to make a decision. In a sense, this is both to police a 'crisis' (*undecidability*) and to give oneself meaning (if 'I' decide something, then 'my' decision says a lot about 'me', too). Meanings are *established*. Thus, the question of how to make sense of 'Writing to Reach You' *and* how to make sense of 'ourselves', our contemporary context (and everything else for that matter), now appear to be different versions of *the same question*.

To understand what this means or how this makes sense, it is helpful to recall that, as John Mowitt puts it, 'what enables [any] reading [any interpretation] to "make sense" reaches well into the institutional field of the social' (1992: 217). So any act of 'sense-making' is never an isolated or 'unconnected' activity. If I decide/interpret a punk song by Crass as being 'just noise', this can be taken to say something about my own values, ways of reading, and investments; just as it does if I make sense of it as being a valid and understandable protest against musical conventions themselves. Examples here are potentially infinite. For, in fact, *all* interpretations derive from and impact upon the 'institutional' context in which they occur. As such, the *way* we make sense of things is more than 'merely academic'. *Sense-making* is both 'forceful' and 'consequential'.

What is often regarded as 'mere interpretation' actually plays a large part in stabilizing and ordering contexts, institutions, disciplines, fields, and practices. The *way* that we interpret is a cultural and political matter. This is one reason Derrida insisted upon and defended *complexity*, refused the idea of simplicity, unity, identity or univocity, and insisted also upon the need for intimate and interminable *reading*: Derrida regarded deconstructive re-reading/rewriting as a kind of *politically consequential non-conformity*:

> I consider it an act of cultural resistance to pay homage publicly to a difficult form of thought, discourse, or writing, one which does not submit easily to normalization by the media, by academics, or by publishers, one which rebels against the restoration currently underway, against the philosophical or theoretical neo-conformism in general (let us not even mention literature) that flattens and levels everything around us .... (Derrida 1998b: 45–6)

The point is not to be 'interpretively passive'. The point is that *re*interpretation can *re*frame, *re*constitute, and draw into question and crisis the *way* we interpret, the way we objectify objects, the way we perceive our values, orientations, and our presuppositions about *what* 'truth', 'proper action' or 'proper practice' should be. Sense doesn't just 'happen': sense is *made*. And 'common sense' is always a powerful political force.

So, how are we to *make* sense, and in the name of what? Any reading, every interpretation, *cannot but* overlook something; it will *privilege* certain questions and features whilst downplaying and even forcefully excluding others. This is why deconstruction argues that the 'most ethical' answer to the question of *how* to orientate one's efforts and *how* to act must involve *putting in question* the established limits of the existing interpretations perpetuated by institutions and taken-for-granted readings. Deconstruction does this 'in the name of the other': the excluded, the subordinated, the silenced. As John Protevi explains:

> But *why* deconstruct . . . ? In the name of what does deconstruction release its forces of rupture? Derrida answers: in the name of justice. Derrida's political physics looks like a 'might makes right' position. And in one sense indeed it is, in the sense that might makes *droit*, that is, the fact that positive law can be analysed in terms of social power. Derrida reminds us, however, that might does not make justice. Instead, 'Force of law' tell[s] us that 'deconstruction is justice'. Institutions, or sets of positive laws [*droits*], are deconstructible because they are not justice. Deconstruction is justice, that is, 'deconstruction is already engaged by this infinite demand of justice'. Deconstruction also finds its 'force, its movement or its motivation' in the 'always unsatisfied appeal' to justice . . . . We might want to say here that *democracy* is the future, the 'to come' of this transformation, intensifying itself to the point where instituted bodies that muffle or distort the calls of others are overflowed and reinscribed in other contexts. Deconstruction is democratic justice, responding to the calls from all others. (Protevi 2001: 69–70)

What is meant by 'the other' is always in question, but it strongly relates to looking for whatever has been 'excluded' by current institutions and the status quo maintained by stable institutional forms. In other words, deconstructive readings look for whatever is *not* present, not *yet* present or not yet *allowed* to be present.

But that's not you

So, what 'others' do we have here? Who or what are the others in or of 'Writing to Reach You'? And what are the 'other' interpretations? As we have already seen, 'Writing to Reach You' begins:

> Every day I wake up and it's Sunday
> Whatever's in my eye won't go away
> The Radio is playing all the usual
> And what's a Wonderwall anyway
> Because my inside is outside
> My right side's on the left side
> 'Cause I'm writing to reach you now but
> I might never reach you
> Only want to teach you
> About you
> But that's not you

Let us re-read this. As well as now appearing uncannily reminiscent of the cultural studies desire to intervene in the world ('to reach you . . . to teach you'), these lyrics also explicitly (even if unintentionally) express some key notions and themes of deconstruction. First we have the inside/outside issue ('My inside is outside'), which we have already encountered. Then comes the uncertainty of destination or reception, the anxiety about 'agency' ('I might never reach you'). This is linked to the desire to 'teach'. (The song desires to reach, to teach, perchance to intervene.) But then it hits an enigmatic non-sequitur: 'But that's not you'. What does this mean? At this precise moment in the song we reach an abyssal lyrical and musical interruption – a hiatus, a pause – with the utterance 'But that's not you'. It runs: 'I'm writing to reach you now but / I might never reach you / Only want to teach you / About you / *But that's not you*'. And then the song pauses. This is the culmination of the first section of the song. A lyrical and musical interruption – a pause – a caesura – and a lament – at the point of a strange and unexpected realisation: 'But *that's* not *you*'. What are we to make of this peculiar twist in which *the lyrics themselves actually 'undecide' the addressee?* For at first they seemed to be treating a known and unambiguous 'you'. But at this moment they stop and announce 'But that's not you'. This interrupts and disorganizes *everything*. For, after everything we have heard about 'you', it turns out that *that's not you*.

There are at least six possible ways to interpret this. Firstly: a 'you' that is 'not you' might be someone imagined – either fictional, or someone onto whom a lot has been projected; so, either a fantasy, or unknowable, or inscrutable. Or secondly: it might be a 'you' that confounds representation – perhaps in the way that God is held to be 'beyond representation' in some sorts of theological doctrine (such as 'negative theology', in which however we try to represent God, it will be inadequate, because God exceeds our mortal minds, words and images). Or thirdly: 'you' might be absent, or even dead, an image. Or fourthly: 'you' might be multiple (a crowd, group, or community). 'You' might never have existed. Or fifthly: 'you' might not exist as such prior to being addressed (perhaps in the way that one 'becomes' something by being addressed, as in: you may never have thought 'It Could Be You' who might win the lottery, or that 'Your Country Needs You', right until the moment of seeing an advert which puts the idea into your head to become a gambler or a soldier). Or sixthly: 'you' might no longer even be the 'same' after being 'reached', in the sense that to 'reach' someone, to 'teach' them, is inevitably to *alter* them in some regard. (As Heisenberg's famous 'Uncertainty Principle' demonstrates, sometimes 'the instrument of measure ... alters the object in the very process of measurement' (Weber 1987: xi)).

These two latter formulations are examples of a process that Louis Althusser called 'interpellation'. 'Inter' means across, between, outside, and 'appeller' means to call; hence 'interpellation' means to be called (up/into) something from elsewhere, from outside. In fact, Travis' line, 'my inside is outside', illustrates an aspect of 'interpellation', however unintentionally. In Althusser's example, when I realise that the policeman shouting 'Hey, you there!' is addressing *me*, I simultaneously recognize lots of different things: I recognize the policeman *as* a policeman, and therefore I recognize my own status as being *subject* to the law; hence, I am literally 'called' into place, 'recognizing' myself as someone in a particular social and political 'place'. So, recognizing oneself in and answering any call amounts to some form of 'being interpellated'. Thus, *education* is arguably profoundly interpellatory. For, in education, subjects are addressed, taught, and if they have been 'reached' successfully, they will have to a greater or lesser extent *changed*. This is the explicit declared intention of the song: 'I *only* want to teach you / *about you*'.

This is the desire expressed in the lyrics. It is also the cause of all the 'problems' they express. Musically too, the song also devolves or 'turns' around this moment. And note the ambiguity of the word 'only': 'only' means either *solely* or *merely*. So therefore, 'only' means both 'merely, slightly, insignificantly, trivially' *and* 'exclusively, entirely, absolutely, singularly, obsessively'. So, it is equally possible to read this singular desire ('I only want to teach you') as something 'mere' *or* as something absolute and single-minded. Is it that 'I *merely* want to teach you (and that's no big deal)' or 'I *solely* want to teach you (and I am single-mindedly obsessed with doing so)'? This deepens the sense of what is potentially most troubling in 'Writing to Reach You': the unusual but plausible interpretation in which the problem hinges on the fact that *if* 'my' call to you is successful, then you would thereby be changed.

Whichever way we approach it, the situation described by the lyrics seems fundamentally paradoxical. For the 'interventional' aspiration of the song is troubled by the possibility that it might 'miss', in two equally bizarre senses. First, the worry seems to be that the effort to 'reach you' might be *resisted*, and hence fail. A second worry seems to be that the letter might actually reach, teach, succeed, *and hence fail* . . . because the 'you' that has been successfully 'reached' is no longer the 'same' *because* 'you' have been reached. So, perhaps what seems to be dramatized here is the theme of the justification of any intervention, of any kind. Reading this text makes it all – *whatever* we think the motivation of the singer or songwriter to be, whether we decide that it is love, desire, philanthropy, care, concern, compassion, fascination, obsession, etc. – start to seem like *a will to power*, bound up in a kind of *appropriative desire* – of wanting to control, to dominate, or indeed to 'colonize' the other (Derrida 1998a: 23–4). The problem in this relation to 'the other' is the ethical ambiguity of wanting to *breach* the other (*any* 'other' at all). The song seems to acknowledge this, and to 'recoil' from it.

But is this reading too much into the song? Maybe. Definitely maybe. This is almost definitely the case if we still cling to the idea that a song must mean what its author may or may not have 'intended'. But we could not *know* this with any certainty. Indeed, neither could the text's author: any author is just another reader, exactly like Phoebe in relation to her song 'Smelly Cat'. Nevertheless, let's merely note the possibility of these 'far-fetched' readings and return to the incontestable observation that 'Writing to Reach You' is clearly about wanting 'to teach you about you'. It states as much, repeatedly. But we can't seem to decide who this 'you' is. Is there any other potential 'you' in the song that it may perhaps be 'writing to reach'?

What's a Wonderwall anyway?

As well as our undecidable 'you', there is one other slightly less enigmatic agency explicitly invoked in the song. We are told: 'The Radio keeps playing all the usual / And what's a Wonderwall anyway'.

In 1999, the 'usual' 'Wonderwall' that radios did in fact 'keep playing' was Oasis' 1995 'classic' of that name (Oasis 1995). 'Wonderwall' begins:

> Today is gonna be the day
> That they're gonna throw it back to you
> By now you should've somehow
> Realised what you gotta do
> I don't believe that anybody
> Feels the way I do about you now
>
> Backbeat the word is on the street
> That the fire in your heart is out
> I'm sure you've heard it all before
> But you never really had a doubt
> I don't believe that anybody feels
> The way I do about you now
>
> And all the roads we have to walk are winding
> And all the lights that lead us there are blinding
> There are many things that I would
> Like to say to you
> But I don't know how
>
> Because maybe
> You're gonna be the one that saves me?
> And after all/You're my wonderwall

Listening to the two songs, one after the other, it becomes immediately apparent that as well as the lyrical intertextual reference that 'Writing to Reach You' makes with Oasis' 'Wonderwall', *musically* it *almost entirely* refers to, draws upon and from, retraces, and is embroiled with Oasis' 'Wonderwall'. They are lyrically, musically, technologically, ideologically, culturally, politically and ethically entwined in ways that far exceed the simple intertextuality of key, tempo, speed, chord structure, genre, etc. They share, exchange, or trade in many similar things. And again, through no necessary fault of its own, 'Wonderwall' rather easily tends to be taken as a simple text that is more or less self-evidently – obviously – 'about love'.

Now, even without the explicit lyrical reference to 'Wonderwall' ('What's a Wonderwall anyway?'), once the songs are heard consecutively, it becomes obvious that the Travis and Oasis songs are in a kind of 'dialogue'. This is one aspect of what is meant by the theoretical term *'discourse'*: texts are in a kind of intertextual 'conversation' with each other. As such, 'Wonderwall' could be taken as a kind of *call* to which 'Writing to Reach You' is a *response*.

This is relevant because – again, despite initial appearances, and *all* protestations to the contrary – the 'about-love' interpretation is even *less* tenable for 'Wonderwall' than for 'Writing to Reach You'. If 'Wonderwall' *is* about love, or about an allegedly 'loving' relation to another, it is perhaps a *more* problematic expression of this than 'Writing to Reach You', as we will see. But it too is far from necessarily 'about love'. (Indeed, the extent to which this *is* ever the way it is made sense of says an awful lot about the invisible and inaudible way meanings and values are imposed from without – 'by us', yet not *properly 'by us'*; the way that we make sense 'ourselves', but without our conscious selves necessarily being involved in the process at all. For we clearly internalize codes, conventions and ways of *making* texts say what they *do not* necessarily say (Macheray 1978: 82). To take this a step further, this has led some theorists to propose that this demonstrates the profound extent to which not only *objects* but also *subjects* arise as the products of institutionally mediated power (Mowitt 1992: 36–7).) So, what's 'Wonderwall' *about*? What's the story, morning glory? Well, what is literally *said* in 'Wonderwall' is actually about as close as you could possibly get to *nothing at all*. It is entirely aphoristic, and accordingly *only calls for* interpretation – interpretation that is generally not forthcoming, when we are 'interpretively passive' and accept the 'about-love-or-something' non- or under-interpretation (see Mowitt 2002: 176). For, lyrically, 'Wonderwall' is more easily 'about' subordination, masculinity, stupidity, refusal to think, subjugation, being working class, religious, or 'certain', *and* manipulation of the other. It is certainly about refusal, denial, and exclusion. But of what?

Well, firstly, 'Wonderwall' appears to be about a refusal to think, or rather, to engage. 'There are many things that I would like to say to you, but I don't know how'. This claim is a masculinist bastion if ever there was one: it is the trope of so many 'manly' moments, from love's young tortured teenager, to the 'properly' conversationally sedulous working-class bloke and beyond. This *apparently* self-deprecating conversational technique (is actually self-aggrandizing and patronizing and) serves as a well-worn way to *avoid* serious or potentially troubling engagement with the other – and with the self. The difference between Travis and Oasis here is significant. For the Travis song seems to carry the sense of doubt, uncertainty and anxiety. This in a sense strikes up an interrogative self-analysis. (The song seems highly introspective and self-reflective.) In short, the desire encountered in the Travis song immediately causes it to confront and apparently to recoil from its own potentially sordid and domineering foundation.

Contrast this with Oasis' 'Wonderwall', a song which seems so much more strident, *'anthemic'* (as music compilation packaging started calling it in about the year 2000) and strenuously hopeful (if only because of a tone of voice) – as in: we're *just simply going* to walk many winding roads, through blinding light, because *maybe* you're *going to be* the one that *saves* me – this song *refuses* doubt and questioning, *affirming* a hope, a belief. This is so even though nothing other than an unspecified messianic telos ('the one that saves me': the messiah, to come (*telos*)) and an unspecified but vaguely intense feeling underpins this determination. (And for Derrida, the work of questioning is always potentially less violent and more ethical than certainty: 'The best liberation from violence is a certain putting into question, which makes the search for an *archia* tremble ... .. *an-archy* ... .' (Derrida 1978: 141).)

Here, the difference between them appears to consist in the fact that the subject of 'Wonderwall' is actually *blinded* by the very thing that lights the way ('all the lights that lead us there are blinding'), whereas the subject of 'Writing to Reach You' only has something in his eye ('whatever's in my eye won't go away'). Now, both facilitate the kind of reading that Paul de Man proposed, about the inevitability of some kind of *blind spot* at the heart of every insight.[4] What is significant here is that Oasis' oxymoronic *blinding guiding light* smacks of the blind fervour of religious zeal. Travis' own 'something in my eye' more readily connotes the Biblical 'mote in thine own eye' that we are enjoined to 'look to' before judging: being aware that we all have an impediment disturbing our perspective and causing discomfort, seems to constitute a significant difference between Travis and Oasis. Not only does the persona of the Travis song have a mote in his eye, he also *knows* it. He nevertheless wants rid of the obstacle. Indeed, he evidently wants *certainty*. In short, he *wants to* 'realise' what Oasis state that they *know*, claiming that they 'realise what you've gotta do', and 'what you're not to do'. Oasis *assert* that there *is* definite certainty: a proper course of action (roads we *have* to walk); proper things to do and not to do; proper action in physical and public reality – on the street (where the word is). And the word on the street is that 'the fire in your heart is out'. So they call for faith so that passion, conviction and certainty in and of certain actions might return.

You're my wonderwall

It seems that *certainty* is what 'Writing to Reach You' is crying out for. This is what 'Wonderwall' has. The fact that the Travis song is in many ways the *thematic antithesis* of 'Wonderwall' suggests that what

'Wonderwall' 'has' represents the impossible desire, remaining forever unacceptable and inaccessible in 'Writing to Reach You'. The obverse of this is that 'Writing to Reach You' stages the 'repressed' or 'excluded' of 'Wonderwall' – what psychoanalytic theorists like Slavoj Žižek might call its unacceptable 'disavowed underside'. But does this sound too far-fetched now? Too indulgently theoretical? Maybe. Definitely maybe. *But*: none of this *needs* to be read as 'theoretical': Oasis are (or were, at this time, during the 90s) *explicitly too 'hard'*, too 'street', too Promethean, and too (authentic) pseudo-working-class (fetishistic) to countenance some wishy-washy middle-class Travis- or Rousseau-like solitary indoors Sunday-morning radio-listening letter-writing you-obsessed reflection. (The 'street'-ness – the references to conversations *on* the street – of Oasis' song, contrasted with Travis' indoors-ness and introspection, adds this class accent (as does, of course, each singer's accent, tone, sneering 'nasality', or timbre); just as the 'religious' element of 'Wonderwall' is massively enhanced by the troubled-agnostic figure traced in Travis' song: For Travis, every day is 'Sunday', the addressee is 'home for Christmas', etc.: Travis seem to have a symptomatic obsession with religion, as if hounded or haunted by, nostalgic for or desirous of, the comforting certainty of *faith* – a faith that they can never hold.) There are definite class and gender issues here. (A discussion of Oasis' manifest aggression towards their erstwhile contemporaries, the clearly college-educated, stylistically dynamic (and hence, presumably, 'inauthentic'), musicians, Blur, would be revealing here. Oasis famously performed a version of Blur's 'Park Life' at a Brit Awards show, changing the refrain 'park life' to 'crap life'. All of the Gallaghers' aggressions come as attacks on the outrageousness of the 'softness' of non-'working-class' bands.) But have I *still* stretched my reading 'too far'? Is what I've got in *my* eye now causing blindness, discomfort? Am I beginning to invent the other, too illegitimately? Let's retreat to firmer ground.

It is at least the case that the Travis song comes in response to and in a sense *transforms* 'Wonderwall'. To *read* 'Writing to Reach You' anything like adequately, one cannot overlook the intertextual connection to 'Wonderwall'. It might be possible to dismiss the reference as casual, irrelevant, or signifying nothing. But, the question is, what grounds are there for such a dismissal? Doing so seems more shaky than exploring the connection. For the connection is strong. Moreover, the intertextual relationship does not simply flow in one direction. The Travis song is a 'reading' of – a 'response' to – 'Wonderwall', one that forever changes the way 'Wonderwall' itself is to be approached or understood. This is because of the unavoidability of what Derrida calls *différance*: constant deferral, transformation of meaning, intertextual displacement and development.

What Travis does to Oasis is much the same as what Oasis' 'Wonderwall' did to a 1960s film of the same name. For after asking the question ('what *is* a Wonderwall anyway?') begged by Oasis' invocation of this mysterious messianic thing, you find two plausible answers: first, 'Wonderwall' is a soundtrack album by George Harrison for, second, a film called *Wonderwall*. Oasis' single revived interest in both: the relatively obscure and accordingly nerdy/cliquey Harrison album, and the largely forgotten film. Original copies (note the oxymoronic character of the term 'original copies') of the album soared even further in value, or at least, in price. The film was re-released. It is now dubbed both a 'cult classic' and an intertextual precedent for *Austin Powers*. In much the same way, Mike Flowers' almost instant cover version of Oasis' 'Wonderwall' and Travis' invocation of it in their song helped consolidate the 'Britpop' canonization of 'Wonderwall' and Harrison's album and the film, *and* the canonization or consolidation of the genre or identity or thing 'Britpop'. (A similar 'afterwardsness' attends the film and the band Kula Shaker, who provided music for elements of the re-release. And so on. This is the hegemonic logic of teleiopoetic call-and-response conjuration conjured up by Derrida in *Specters of Marx* and *Politics of Friendship* (Derrida 1994, 1997b).) Appropriately, perhaps, given the potentially violent subjugatory sexual or interpersonal politics of these songs, the film *Wonderwall* deals with a man who becomes a voyeur, spying through holes in his wall into the sexually and psychedelically fascinating life of a model – hence, the 'wonder wall' is a deeply problematic agency. After having been forgotten (written off) the film was reclaimed, value added, and even substantially reconstituted through the intervention or agency of psychobabblistic film commentary (in which any pseudo-Lacanian likeness to Hitchcock seems automatically to equal 'value'). Such is canon-formation – always in the post.

In many ways, popular culture can be understood as an *intertextual* process of unending *discourse* because of the unavoidability of *différance*. The question is: does any of this have any bearing on *our* identities?

Ghost Dog: The Deconstruction of Identity

I'll be giving birth to centaurs one day.

Friedrich Nietzsche

there is no such thing as x, there is nothing but x

Jacques Derrida (1998a: 21)

I want to transform into a Tyrannosaurus Rex

The surprise pop hit of Christmas and New Year 2005–06 in the UK was 'JCB Song' by the band Nizlopi (2005).[1] Everything about it can be regarded as surprising. Released by a hitherto largely unknown band, 'JCB Song' reached number 2 in the BBC Radio One singles chart. Commentators deemed this event particularly remarkable because the song was successful apparently without very much in the way of a marketing campaign or commercial apparatus behind it. So its success seemed to relate largely to its inherent appeal. The question of where the source of such an appeal might lie would seem difficult to ascertain, given that musically the song is simple and unremarkable, lyrically it is childlike (it is sung by an adult but in the first person of a five-year-old boy), and it is arguably neither particularly innovative, trailblazing, nor indeed even of its moment (nor even fashionably out of step with its moment). Indeed, it could not really be said to enact the norms or fantasies either of most popular music of the time or those of most typical 'Christmas' hits in particular.

Nevertheless, what the song lacked in terms of fashionableness it more than made up for in terms of what might be called a certain recognizable 'fantasy structure', a 'fantasy structure' that is played out in the mode of nostalgia. Predominantly played in melancholic minor chords, except during the final jubilant refrains, 'JCB Song' tells the story of a short journey. It is unclear whether the account is of only *one* moment within *one* journey, or whether it is a memory of regular childhood journeys merged into one emotional recollection. Either way, the song is about a momentous moment: one small step in a subjective process that is also a giant leap in terms of a relation to reality. The song begins, slowly:

> Well I'm rumbling in this JCB
> I'm five years old and my dad's a giant sitting beside me
> And the engine rattles my bum like berserk
> While we're singing 'Don't forget your shovel if you want to go
>   to work'
> My dad's probably had a bloody hard day
> But he's being good fun and bubbling and joking away
> And the procession of cars stuck behind
> Are getting all impatient and angry but we don't mind

Then the chorus – nostalgic in the extreme for most adults, even those whose fathers didn't drive a big yellow digger:

> We're holding up the bypass, oh
> Me and my dad having a top laugh, oh-whoa
> I'm sitting on the toolbox, oh
> And I'm so glad I'm not in school boss
> I'm so glad I'm not in school, oh no

Even the literally 'so glad' and therefore putatively 'happy' lyrics of the chorus are coloured melancholy by the minor mood of the music and the timbre of the singer's voice. Again, the fact that the singer is an adult using the words of himself as (if) a five year old reinforces the nostalgia. The emphatic negative 'oh no' after the assertion of being 'glad' not to be in school introduces the likelihood that the five year old, who we soon learn is called Luke, is particularly happy *here* also because *here* is *not there*. The next verse explains why this might be:

> And we pull over to let the cars pass
> And pull off again, speeding by this summer green grass
> And we're like giants up here in our big yellow digger
> Like Zoids or Transformers or maybe even bigger
> And I want to transform into a Tyrannosaurus Rex
> And eat up all the bullies and the teachers and their pets

And I'll tell all my mates 'my dad's BA Baracus
Only with a JCB and Bruce Lee's nunchakus'

So, the problem is 'the bullies and the teachers and their pets'. One more chorus, this time lengthened by an extended reflection on being 'glad I'm not in school, boss / So glad I'm not in school'; and then the song stops. A caesura. A musical and lyrical hiatus. Key change. Tempo change – like a gear change. And a jubilant final section, beginning with an unaccompanied, upbeat chant ('Said, I'm Luke, I'm five and my dad's Bruce Lee / Drives me round in his JCB'), shortly joined by upbeat and up-tempo skiffle drumming, and then the rest of the musical accompaniment (guitar plus a lively new aspect offered by a banjo). The victory chant continues, merging straight into one more upbeat rendition of the chorus, then one more series of jubilant chants, and then the song ends.

Arguably, then, the song recounts – actually, *performs* – something like a Freudian 'screen memory': a childhood event, scene, scenario or detail recalled with incredibly strong affective intensity and clarity in adulthood. For Freud, screen memories serve the function of defending against, by blotting out or covering over, pain or trauma. As we have just heard, these lyrics not only recount but actually perform, in the present tense, this child's extreme happiness at being *here*, in the JCB, with dad. But this intensely declared happiness is not just because dad is being a 'top laugh'. The lyrics also reveal that the *other* reason for the intensity of the happiness is directly related to an anxiety and an unhappiness elsewhere (another scene of interpellation). This other scene is school, with 'all the bullies and the teachers and their pets'. So, the scenario set out in this song is basically the working out of a psychic drama. School is where the problem lies. School is the big problem.

This is his big problem: the big bullies, the big teachers and their pets. His dad is also big. JCBs are big. Being in the JCB with his dad makes him part of the 'good big' and also equals womblike sanctuary, safety. This is all rendered through the trope of *size*. The song is at first all about size. Largeness first stands for invulnerability. First of all, 'dad is a giant sitting beside me'. Then, next, *'we're* like giants up here in our big yellow digger'. Then a transformation into the fantasy (or 'phantasy') world expressed in the lexicon of a child: to Luke, thanks to being 'up here' in the digger, it feels like they are 'like Zoids or Transformers or maybe even bigger'. ('Phantasy' is the (usually British) spelling for a psychoanalytic notion often used in cultural theory. This spelling is sometimes preferred to 'fantasy' in order to indicate that the word is being used in a precise technical sense, rather than in a casual or everyday sense.) And this feels good. Size matters. This is because of what you can do with it: if he could only *be* a Tyrannosaurus Rex, then he really could 'eat up all the bullies and the teachers and their pets'.

This is why Luke declares that he wants to 'transform into a Tyrannosaurus Rex'. It is a fantasy solution to a practical problem. A Tyrannosaurus Rex would be able to 'eat up all the bullies and the teachers and their pets'. But even the five year old knows that such a thing is an impossible fantasy, and that there remains a harsh reality to be lived in, a real problem to be faced. Then the penny starts to drop, he starts to come to a realisation, solves a riddle, and makes a decision – and the song consists effectively in the performative moment of the making of this decision, the realisation of a solution: seeing as he can't really do the impossible phantasmatic transformation into the ultimate 'big daddy', the Tyrant King, Tyrannosaurus Rex, he'll do the next best thing: 'I'll *tell* all my mates my dad's BA Baracus / Only with a JCB and Bruce Lee's nunchakus'. He's nearly there. The full solution appears only in the final jubilant section of the song, after the hiatus, the long pause. The jubilant, upbeat quality of this final section performs the relief and release of realising how to solve the problem, 'in reality'.

It all happens very quickly and economically in the song: competing interpellations, the journey from the relief of escape and enclosure, to fantasy, on to phantasmatic wish fulfilment, and finally to a pragmatic decision. First, imaginary fantasy: 'we're like giants up here in our big yellow digger / Like Zoids or transformers or maybe even bigger'. Second, phantasmatic wish fulfilment: 'And I want to transform into a Tyrannosaurus Rex / And eat up all the bullies and the teachers and their pets'. Third, decision: a compromise formation, but a way to incorporate fantasy into reality in a way that modifies (an orientation within) reality: 'And I'll tell all my mates 'my dad's BA Baracus / Only with a JCB and Bruce Lee's nunchakus'. After one final reiteration of the present situation – one that is entirely Oedipally overdetermined and overcoded – 'we're holding up the bypass / Me and my dad having a top laugh . . . And I'm so glad I'm not in school boss', the song pauses, as if in the moment of impact, the full realisation of the solution, and then becomes jubilant, a chant, almost a mantra: the riddle is solved: to sort out the bullies and the teachers and their pets, Luke will actually go one better than telling all his mates that his dad's BA Baracus with a JCB and Bruce Lee's nunchakus – better than this, he will tell them, as he repeats, chants, jubilantly, over and over again, that his dad *is* Bruce Lee. His refrain – 'I said I'm Luke, I'm five and my dad's Bruce Lee / Drives me round in his JCB. / I'm Luke, I'm five and my dad's Bruce Lee / Drives me round in his JCB' – equals a solution, a resolution, a dissolution of the problem; an orientation in the face of the problem, a way to defend against the pain it formerly caused. And this solution involves a profound and multi-layered identification, at once real and phantasmatic, personal and social; a victory for a hybrid of the competing interpellations. For his dad is to him already as good as Bruce Lee, invincible, invulnerable. (Recall: 'the procession of cars stuck behind / Are getting all impatient and angry *but we don't mind*'. This is important: others become angry, yet dad remains unruffled.) To tell his mates that his dad *is* Bruce Lee will serve many functions. If the gamble pays off, this will be the way that he can retain them as allies, recruiting them to his fantasy, as well as opening up a space for subsequently *handling* the bullies and teachers and teachers' pets. His mates may even be able to understand the 'real' reason why if and when he is attacked he need not even fight back or get his dad to fight for him: it is because – in the manner of all good martial arts and action-hero movies – he would certainly win – he has always already won. *Obviously*. His dad's Bruce Lee: how could you *ever* beat that? Indeed, to quote Bruce Lee's famous reply to a bully in *Enter the Dragon*, Luke has just learned 'the art of fighting without fighting'.

What seems particularly pertinent here is the way that a *fantasy* becomes part of *reality*. It clearly illustrates the way that 'Bruce Lee' entered the consciousness of many people: entirely as what postmodernists called a *simulation*, or what psychoanalytical cultural theory calls *fantasy* (or, sometimes, *phantasy*). It is important to consider the significance of the ways in which material from the 'outside', from popular culture, can *supplement* our identity – *intervening* in our identity, offering new points of identification, and playing complex roles in the construction of identity. But it is not just humans who are said to have an identity. Cultural practices are often held to have a stable identity. Moreover, *cultures 'themselves'* are often said to have an identity. There are debates about 'national identities', 'cultural identities', 'regional identities', 'class identity', 'ethnic identity', 'gender identity', and so on. There are also said to be distinct sorts of 'Eastern' and 'Western' cultural identity. However, by looking at the way that Bruce Lee intervened in so many realms of popular culture in so many international contexts, this chapter seeks to short-circuit many of the assumptions about not only subjective identity but also the supposed identity of cultural practices and indeed cultures themselves.

Enter the fantasy

The entrance of the dragon, Bruce Lee, was primarily of the order of what postmodernists called the simulacrum, or indeed fantasy (phantasy). Now, fantasy and physical reality cannot be divorced, given that even 'in what makes reality seem original to us, fantasy is at work' (Mowitt 2002: 143). So, fantasies are both social and psychic, frustrating the possibility of a simple or sharp distinction between objective and subjective, and indeed between the inside and the outside of the subject. Fantasies *supplement* the subject: they are an element from *outside* that is also at the heart of the *inside* (Derrida 1981, 1998a). According to Judith Butler, fantasies are dynamically linked with what she calls 'social norms', values and practices that 'are variously lived as psychic reality' (2000: 154). Crucial here is the word 'variously'. For identity is always performative: one is not born a subject, one becomes one, and there is no essential 'being' behind this doing, effecting, and becoming. In Butler's words: 'Norms are not only embodied . . . , but embodiment is itself a mode of interpretation, not always conscious, which subjects normativity itself to an iterable temporality' (2000: 152). Reciprocally, therefore: 'Norms are not static entities, but [are] incorporated and interpreted features of existence that are sustained by the idealizations furnished by fantasy' (152).

In this respect, the fantasy offered by Bruce Lee is in one regard *perfectly normal*: as a point of identification, the heroic (phallic) subjectivity that Lee offers is straightforwardly patriarchal or heteronormative. Yet, in another respect, this particular fantasy was a *reinterpretation* of such norms, a very particular *reiteration*: a reiteration that did not simply *repeat*, but at a particular historical moment actually *transformed* norms, fantasies and discourses (Derrida 1982: 318; Butler 2000: 152). In other words, Bruce Lee intervened in the fantasy life, discourses and lived practices of international culture in a particularly remarkable way. This not only enables us to grasp the sense in which it is possible to 'place the body-in-cultivation in a specific historical context' and see how 'the individual, physical body both registers and reveals the . . . sociopolitical landscape' (Xu 1999: 961). It also helps to clarify the connections and complex 'communications' between signification, semiosis, identification, desire, bodily practice, and the discursive shifts of the movements of history. It enables us to engage with questions of identity, both personal and cultural, in a tangential but enlightening way.

The historical moment of the 'entrance' of Bruce Lee can be regarded as the tail end of the first generation of a counterculture whose seeds had been sown in World War Two, which emerged in the 1950s and proliferated in the 1960s (Heath and Potter 2005). The 'mechanics' of this entrance – or rather of the transformations that it precipitated – can again be approached most concisely in terms of 'interpellation' (Althusser 1971; Mowitt 2002).[2] For what this simulation of physical prowess 'did' was to simply call out to viewers: *'Hey, you! This could be you! All you need to do is train in kung fu, and you too can become (closer to) invincible!'* Thus, the event of Bruce Lee is first that of a simulacrum conjuring up a fantasy. But what it explicitly called out for was a very physical encounter with the bizarre new/ancient Oriental thing called kung fu. In itself, this new 'lifestyle option' can be viewed as culturally significant. As one biographer of Bruce Lee reflects, it was entirely down to Bruce Lee films that he, 'an Englishman ... was able to begin learning a Chinese martial art from a Welshman' (Thomas 2002: xii). This is both *subjectively* and *socio-culturally* significant. For, subjectively, such training leads to the 'transformation of the novice, the change of his or her muscles, attention patterns, motor control, neurological systems, emotional reactions, interaction patterns, top-down self-management techniques, and other anatomical changes' (Downey 2006). Moreover, as Lee's biographer claims, Bruce Lee's intervention was one which apparently 'bridged cultures, revolutionized the martial arts, taught a fierce philosophy of individualism, ... and remade the image of the Asian man in the West' (Thomas 2002: xi).

We will need to consider further these claims about 'culture bridging' in due course. For, this is where the question of *personal* identity merges into that of *cultural* identity. But, first, we should note the link between *the simulation*, the *subjective fantasy* and *bodily practice*. As many have argued in different ways, bodily practices are what literally make us, and they are what can remake and change us. According to Bourdieu:

> The body believes in what it plays at: it weeps if it mimes grief. It does not represent what it performs, it does not memorize the past, it *enacts* the past, bringing it back to life. What is 'learned by body' is not something that one has, like knowledge that can be brandished, but something that one is. (Bourdieu 1990: 73)

Ultimately, what the event of Bruce Lee precipitated was a virtually global popular encounter with kung fu. Or, more correctly: *with the fantasy of kung fu*. For, as is well known, the 'Shaolin kung fu' of *Enter the Dragon* bears little if any relation to the actual 'kung fu' that may have been practised in any of the Shaolin monasteries or elsewhere. Indeed, even the term 'kung fu' itself is acknowledged to be a misnomer, and moreover a *Western imposition*, the synecdochic transformation of a general term for 'effort' or 'discipline' into the name for 'all Chinese martial practices'. But to the accusation of the lack of 'reality' of Lee's cinematic kung fu, disciples of Bruce Lee themselves made plain that what is seen in Bruce Lee films is *knowingly* spectacular and *deliberately* hyperbolic choreography. What Bruce Lee 'really practised', they continue, was *his own brand* of innovative and trailblazing fighting: *jeet kune do* (Inosanto 1980). The 'real practice' of *jeet kune do* is considered by fans and disciples as proving Lee's combative genius, and as evidence of his having *sublated and surpassed* 'traditional' martial arts by inventing a superior hybrid. Of course, this hybrid identity is construed by others as merely reflecting the fact that Lee never actually completed any formal training syllabus in any one martial art (Smith 1999). Either way, the point here is that, in any and every eventuality, what Bruce Lee offered was *a fantasy* of kung fu.[3]

Of course, Bruce Lee is certainly not responsible for *the* fantasies of kung fu. Indeed the Shaolin warrior monk that he plays in *Enter the Dragon* is a mythical figure of dubious historical status, which antedates Bruce Lee. Historians have always cast doubt on the origin myth of Shaolin kung fu, in which wandering monk Bodhidharma introduced Zen meditation to the unfit monks of the Shaolin Temple and, as a result of the physical discipline required for Zen meditation, also inadvertently invented kung fu. Historians also consistently challenge the subsequent myths of the improbable physical abilities of Shaolin monks. For instance, Kennedy and Guo suggest that the myths of Shaolin were 'largely created in two books': a popular turn-of-the-century novel, *The Travels of Lao Ts'an* (Liu 2005), and an apparently totally fabricated and instantly debunked 1915 training manual entitled *Secrets of Shaolin Boxing* (Unknown 1971; Kennedy and Guo 2005: 70–1). Henning points out that the origins of the Shaolin myth 'cannot be traced back earlier than its appearance in the popular novel, *The Travels of Lao Ts'an*, written between 1904 and 1907, and there is no indication that it was ever part of an earlier oral tradition' (quoted in Kennedy and Guo 2005: 70). *Secrets of Shaolin Boxing* contained accounts of improbable/impossible processes and end results of Shaolin training. It was instantly debunked by the leading contemporary martial arts historians of the time (Tang Hao and Xu Je Dong). Yet this book in particular had a significant impact. For, even though quickly exposed, 'unfortunately [it] became popularly accepted as a key source for Chinese martial arts history enthusiasts, and its pernicious influence has permeated literature on the subject to this day' (Henning quoted in Kennedy and Guo 2005: 70–1).

Pernicious influence? Utter fantasy? Little relation to reality? Maybe. But, in terms of physical practice, *nothing about this distance from 'reality' really matters*. The 'Western' encounter with kung fu may have been an encounter with a fantasy, but it was a cinematically mediated fantasy which *called primarily to the imagination in ways leading to new practices and new transformations of mind and body*. Those subjects called, hailed or interpellated into position did not feel any need to distinguish, discriminate between or indeed even know about or care about the vast internal, external, political, cultural, ideological and cosmological differences between, say (Chinese) 'kung fu' and (Japanese) 'Samurai'. Historical truth is by-the-by here. What *matters* is a fantasy about physicality. As the lyrics to the song 'Strange Eyes' on the soundtrack to the film *Ghost Dog: The Way of the Samurai* put it:

> ... Let's go steal a coup
> and practice kung fu on the roof next to the pigeon coup
> and keep the stack like the big boy Cadillac
> Forty eight tracks, got my voice on the DAT
> Samurai style for them niggas actin' wild

(Japanese) 'Samurai' did not practise (Chinese) 'kung fu'. But this need not matter in the hybrid spaces of popular cultural practice. The fantasy here happily connects elements, ideas and practices that hitherto have been geographically, culturally, politically and otherwise distinct but that can be appropriated as emotionally, semiotically or affectively intimate or identical. It evidently does not matter to The Wu Tang Clan, Sunz of Man, or others who have been 'inspired' by Shaolin and Samurai myths, nor indeed, as Stephen Chan puts it, to the millions 'worldwide who practice [certain] martial arts and believe that these arts have antique and spiritual values beyond what passes for history and cultural value in the constructions of their own cultures' (Chan 2000: 69).

However, Chan's argument is slightly different. For him, myths of 'ancientness' *do* matter. But they still need not be related to any 'truth'. Of course, this is a controversial view. As he explains, 'a UNESCO survey of the world's martial arts' that he was involved with had to be abandoned 'because the various authors could not agree on the nature of the project' (Chan 2000: 69). They could not agree on a workable definition or delimitation of their shared object of study, 'the martial arts'. In other words, this putatively obvious and stable identity ('martial arts') itself immediately turned out to be a rather deceptive signifier, something that can be drastically differently construed depending on one's standpoint. The UNESCO group was unable to agree on *how* to conceive of the martial arts: how to contextualize them, how to establish and assess their limits, their 'essence', and indeed how to ascertain what constitutes their 'reality'. They were especially unable to agree on whether the 'reality' of martial arts should include or exclude the myths, fictions, fantasies, and fabrications that constantly blur the edges and muddy the waters of this subject.

Chan's area in the UNESCO study was to have been Japanese martial arts. On this topic, he offered the view that 'mythology plays a large role in the internationalization of Japanese martial arts' (Chan 2000: 69). However, this proposition, he observes, 'seemed particularly contentious' to the other authors; who, holding different notions of what constitutes the reality of a martial art (and implicitly therefore a different notion of what constitutes reality as such), wanted to downplay or ignore myth. According to Chan, however, 'little progress seem[s] possible in separating histories from mythologies', when it comes to martial arts (2000: 69). This is because in their formation, dissemination and proliferation, myth demonstrably often trumps history. We might merely consider the explosive impact that a film like *Enter the Dragon* had on the fantasy life and martial arts practice the world over to see Chan's point: namely that when it comes to the martial arts, myths and fictions can be far more influential and orientating than truth.

As mentioned, it is widely known that the choreography seen in *Enter the Dragon* has little direct relation with the 'real' Shaolin kung fu that the character of Lee in *Enter the Dragon* 'would really' have practised; just as the 'celluloid' cinematic choreography in Bruce Lee films had little in common with the interdisciplinary bricolage of different approaches to combat actually developed and taught by Bruce Lee himself. (Both of these points are regularly clarified in the extensive literature on Bruce Lee. One good discussion can be found in Inosanto (1980).) But it was not just Hollywood and Hong Kong cinema that unleashed 'myth' by manipulating fantasies worldwide, conjuring up spurious yet putatively ancient arts (now called 'wu shu' and 'wire fu': namely, the dramatic athletic kung fu of film choreography). Chan himself lists a whole host of Japanese martial arts that are often deliberately represented, exported and consumed as if they are authentically ancient warrior arts, but which are in fact relatively recent, often 20th-century inventions.

His point is simple: what he calls 'mythologizing' more than muddies the waters of reality: it actually constitutes it. As he points out, there are millions 'worldwide who practice the Japanese martial arts and believe that these arts have antique and spiritual values beyond what passes for history and cultural value in the constructions of their own cultures' (Chan 2000: 71). Indeed, he suggests that those who have bought into many of the myths of Japanese martial arts have in a sense been duped by the cynical ministrations of what he calls 'the Japanese cultural authorities'. These, he argues, have deliberately worked as the 'editor of mythologies' (71) in order to make Japanese culture into a commodified artefact. This mythology is commodified in myriad ways: both 'in fact' (through the production of new 'ancient' martial arts) and 'in fiction' (through film, literature and other such productions). These artefacts are produced and consumed as if authentically ancient culture, when in actual fact they have been deliberately produced: conjured up, exported (re)imported and consumed.

The way of identifying

Given this complexity, the question of how to define, delimit and make sense of the identity of 'martial arts' inevitably encounters the problem that 'martial arts' exceed simple categorization. So, in order to try to adequately or exhaustively approach and to attempt to understand *fully* what martial arts 'are', one would have to cover a vast interdisciplinary breadth. For to grasp the 'whole truth' would seem to demand mastery of realms as diverse as archival research, history and historiography, translation, comparative philosophy, culture and religion, psychology, sociology, political economy, marketing, aesthetics, politics, cinematography, and popular culture, to say the least. Given the multiple dimensions of 'martial arts', the question is: what sort of a paradigm could possibly hope to be adequate to the task? The problem here is that any approach will privilege certain dimensions and subordinate, be ignorant of or otherwise exclude others. Every version of 'interdisciplinarity' cannot but be led by a *particular* disciplinary preference, and so will differ from other possible versions of interdisciplinarity, and therefore produce different (often utterly contradictory forms of) knowledge. Omniscience is not possible. Every account or manner of 'understanding' will be enabled and limited by a particular partial bias.

Given Chan's argument about the ensnarement of Japanese martial arts within a commodifying process, then, from a Marxian perspective, such as that recently (re)developed by the influential Slovenian cultural critic, Slavoj Žižek, Chan's observations might immediately be taken to be the start and end-point – the *culmination* – of an argument. That is, from the perspective of Marxian economism (the view that the dictates of the economy determine in the last instance the beliefs and practices of culture and society), then the point about commodification may be regarded as the last word on the matter – as if proving that culture has been decisively colonized by capitalism, and that all beliefs and practices are ideological (because they are commodified myths that we have bought into), and that cultural practices like martial arts are simply a kind of modern 'opium of the masses'.

However, Chan himself is evidently neither a Žižekian nor any other kind of economic reductionist, as he does not propound such a view.

On the contrary, he contends that whilst, on the one hand, one cannot simply or uncritically believe all of their 'history' ('Much of what seems to be antique is not' (2000: 71)), on the other hand, martial arts cannot just be viewed as commodity pure and simple. In this respect, he gives examples of martial arts in 'African shanty townships', where karate has become 'an alternative source of values and cultural shelter to those shut outside the wealth of the Western economy, and who have been divorced by location and the exigencies of poverty from a deep indigenous sense of culture' (70). Here, there is something strongly 'cultural', indeed even *political* about martial arts. They become bound up in identity, in identification, in organic community, and can be construed as taking on a place and significance that is far from simply consumerist.

So, an overly economistic or reductively Marxian take on culture as capitalist-colonized seems limited. What alternative paradigms are available that we might bring to bear on the identity of martial arts? Any answer will already be biased and therefore in every way 'partial'. But, from the point of view of the contemporary interdisciplinary arts and humanities, there is 'obviously' much that is psychoanalysable in martial arts (given the palpable presence of masculine desire, fantasy and fear, as well as cultural projections about 'the other', for instance). There is also much that seems to cry out for Foucauldian styles of analysis of the body in discourses and relations of power – not forgetting post-Foucauldian and postcolonial considerations of 'orientalist discourse'. Martial arts phenomena demand historicization, too, of course. But even if something universal is discerned in the impetus to begin martial arts training – perhaps the sense of 'lack' that might precipitate in the subjective desire to become powerful or invincible – such a symptom can of course be treated in many manners: reiterated or recurring symptoms need not necessarily be approached through Freudian or Lacanian optics. There are vastly differing ways to interpret even a universal or general feature, from the most positivist, behaviourist or empirical paradigms to the most postmodern or deconstructive. In terms of the latter, for instance, Jacques Derrida's ruminations on death and its relation to questions of responsibility (in *The Gift of Death* (1995)) almost call out be applied to a consideration of the martial arts. Or, to put this another way: surely consideration of the martial arts should be accorded the dignity and seriousness of philosophy, especially insofar as they seem so closely related to questions of death, desire, responsibility, discipline, mortality and purpose. As Derrida argues at one point:

> ... a concept of *discipline* covers a number of senses ...: that of training, first of all, or exercise, the idea of the work necessary to maintain control over orgiastic mystery .... Secondly, this discipline is also philosophy, or the

dialectic, to the extent that it can be taught, precisely as a discipline, at the same time exoteric and esoteric; as well as that of the exercise that consists in learning to die in order to attain the new immortality, ... the care taken with death, the exercise of death, the 'practicing (for) death' that Socrates speaks of in the *Phaedo*. (Derrida 1995: 12)

The way of hybridity

To regard Derrida or even Socrates as Samurai/martial theorists may not turn out to be as preposterous as it might at first sound. For many things come in response to knowledge of the inevitability of death and the problem of responsibility: philosophy and discipline are but two. This comes to light, for instance, in the film *Ghost Dog: The Way of The Samurai* (Dir. Jim Jarmusch 1999), where the similarities between Hegel's master-and-slave dialectic (which proposes that identities are constructed through identifications and relations with significant others (Hegel 1977)) and Tsunetomo Yamamoto's *Hagakure: The Book of the Samurai* (1979) are in a sense played out in exemplary fashion. For, in this film, the life of a black youth (Forrest Whittaker) is saved by a Mafia gangster who shoots two white teenagers who were beating him apparently to death. The youth subsequently devotes his life to the 'Samurai code' and hence to martial arts training. As an adult, he becomes 'Ghost Dog', an enigmatic assassin, who works exclusively, invisibly and anonymously for his gangster saviour. Yet, despite this, he has attained a paradoxical and improbable status within the local ghetto community: Ghost Dog is both *well-known* and well-respected in the community (moreover, by gangs and rappers of all colours – a surely impossible fantasy), and yet he remains secretive, *unknown* and often effectively invisible. Throughout the film, Ghost Dog regularly refers to *Hagakure: The Way of the Samurai*, and quotations from this book intersperse the film and (especially) the soundtrack. These enlighten viewers and listeners as to precisely what the 'Samurai code' may be or entail. Thus, the film directly proposes that through an encounter with a *translated* Japanese text, and through *fantasy* (identification with a fantasy social position – one *cannot be* a Samurai outside of feudal Japanese social relations), and the *discipline* of martial arts, a black youth from violent ghetto streets can 'become', to all intents and purposes, a ninja. The ninja were a legendary/mythological clan of Samurai forced into hiding and turned assassin. This is precisely what Ghost Dog has become.

So, the film proposes that identity is formed through a complex and hybrid process of identification – processes of fantasy and self-invention, processes of *'seeing oneself as'* this or that. The premise of the film is best illustrated in a scene in which Ghost Dog encounters two redneck hunters who have illegally killed a black bear and who seem more than prepared to do exactly the same thing to the very palpably black man who is questioning them about their actions:

Hunter:	You see, there aren't too many of these big black fuckers left around here, so when you get a good, clear shot at it, you sure as hell take it.
Ghost Dog:	That's why you shoot them, 'cause there's not that many left?
Hunter:	There ain't all that many coloured people round here, neither.
Ghost Dog:	In ancient cultures, bears were considered equal with men.
Hunter:	This ain't no ancient culture, mister.
	[Hunter reaches for a gun. Ghost Dog shoots both hunters]
Ghost Dog:	Sometimes it is.

So, the controversial proposition of *Ghost Dog* is this: *sometimes, at least, this culture can be or could become another culture – and even when the only 'direct access' to or 'contact with' that other culture is 'translated', 'mediated', 'packaged' and reliant upon a (phantasmatic) identification with a fantasy.* This is a significant idea, which both plays and erases the notion of 'identity'. For if identity is not fixed but transformable, then it is not 'one': there may be no identity as such. Such films, as points of identification, may constitute very peculiar kinds of cross-cultural 'encounters' engendering unexpected transformations in 'identities' of all orders. What is the status of these texts as 'cultural encounters'?

Cultural identity or cross-cultural hybridity

Although it is possible to construct what J. J. Clarke calls a long list of 'the West's intellectual encounters with Eastern thought', it remains equally valid and necessary to 'ask philosophical questions about the very possibility of crossing linguistic and cultural boundaries, and about the adequacy of inter-cultural communication, and [to] reflect on the nature of the hermeneutical process which . . . is at the heart of these encounters' (Clarke 1997: 181). But, what is at the heart of *simulated* 'East–West encounters', so many of which are initiated or organized by (fantasies about) martial arts?

On the one hand, there have been some extremely positive interpretations of any kind of Western interest in other cultures. This perspective was exemplified by Alan Watts who, writing in the 1950s, at the cutting edge of the emerging counterculture, began his enormously influential book, *The Way of Zen* (1957), by remarking on the 'extraordinary growth of interest in Zen Buddhism' and in East Asian culture and thought in the West: 'this interest has increased so much that it seems to be becoming a considerable force in the intellectual and artistic world of the West'. He suggests that the reason for its growth 'is concerned, no doubt, with the prevalent enthusiasm for Japanese culture which is one of the constructive results of the late war' (Watts 1957: 9). In other words, Watts suggests, because what the counterculture (of beatniks, peaceniks, hippies and New Agers) was *counter to* was the *Western* culture which went to war with the East, therefore the counterculture chose to adore the East. The post-Second World War and then the Vietnam War countercultural turns away from faith in Western institutions (and away from *institutions* and *the West per se*) and towards the 'mystical' and the Oriental were doubtless bolstered by the sense that (as Watts discusses at the very beginning of Chapter 1 of *The Way of Zen*) 'Zen Buddhism is a way and a view of life which does not belong to any of the formal categories of modern Western thought', and particularly because it 'is not a religion or philosophy; it is not a psychology or a type of science', but rather 'an example of what is known in India and China as a "way of liberation", and is similar in this respect to Taoism, Vedanta, and Yoga' (1957: 23). Hence, Watts offers an exemplary version of the belief in the emancipatory cultural implications of the Western interest in changing the 'formal categories of modern Western thought' through an encounter with Eastern thought.

On the other hand, though, and writing at roughly the same time as Watts, another philosopher offers a very different interpretation of the effects on a culture's 'identity' of cross-cultural encounters between East and West. This can be seen in the Socratic-style (question and answer) text, 'A Dialogue on Language: Between a Japanese and an Inquirer' (1971), first published in 1958, in which the philosopher Martin Heidegger portrays himself as an inestimable 'Inquirer' being interviewed by an adoring Japanese guest. The Inquirer (Heidegger) suggests that perhaps 'a true encounter [between East Asian and] European existence is still not taking place, in spite of all assimilations and intermixtures' (1971: 3). Indeed, 'Perhaps [a true encounter] cannot take place' (3), suggests the Inquirer's Japanese guest. The 'Dialogue on Language' proposes that this is because the modern world is *dominated* by what it calls American-led 'Europeanization'. This has resulted in the 'modern technicalization and industrialization of every continent', from which 'there would seem to be no escape any longer' (3). So, the fundamental problem with this process is said to be that 'technicalization and industrialization' brings with it what the 'Dialogue' calls the dominance of

'European conceptual systems' (3); in other words, the technologically determined dominance of 'European' ways of thinking that threaten to extinguish all true cultural alterity – namely, everything 'Eastern'.

The question of the role that film plays in all of this raises its head in Heidegger's philosophical text. Indeed, the 'Dialogue' actually proposes that the most culturally problematic aspects of 'European conceptual systems' are most present in the synthesis of 'Western' aesthetics and 'Western' technics that is *the film camera*. 'Perhaps you have seen' Kurosawa's film, *Rashomon* (1950), says Heidegger's Japanese guest. 'Fortunately, yes; unfortunately, only once', responds the Inquirer: 'I believed that I was experiencing the enchantment of the Japanese world, the enchantment that carries us away into the mysterious. And so I do not understand why you offer just this film as an example of an all-consuming Europeanization' (Heidegger 1971: 16). But, for Heidegger's imaginary Japanese visitor, the film *Rashomon* is an index of Europeanization because as soon as something – *anything* – is captured on camera, it is committed to what Heidegger's 'Dialogue' calls a fully Western 'objectness' (17), an 'objectness' that is apparently alien to all things essentially East Asian.

This 'objectness' refers to the dividing up of the world into subject and object relationships, which involves ways of thinking, conventions of representation and conventions of *reading* representations that are irreducibly European. Hence, says Heidegger's Japanese guest, this means that 'seen from the point of view of our Eastasian existence, the technical world which sweeps us along must confine itself to surface matters, and . . . that . . .'. He tails off, unable to complete his thought. The Inquirer finds the right words for him and suggests: ' . . . that for this reason alone a true encounter with European existence is still not taking place, in spite of all assimilations and intermixtures'. Indeed: 'Perhaps cannot take place', concludes the Japanese, perhaps glumly (Heidegger 1971: 3).

And here's the rub: the 'Dialogue on Language' suggests that even for the Japanese *to be able to conceptualize* any of this 'I need precisely your [European] language' (Heidegger 1971: 16). So, under the Western gaze, 'the Japanese world is captured and imprisoned . . . in the objectness of photography, and is in fact especially framed for photography' (16). Furthermore, 'photographic objectification is already a consequence of the ever wider outreach of Europeanization' (17). Ultimately, therefore, proposes the 'Dialogue', 'the Eastasian world, and the technical-aesthetic product of the film industry, are incompatible' (16). Thus, suggests Stella Sandford, Heidegger's 'Dialogue on Language' is fundamentally 'preoccupied with the issue of the possibility or impossibility of an East–West dialogue', and that while scholars like

Reinhard May (1996) have read it 'as proof both of Heidegger's indebtedness to East Asian sources and his attempts to cover this over', she concludes that:

> it is equally plausibly read as a statement of Heidegger's belief in the fundamental and incommensurable *differences* between philosophical traditions, and of the extraordinary difficulty, if not the outright impossibility, of a true dialogue, despite the best intentions of the interlocutors. (Sandford 2003: 14)

So these are, in effect, the two opposing interpretations of the question of cultural identity. On the one hand, cultural identity is to be regarded as incomplete, mutable, transformable. On the other hand, cultural identities are to be regarded as *incommunicable*. This is, in a sense, the Heideggerian position. Yet there is a paradoxical element to Heidegger's text. This can be observed in the ambivalence of the speaking position of the Japanese guest, when it comes to the possibility of an authentic encounter of any kind. For, again speaking of *Rashomon*, the dialogue runs:

J: We Japanese consider the presentation frequently too realistic, for example in the duelling scenes.

I: But are there not also subdued gestures?

J: Inconspicuities of this kind flow abundantly and hardly noticeable to a European observer. I recall a hand resting on another person, in which there is concentrated a contact that remains infinitely remote from any touch, something that may not even be called gesture any longer in the sense in which I understand your usage. For this hand is suffused and borne by a call calling from afar and calling still farther onward, because stillness has brought it. (Heidegger 1971: 16)

The claim here and elsewhere throughout the 'Dialogue' is that this trace of an authenticity which allegedly *escapes* Western technics, aesthetics, and Western forms of reading (ways of seeing) *nevertheless escapes from the film*. We know this because we have just been informed that it *remains perceptible* to this Japanese viewer. Much could be made of this paradoxical claim, which boils down to the tautology: the imperceptible, untranslatable, ungraspable thing is nevertheless there, perceptible and graspable, albeit only to those who are able to perceive it thanks to their enculturation. For, in fact, one could say this about *anything 'in' any text at all*.

So, rather than the Heideggerian conclusion (of *you can't see what I can because you're essentially different*), J. J. Clarke proposes that 'arguments which apply to [the impossibility of] communication between Europe and China apply with equal force, not only between modern and mediaeval Europe, but also between any two individuals attempting to communicate with one another' (1997: 182). In this case, then, what needs to be enquired into is the *nature of* the 'possibility of crossing linguistic and cultural boundaries' and the *nature* of 'inter-cultural communication' (181). As we have seen, as Clarke has argued, it is important to 'reflect on the nature of the hermeneutical process which . . . is at the heart of these encounters' (181). But, it is equally important to ask: *is* 'the hermeneutical process' necessarily 'at the heart' of intercultural (or any other) encounters? Or rather, is 'interpretation' all there is? Our opening consideration of the *fantasy structure* of identifications might lead us to doubt this.

For, *what is there* in such films as *Enter the Dragon* or *Ghost Dog*? These encounters are not 'authentic', of course. But nor are they 'hermeneutical' in the dry intellectual (logocentric) sense. Rather, the encounters are with fantasies. At their heart is not an intellectual 'hermeneutical process'. And even though all that is 'there' is obviously a semiotic simulacrum which may be deemed anything from patriarchal to orientalist to fetishistic to commodifying, the *spectacle* of Bruce Lee *calls to the body directly*, in precisely the same way music calls to the body directly (Gilbert and Pearson 1999: 44–7; Mowitt 2002). For, when music starts playing, it is not a 'hermeneutical process' that makes your feet start tapping and your body start moving. In exactly the same way, Bruce Lee is *music to the eyes*.[4]

What is really communicated by the simulation?

A key instance of this occurs at the end of the most spectacular fight sequence of *Enter the Dragon*: Bruce Lee's prolonged battle with hordes of the evil Han's guards. During this frenetic and protracted fight, Lee systematically and artfully bests wave after wave of assailants with bare hands and a range of traditional martial arts weapons. The fight ends abruptly when Lee runs into a vault and thick steel doors slam down all around him, preventing his exit. Instantly realising there is nowhere to go, the sweating and bleeding Bruce Lee simply sits straight down, crosses his legs, hangs his nunchakus around his neck, and pulls his heels onto his thighs, adopting the classic meditative lotus position. Now, *this* is what 'enters' with *Enter the Dragon*. In the instant switch

from amazing fighting to meditative calm sitting, a clear and unequivocal connection is made between 'mystical', 'spiritual' alterity and the
disciplined body. And *this* is a *rearticulation* – a *rewiring*, a *rearrangement* –
of the usual connections made in Western discourses, in which the spiritual is (or was) *opposed* to the physical, or the body. In *Enter the Dragon*,
audiences are repeatedly shown an entirely novel transformation of this
traditional relation.

Of course, this rearticulation is not at first entirely intelligible. This
is perhaps why the film needs to introduce it several times, in different
ways: to reiterate it rapidly in the first three scenes, and intermittently
throughout the film. Thus, before introducing plot, before any characterization, and in fact, before anything else, the beginning of *Enter the
Dragon* aims at delivering the lesson of this new equation. Perhaps most
clearly, scene three is entirely pedagogical: the young Shaolin monk
kung fu master, Lee (Bruce Lee) gives a lesson to a student, a young
boy called Lau. This scene actually begins with Lee meeting the British
agent, Mr Braithwaite, in a garden. They are served tea. 'This is very
pleasant', observes Mr Braithwaite. But before they can get down to the
business of discussing the mission that Braithwaite has for Lee (the mission that will drive the plot), they are interrupted. A young boy turns
up. Seeing him, Lee says:

Lee: It's Lau's time.
    Braithwaite [slightly confused]: . . . . Yes, of course . . .
    [*Lee walks over to Lau. They bow to each other*]
Lee: Kick me . . . . Kick me. [*Lau throws a kick*] What was that? An exhi-
    bition? We need [*pointing to his head*] emotional content. Try
    again . . . . [*Lau kicks again*] I said emotional content. Not anger!
    Now try again! With *me*! [*Lau throws two more kicks, causing Lee to
    respond, moving and blocking*] That's it! How did it feel to you?
Lau: Let me think.
Lee: [*slaps Lau's head*] Don't think! *Feel!* It is like a finger pointing away
    to the moon. [*slaps Lau's head*] Don't concentrate on the finger or
    you will miss all that heavenly glory. Do you understand?
Lau: [*smiles, nods, bows*]
Lee: [*Slaps the back of Lau's head*] Never take your eyes off your oppo-
    nent, even when you bow . . . . [*Lau bows again, very cautiously*]
    That's it.

The camera cuts back to Braithwaite, who is smiling and nodding (*our*)
approval. For, even though this lesson has delayed his delivery of the
plot, all is forgiven: this peculiar lesson feels much more important.
But what has been learned? Certainly nothing *logocentric*, or to do with

words, statements or meanings. So what is 'it'? In fact, in the preceding scenes, we have already been shown what Lee 'knows'. Immediately before this pedagogical scene, for instance, we have seen Lee with his own teacher. This is the second scene of the film. The first scene saw Lee winning a ceremonial – apparently graduation-like – fight in the Shaolin Temple. After passing that physical test, Lee goes to his own teacher (as if for the *viva voce*):

> [*Lee approaches an elderly monk on a path*]
> Lee: [*bowing*] Teacher?
> Teacher: Hmm. I see your talents have gone beyond the mere physical level. Your skills are now at the point of spiritual insight. I have several questions. What is the highest technique you hope to achieve?
> Lee: To have no technique.
> Teacher: Very good. What are your thoughts when facing an opponent?
> Lee: There is no opponent.
> Teacher: And why is that?
> Lee: Because the word 'I' does not exist.
> Teacher: So. Continue.
> Lee: A good fight should be like a small play, *but* played seriously. A good martial artist does not become tense, but ready. Not thinking, yet not dreaming: ready for whatever may come. When the opponent expands, I contract; when he contracts, I expand; and when there is an opportunity, I do not hit: [*he raises his fist, but does not look at it*] *it* hits all by itself.

So, we have seen: a rite-of-passage ceremonial fight; Lee with his teacher; Lee with his student. The second and third scenes are lessons, *showing* (but not *explaining*) what Lee 'knows'/is. Now, it may be clear to our post-Foucauldian academic eyes that what subtends all of this going 'beyond the mere physical level' is *not* disembodied 'spirituality' but physical *discipline* (with Lee amounting to the highest production of Shaolin discipline – indeed, the most perfect example of a Foucauldian 'docile body'). Nevertheless, what this strange pedagogy is actually at pains to emphasize is an entirely unequivocal yet still unusual equation between subject, body and 'spirituality'. And this is a difficult lesson to 'show' (let alone to 'explain'). For, as Smith and Novak point out:

> Because meditation is commonly linked to the vague term 'spirituality', it is sometimes tarred with that term's negative connotations toward the body. Those who have not undertaken Buddhist meditative training, therefore, can

hardly be expected to guess how intimately connected it is to an awareness of one's own body. The body may be the site of our bondage, but it is also the means of our extrication. Thus, it is not surprising to find the Buddha suggesting that having been born into a human body is one of the three things for which we should give thanks daily.

Indeed, it barely exaggerates the matter to regard Buddhist meditation as a lifelong training in right body awareness. (Smith and Novak 2003: 80)

Enter the Dragon constructs and conveys this particular connection and introduces the key indices of this 'new mystical Eastern' discursive constellation extremely efficiently. Indeed, what it proposes, through the model of Lee, is an inversion and displacement of Freud's Enlightenment motto *'Wo Es war, soll Ich werden'* ('where id was, there ego shall be'): in other words, let the light of conscious knowledge replace the darkness of ignorance. Instead, in Lee's physical spirituality, the path to insight that is proposed follows almost the opposite maxim: *where ego was, let 'it' be*. But *'it'* is no longer the barbaric primary impulses of an id that must be repressed. Rather it is a fundamental harmony and enlightenment achieved through a non-egotistical but disciplined mastery of the mind and body. In other words, whilst meditation *per se* may not be much of a spectator sport, nor make for very exciting viewing, Hollywood nevertheless managed to represent a strong trait of the 60s countercultural interest in oriental alterity through the mystical and spiritual 'way of liberation' and 'enlightenment' produced by the 'training in right body awareness' embodied in the spectacular character of Lee's mythical Shaolin Temple warrior monk. *There is thus the potential of a 'communication' between physical bodies induced by an interpellation that is mediated – disseminated – by the cinematic apparatus.* In other words, this is a *simulation* which engages *fantasy* which precipitates in *practice* that leads to subjective, physical and discursive *transformation*. For such practice may well be or become Zen or Buddhist meditation, Taoist chi gung, or any number of other bodily technologies. Thus, the simulacrum may well offer an 'entrée into Chinese philosophy, medicine, meditation, and even language' (Wile 1996: xv). *Or it may of course produce chimeras, fictions, fantasies, and absurdities, such as the wonderfully ridiculous invented 'martial art' of 'Rex Kwon Do' in *Napoleon Dynamite* (2004).[5]

What is there?

What is there to be learned from this? This is just another way of asking: What is there? To think about the lesson, let's rewind to the touching pedagogical scene in which Lee points Lau to the physically graspable, metaphorically evocable but linguistically unsayable 'it'. As you will recall, Lee tests Lau by gesturing and saying 'It is like a finger pointing away to the moon'. Then he slaps Lau and says: 'Don't concentrate on the finger or you will miss all that heavenly glory'. Lesson learned. But, what is it? As we are not simply Lee's Shaolin disciples, let's allow ourselves the luxury of one last quick furtive look at Lau looking at the pointing finger, for which he was sternly reprimanded.

In an essay entitled 'What Is There?' (2001), Maurizio Ferraris proposes that *any* response to the ontological question of 'what is there?' always boils down to the work of 'A finger, generally the index, [which] gives a sign towards something, and indicates it as *this*'. And this, he points out, 'is *presence*, ontology in the simple and hyperbolic sense' (96). Then Ferraris goes on to consider what he calls that 'obstinate superstition that holds [that children are] incapable of abstraction [because they] look at the finger ... instead of what the index is pointing to' (100). He notes that the conventional interpretation of the classic child's mistake is that it shows children are *incapable* of abstraction. (Similar statements have been made about the so-called 'Chinese Mind', of course.) But Ferraris suggests that surely children who look at the finger and not at what it points to 'are if anything *more* abstract [than adults], since they produce an inflation of presences' (100). For what they are staring at (if not 'seeing') is *the agency which designates – the act of designation* – rather than that which is intended. Thus the over-attention of the naïve, captive and attentive disciple inadvertently and unintentionally points to the fact that we are always guided, led, directed, pointed to something, by some guide or guiding act of designation. Designation is determined by a designator. Disciples are taught what to look at and see and what not to see. What disciples *see* is what they are in a sense *shown* (or trained) *how to see*. Thus, as Ferraris puts it: 'the presence of the index is no less problematic than everything it points to' (98).

Of course, Lee's character is seeking to dissolve the 'Western' problematic in which, behind the index (the finger pointing us to what *is*), 'there is first of all a *cogito* with respect to which [things] are present' (Ferraris 2001: 98). As Lee has already told us, 'the word "I" does not exist'. Similarly, Alan Watts once asked: 'What happens to my fist (noun-object) when I open my hand?' (1957: 25) The question sought to suggest that ways of thinking determine what can be seen, understood, or communicated. Thus, what may seem like an *object* may perhaps be better construed as an *event* or a *process*. In a similar sense, the concept-metaphors used to think about 'culture' have themselves shifted from conceiving of it as a fixed or essential *thing* towards thinking of it as an *event*, a *process*, or – overwhelmingly nowadays – as *communication*. But, what is communication? And how is 'it' communicated? As Jacques Derrida once asked: what does the word *communication* communicate? We tend to 'anticipate the meaning of the word *communication*' and to 'predetermine communication as the vehicle, transport, or site of passage of a meaning, and of a meaning that is *one*' (1982: 309). But, he observes:

> To the semantic field of the word *communication* belongs the fact that it also designates nonsemantic movements ... [O]ne may, for example, *communicate a movement*, or ... a tremor, a shock, a displacement of *force* can be communicated – that is, propagated, transmitted. ... What happens in this case, what is transmitted or communicated, are not just phenomena of meaning or signification. In these cases we are dealing neither with a semantic or conceptual content, nor with a semiotic operation, and even less with a linguistic exchange. (Derrida 1982: 309)

One may also communicate identities through *ghosts*, and as we will see in the following chapter, one may also communicate through and with *spirits*.

Street-fetishism: Popular Politics and Deconstruction

I am a monster of fidelity, the most perverse infidel.

Jacques Derrida (1987: 24)

Popular action in deconstruction

On 1 August 2000, the Conservative Party in Britain urged motorists to 'dump the pump' – to stop buying fuel for their cars. One might immediately imagine many conceivable reasons why such a course of action could be advocated. For instance, we may have concerns related to ecology, care for the environment, worries about the damage caused by fossil fuels, concerns about health, air quality, or congestion. We may be concerned about what is going to happen when the world inevitably runs out of the fossil fuel that drives not just vehicles but virtually all major industries and forms of transport. In other words, we might be concerned about the consequences of the entire world's reliance on fossil fuels. But in August 2000, the Conservatives – who were at that time the main opposition party in the UK – were not motivated by any of these. Instead, they suggested that the public should 'dump the pump' in a protest about the *high price* consumers were paying for fuel.

By 5 September, further price rises led to protests on the streets. In these, protestors organized blockades of oil refineries, ports and oil storage terminals all over the UK. This caused widespread panic buying, leading to the rapid emptying of petrol stations, fuel shortages, and then, quite quickly – perhaps because people couldn't get any fuel for their cars – public support for the blockades rapidly diminished. The blockades were soon lifted, although with what sounded like an ominous ultimatum: the protestors 'gave' the government 60 days to come up with a solution. Then the whole thing fizzled out, without much in the way of a deliberate solution and without much in the way of further protests.

Nevertheless, perhaps these peculiar 'political' events are still significant. For it *looked like* the UK was experiencing a kind of apparently radical direct political activism. This was organized at grass-roots level by activists. It was action that was supported in principle by opposition politicians as well as large portions of the public. The action was implemented on the street and was designed to give voice to a demand and to put pressure on the powers that be (the government and petrochemical companies) to respond to that demand. Indeed, what was seen here might seem to be exemplary political action. It certainly seemed to tick a lot of the boxes that are used to decide whether or not something is political: Was there a clear issue? Check. Was there a clear demand? Check. Was there a unified group in conflict with more powerful parties and interests? Check. Could this group feasibly be called 'the workers' or 'the people'? Check. Was public opinion divided? Check. Was there widespread and coordinated mobilization, involving different sorts of protest, from direct action to lobbying and awareness-raising, and including some principled civil disobedience? Check. Was it presented or represented as an issue that 'they' (the 'powers that be') caused, an issue that bore directly on all of 'us' ('the people'), and that 'we' demanded that 'they' solve? Check.

But, hold on. Let's just check something else. What are we to make of the fact that this apparent *radicalism* was supported by a political party who claim to be *conservative*? And what about the fact that this action was not calling for a radical rethink or reorganization of anything to do with fossil fuels in society *per se*, nor for redistribution of rights, laws, social relations or responsibilities, but was instead merely calling for – drum roll . . . wait for it – the price of fuel to be brought down, a bit? When cast in this light, it seems considerably less radical. It was not in fact calling for a *change*, or even a *rethink*, but rather for a defensive protection of the status quo.

According to Jacques Rancière, this kind of activity is not really worthy of the name politics at all. Instead, it is what he refers to as a kind of *police* activity: although it is not carried out by the police force, such actions and orientations are nevertheless a defensive preservation of the status quo. As Rancière sees it, a strike, for example, or a blockade

> is not political when it calls for reforms rather than a better deal or when it attacks the relationships of authority rather than the inadequacy of wages. It is political when it reconfigures the relationships that determine the workplace in its relation to the community. (Rancière 1999: 32–3)

In the UK fuel protests of 2000, there was no kind of reconfiguring of the relationships between 'the workers' and 'the community'. Even though those who led the protests were predominantly workers and haulage companies who were heavily reliant on fuel, there was no call for a social or political rethink. In fact, there was no real programme for political change at all. In other words, and using Rancière's insights: just because something *looks like* political action or just because certain calls may *sound like* political demands, there is no guarantee that any of this actually *is* political. As Rancière puts it, 'nothing is political in itself . . . . The same thing – an election, a strike, a demonstration – can give rise to politics or not give rise to politics' (1999: 32).

Street-fetishism

This has implications for our understanding of what politics *is* and how to *do* politics. For, in this thinking, politics boils down to the precipitation of an *event*, which changes things, rather than to ineffectual gestures. In other words, politics – and, in particular, political action – may well be a lot rarer than we think. For what is political action? Voting? Marching? Signing a petition? Wearing a ribbon 'in support' of this or that? Some of these may make us raise a sceptical eyebrow. So what is political action? As we have already seen, *political* action is often equated with *direct* action, on the *street*. The reasons for this relate to a very long history, in which now-familiar forms of action such as protest, marching, demonstration, and particular sorts of language use, gestures and discourses, etc., have come to be recognizable *as* political action *per se*.

But deconstruction suggests that there are also profoundly ingrained 'philosophical' reasons for this preference – or rather, a particular type of *bias* inscribed in 'Western', 'metaphysical' forms of thinking, which can be seen to be at work guiding and skewing the dominant tendencies even of Western philosophy. What this 'metaphysical bias' is – what it boils down to – centres on the tendency for the central focus and hence the central concept of politics to be on what is presumed to be the hard stuff of material reality. *Reality* is often taken to be the *ground* – both philosophically and 'literally'. It is that upon which all of our constructions are *based*. It is the *foundation* upon which everything must *stand*. Hence, the most perfect 'concrete example' of material reality has a tendency to be *the street*.

Of course, when the cause in question has an ecological flavour, then it is likely that the preferred terms and types of imagery will not be about 'concrete' or 'the street', but rather about 'the grass roots'. The point is that, in all cases, what is most valued is what is taken to be the ultimate sign of *material reality*: the *ground*, the *foundation*, the *bedrock*, the *base*, the *real*. As Martin McQuillan puts it: in (metaphysical) political discourse, 'The material is the concept against which all other concepts must be judged and inevitably be found wanting in contrast' (2001: 123). For how could anything be as real, as important, as valuable as 'concrete reality'? The implication lurking in the wings here is, of course, that there is therefore a hierarchy, a spectrum of descending value, ranging from *best* (base/ground/foundation/nature/real) to *right* (that which is built on it) to *suspect* (that which is not yet fully 'real' – words, conversations, etc.) to *worst* (that which is flight of fancy, thought, imagined – furthest from 'real': useless). According to this line of thinking, 'really doing' is most likely to be construed as involving 'really being there', 'getting down and dirty', involving physical presence, physical activity, physical action.

This is the bias that Jacques Derrida characterized as a large part of what he called 'the metaphysics of presence'. In this kind of 'metaphysical' thinking, it can be very easy to forget that the physical, the material (that which is physically *present*), is not the sum total of 'reality' – and is in fact only a very small part of it. For, the physical – or even the bodily – does not hold the monopoly on reality. 'Action' is not more real than thinking. 'Doing' is not something that can be opposed to 'speech'. 'Thinking' is not distinct from 'doing'. Nevertheless, there is often an assumed hierarchy in which what is deemed *most 'real'* is physical action, what is deemed *less 'real'* are words; and in which the best words are those leading to or closely related to action, while what is considerably inferior and somewhat worse are words which are deemed to be 'empty' or 'abstract', not directly related to action, or the mere sounds of thoughts. This hierarchy is all part of Derrida's notion of the 'metaphysics of presence': the fervent belief and regularly returning presumption that *being physically present in the present* has the monopoly on reality. But does it? There are many ways to deconstruct this.

Derrida starts one such deconstruction by observing that the privilege given to the value of *really being there in the present* leads to a privileging of speech over writing. For, obviously, speech (often) happens in face-to-face situations, in which real people are really present to each other. Derrida claims that this leads to a bias in thinking which can be observed in many Western philosophers. For instance, Derrida reads the work of Condillac, who proposed that 'because men are *already* capable of communicating and of communicating their thought to each other [then], in continuous fashion, they invent the means of communicating that is writing' (Derrida 1982: 312). Thus, speech is regarded as *primary*, while writing is a *secondary* addition. According to Derrida, the consequences of this line of thinking have been enormous. He calls it *phonocentrism*: the preference given to speech (and presence) over writing (and absence).

Now, Derrida's argument suggests that this line of thinking has had enormous effects on the conclusions arrived at, and hence on the actions taken as a consequence. Already, then, this inverts the usual hierarchy. For it suggests that *thinking* guides *what we do*. This may not seem like a controversial observation. But the point is, it shows that the usual preference given to 'action' or 'real practice' over 'thinking' or 'mere theory' is somewhat misguided – because all deliberate action is in some sense informed by a theory. Action may be preferred over mere thought, but it must be *supplemented* by it. We will deal more directly with Derrida's own deconstruction of phonocentrism in due course. At this point, we need merely note that words are not opposed to action. Words can be actions. Thinking is not opposed to the physical or the material or any other type of 'reality'. Thinking and speaking are irreducibly parts of doing. They are influential and orienting parts, too – without which there could arguably be no 'real doing' as we know it.

Every possible 'key component' of reality is supplemented by the others. So, even if what is desired is action, it must be remembered that not all talk is just empty noise. Indeed, if all talk *is* deemed to be empty and inferior to 'proper activity', then even 'straight talking', even 'keeping-it-real talk', even fighting talk, even if it is in the language of the street or indeed of the gutter, even if it is shouting, would still therefore be mere talk. The question would be: what makes one type of speech in one type of situation any more or less real or 'politically effective' than another? What would make the conversation among activists on the street more real or effective than, say, academic argumentation or philosophical speculation? Now, there *are* differences. Not all statements in not all contexts have the same effects. But, although it is true that there is a *difference* between different types of discourse in different contexts, the point is that even in direct action or on the street, when it comes to getting things done, there is no getting away not only from talk but also from *theory*. So, even though 'talking street' at grass roots *seems* really real, really active, really engaged, it is not *necessarily* so, and certainly not 'directly'. This is because the action of politics is not direct.

Indeed, there is the possibility that direct action 'on the street' can be a complete cul-de-sac. As Jeremy Gilbert points out, sometimes street politics can actually flip over and become the opposite of what it may initially have intended to be, when 'an insistence on and faith in autonomy' (an insistence on individual direct action in the present) becomes a kind of 'refusal to adopt *any* strategy, a metaphysical refusal of politics itself. In this movement "direct-action" is seen often not as a political tactic but as a substitute *for* politics' (2001b: 111). In a sense, such an ironic twist, in which an activity becomes the opposite of what its authors may have intended, could be regarded as a consequence of this 'metaphysical' bias in favour of the street – a result of overvaluing the physical, face-to-face version of what reality is – and because of the way in which too much focus can flip over and become a kind of myopia.

Another way to formulate this would be to suggest that too much fixation can become fetish. Indeed, Slavoj Žižek suggests that there is a fetishistic character to certain dispositions and types of subjectivity in the contemporary world. The Freudian formula for the fetishistic attachment is 'I know very well, but ...'. That is, although a foot-fetishist knows very well that high-heeled shoes are just an inessential adornment, nevertheless the fetishist needs them to attain full enjoyment (orgasm). As Žižek puts it:

> ... fetishists are not dreamers lost in their private worlds, they are thoroughly 'realists', able to accept the way things effectively are – since they have their fetish to which they can cling in order to cancel the full impact of reality. (Žižek 2001a: 13–14)

Fetishists know very well what they are doing, and the problems, limitations, failures, and arguments against their activity. Nevertheless they keep doing it. So, just as foot-fetishists need feet to reach sexual satisfaction, street-fetishists need the street for political satisfaction. Both are gratifications (mediated by shoes). The obsessive direct-action focus, the street-fetish, would in Žižek's theory be 'the embodiment of the Lie which enables [them] to sustain the unbearable truth' – 'their fetish to which they can cling in order to cancel the full impact of reality' (2001a: 13–14). In other words, people can acquire an obsessive attachment to endlessly repeating certain types of activity. As Judith Butler suggests:

> Clearly, the fear of political paralysis is precisely what prompts the anti-theoretical animus in certain activist circles. Paradoxically, such positions require the paralysis of critical reflection in order to avoid the prospect of paralysis on the level of action. In other words, those who fear the retarding effects of theory do not want to think too hard about what it is they are doing, what kind of discourse they are using; for if they think too hard about what it is they are doing, they fear that they will no longer do it. (Butler 2000: 265)

That is to suggest that the resistance to theory in some quarters is a resistance to thinking itself. Certain forms of political action may be the repetition of ineffectual gestures, but how would one be able to work this out without studying, rethinking, and retheorizing? Butler suggests that sometimes repeating these gestures may boil down to an enjoyment of doing them, or a blind zeal, like religious faith.

Interestingly, however, even Butler can be very attached to the idea (or fantasy) of making a real difference 'on the street'. For instance, in one anecdote, Butler tells us she was walking along the street one day when a 'kid' called from a window asking if she was a lesbian. She was not ashamed to reply that she was. This, she believed, shocked her harasser (but this is already an interpretation, and the most that can perhaps be said is that it momentarily silenced him). Her interpretation?

> ... it's as if the interrogator hanging out the window were saying 'Hey, do you think the word *lesbian* can only be used in a derogatory way on the street?' And I said 'No, it can be claimed on the street! Come join me!' We were having a negotiation. (cited in Salih 2002: 760)

Now, I'm not very convinced about this interpretation of what happened in this exchange, nor of its status as a good example of politics happening 'on the street'. Indeed, I would rather suggest that, if anything at all 'happened', then it was not quite the event that Butler hastily decides it was. Rather, *if* something happened here, it seems more likely that at least two different things did. First, there is what Butler seems to think happened: her experience. Then there is what her harasser may have thought happened: his experience. But there is no guarantee that this exchange needs to be interpreted as an event in which something changed as the result of a dialogue or a negotiation. For perhaps nothing changed either for Butler or for her interrogator. Perhaps both remain agencies divided by different understandings of a common word, in this case 'lesbian'. In other words, perhaps it was a failed encounter. It was certainly evidence of a *disagreement* – and, according to Rancière, 'disagreement' ought to be understood as a particular 'kind of speech situation':

> ... one in which one of the interlocutors at once understands and does not understand what the other is saying. Disagreement is not the conflict between one who says white and another who says black. It is the conflict between one who says white and another who also says white but does not understand the same thing by it or does not understand that the other is saying the same thing in the name of whiteness. (Rancière 1999: x)

Both Butler and her interrogator understand the term 'lesbian' but surely do 'not understand the same thing by it'. So there is the potential for politics to flare up here. However, in Rancièrean terms, this disagreement is not yet political. This is because, as Benjamin Arditi explains:

> ... a disagreement is less a confrontation between two established positions – as in the case of a debating society – than an engagement between 'parties' that do not antedate their confrontation. A disagreement constructs the object of argumentation and the field of argumentation itself. (Arditi 2007: 115)

For Rancière, the political relation is born when there is an inkling that there is an equal who is addressing us and trying to make sense (or vice versa). What makes this person *equal* is the realisation that they are *like us*, in command of reason, sense, or *logos*, as opposed to being some kind of ignorant grunting animal. Is it entirely certain that both of the parties to the Butler–Interrogator encounter have yet acknowledged the other as fully equal? Is it entirely certain that either is prepared to compromise their position by listening to the other and changing their position as a result of a dialogue? Maybe not. For 'the street' is not necessarily where differences can be made. There are other scenes that are surely just as important: educational contexts, institutional contexts, legal and legislative contexts, and so on. None of these need be on the street. Of course, some face-to-face contexts are indeed crucial places to secure change. But the street is not necessarily one of them. Indeed, since the 70s, Western governments have not even pretended that they will respond to mass street protests. So why bother with them? 'I know very well, but ...'.

In more considered moments, Butler clearly knows that conventional forms of political practice might be ineffectual knee-jerk responses. But, given the demonstrable centrality of *the idea of* the street to thinking and doing politics, it is easy to see why one might want to focus on it. Indeed, during the 1990s, there were even mass efforts to *reclaim the streets* – to occupy them, inhabit them, to use them differently. But, to what ends? What else is there to be done after reclaiming a street from the cars, the pollution, the industry, the journeys to work, the boring regimentation and routine that this journey symbolizes? One answer is in the question: you have a party!

Such a rationale (that reclaiming the street plus partying equals direct radical political action) is arguably one version of a wider countercultural logic whose most basic form or most common caricature involves the equation 'the way it is now equals bad, therefore the opposite of this equals good'. (We will be looking at this a bit more in the next chapter.) In the student protests, occupations and blockades in Paris in May 1968, such slogans as 'La beauté est dans la rue!' or 'Under the street, the beach!' were widespread. However, Joseph Heath and Andrew Potter (2005) contend that this line of countercultural thinking is misguided. They note that you might reclaim, occupy or tear up the street because it is a symbol of our channelled lives, our domination, our regulation through domestication, our slavery to cars, part of the apparatuses and mechanisms of exploitation, and so on; and that instead of a life of mediocrity, routine, regulation and channelling, the countercultural sentiment has always been the belief that through the destruction of the basic routes and arteries of subjugation we will get to, well, *lie on a beach instead*. Heath and Potter point out that although this sounds great, such a desire is arguably the purest possible example of the normal aspirations of 'hegemonic' neoliberalist individualism: the desire for an eternal California beach holiday; an exemplary consumerist fantasy. Hence, they conclude that this kind of radical thinking is not so radical, dude.

Similarly, in the 1980s and early 1990s, in the era when the British Prime Minister Margaret Thatcher claimed to be implementing Adam Smith's economic policies, Robert J. C. Young wondered why so many cultural and political theorists seemed to think (implicitly following Bakhtin) that carnival and the carnivalesque was politically radical. Young wrote: '... it is hard to understand why it is that those on the left who make great claims for carnival as radically subversive of the social order always seem to forget to mention that Adam Smith shared their enthusiasm'. Indeed, observes Young, Adam Smith proposed that 'the state should also encourage regular carnivals ... as a way of easing the ills of alienation' (Young 1992: 117–18). So, perhaps dramatic actions on the street are not necessarily radical or political. Indeed, perhaps sometimes the royal road to political fetishism is fixation on the street.

Rather than the drive for immediate and physically present satisfactions, surely the aim of making political change and intervention involves a long and winding ('discursive') road. As Stuart Hall proposes, political action is that which 'tries to make a difference in the *institutional* world in which it is located' (Hall, Morley and Chen 1996: 271). This is a theoretical aim, in which one's focus is on another aspect of the street, as it were, crossing over or moving on from fetishizing the (meta)physical street as the tautological start and endpoint of politics – the presumed starting point and ultimate destination of all efforts. Rather, one should perhaps think of the street as a *link* in a social chain, as part of a *process*, as *connection* in a structure, as an institution among and between institutions; in short, a mode of *articulation* (Laclau and Mouffe 1985). Perhaps this will help us to get somewhere.

The long and winding road

The displacement that is politics can be grasped using an example given by Jacques Rancière. In Rancière's thinking, *politics* only happens when a group demands its right to *equality*. For equality is something that we are all said to have in common. But because societies are structured and hierarchical, there are any number of ways in which inequality can come to be perceived. For Rancière, politics happens when what he calls 'egalitarian logic' – the claim for equality made on the basis of the fact that we are all *already supposed* to be equals – clashes with 'police logic' – the logic of keeping the status quo unchanged, the reasoning which says that the way it is now is the way it should always be. In this light, Rancière discusses feminism. One of the tenets of feminism, of course, is that 'the personal is political': that there are power relations and hierarchies, classifications and judgements made all of the time, and they are often sexist. This is why feminism so often battles with gender distinctions and fights to change the gender roles that feminists perceive to be inegalitarian. After all, if we are all equal, why should women be required to do all of the domestic labour, why should men enjoy greater economic success, and so on? So, feminism focuses on the power relations between the sexes. However, Rancière adds to this:

> The domestic household has been turned into a political space not through the simple fact that power relationships are at work in it but because it was the subject of an argument in a dispute over the capacity of women in the community. (Rancière 1999: 33)

For there are 'power relationships' everywhere. In our relationships with each other and all of the relationships we enter into with institutions (family, education, employment, clubs, etc.), power relations can be said to be present. But they do not necessarily ever become *political*. They only do so when a disagreement or dispute flares up. So, Rancière's essential proposition is that *politics* is actually *rare*, while what is *common* is *police* (Rancière 1999: 17, 139). By police, what Rancière refers to is work and actions which protect the status quo. As such, what is normally thought of as *politics* is in Rancière's terms most often *policing*. Ironically, the best example of this police work is the administrative tinkering of politicians' 'political' actions. So, for Rancière, 'Politics, in its specificity, is rare. It is always local and occasional' (1999: 139). Politics is *momentous*, in every sense of the word. For, according to Rancière, politics always reflects a social *convulsion*, a social *conflict* around a wider dispute.

Thus, using Rancière's construction of the terms of the debate, the direct action and demand-making of the fuel protests of 2000 perhaps should not be regarded as political. This is not because it was a sham. It is because it did not precipitate a wider debate or convulsion around any of the issues that organized it: fuel, fuel prices, UK industry, consumption, the global economy, dependence on oil-producing nations and companies, the environment or pollution. Others have tried in various ways to stimulate debate, action and change on all of these and many more points. But the fuel protests did not.

Yet the *political* question is always how to *cause* a wider debate and how to *induce* a social convulsion. In other words: *how* to change things. Street-fetishists may demand that the question be how we change things on the street. And this sounds very noble. But it is important to note that, in this sense, 'the street' *itself* is 'really' a metaphor; a metaphor that is structured by a metaphysical conception of reality, that is not necessarily realistic.

De-class-ifying politics

For what do we *mean* when we evoke 'the street' or being 'on the street'? Like saying 'back in the day', it is a rhetorical construction for a fantasy that may never have really existed. In discourse, argument or conversation, 'the street' can function as a metaphor, as opposed to a 'real thing' (aka: a *referent*). Or, as Derrida once put it, 'The absence of the referent is a possibility rather easily admitted today' (1982: 318). That is, we can quite easily accept that words do not necessarily *refer* to real things. We can, for instance, speak of unicorns, fairies, Santa Claus, and so on, and understand that such things both do and do not exist. They exist within certain discourses, certain imaginary universes and particular narratives. But we don't think that they exist in the same way that, say, 'the street' exists: there really are real streets. This may be so, but the point here is that words, concepts or notions can be deployed in different ways, to do certain jobs. 'The street' can function as a *rhetorical device*, such as a *metonym*, in which the word 'street' stands for a larger entity – 'reality', 'real life', etc. In other words, different styles of language and representation create different effects, and can even conjure up different objects. This is perhaps particularly so in the case of arguments. As Hindess and Hirst once argued, in any given argument:

> Concepts are deployed in ordered successions to produce [the] effects [of analysis and solutions]. This order is the order created *by the practice of theoretical work itself*: it is guaranteed by no necessary 'logic' or 'dialectic' nor by

any necessary mechanism of correspondence with the real itself. (quoted in Spivak 1999: 316)

In other words, language and the construction of worldviews is not a neutral or natural process. Rather, when it comes to making inter- pretations, classifications, and decisions, it is true to say that there is a complex relationship between what is being interpreted, classed, or decided, and the work of the classifier – the person doing the interpret- ing. The productive and inventive character of the relationship between what is being engaged with or interpreted and the *way* this is being done means that interpretation is a work of *invention* rather than 'discov- ery'. Deconstruction suggests that interpretations chiefly involve not the uncovering of truths but rather the making of decisions – decisions about the way to connect and associate objects and features – in order, as it were, to come up with the conclusions desired or required.

This can be seen for example in the case of that most central of polit- ical referents: the idea of *class* itself. Traditionally, left political thinking was organized by the observable existence of different classes in society. This led Marxist and materialist political thinking to insist upon what Ernesto Laclau and Chantal Mouffe call the belief in the 'ontological centrality of the working class' (1985: 2). What they mean by this is the belief that there is such a *thing* as the working class, that it is *one identity* and that it has *one* true, correct, necessary, inevitable and real *place* and *function*. A belief in the 'ontological centrality of the working class', they claim, has been a core belief of Marxism, workers' movements, socialist, communist and generally left-wing thinking since at least the 19th cen- tury. Laclau and Mouffe deconstructed this belief in the *centrality* of the working class for politics. They did not simply say, 'class does not exist'. Rather, they retheorized politics and the mechanisms of political causal- ity in an argument that has profound implications for the understanding of politics and the political dimensions of popular culture.

What they did was to target the 'ontological argument', and to point out that one should not really take the existence of a *concept* as proof of the existence of the *thing* conceptualized. In other words, we might speak of 'classes', but what do we mean? How are we to understand what a class is, how it works, what it might do, etc.? Upon posing these questions to the notion of 'class', Laclau and Mouffe started to retheorize 'class' as having always been a *contingent articulation* – that is, a *partic- ular sort of connection* between people. Thus, they concluded, politics is specifically about 'articulation' (linkages, connections, bonds), rather than necessarily about class *per se*. As John Mowitt explains, this rethink- ing 'registers the fact that the present historical conjuncture is marked by an eruption of conflicts among groups whose social identities are torn by the contradictory interpretation of race, class, sexuality and gender' (1992: 78).

Now, this process of deconstructing class led to some considerable controversy. Marxists, socialists, and those on the left accused Laclau and Mouffe of attempting (or inadvertently working) to destroy left politics by questioning its core categories. But, Laclau argued, it is surely *more* problematic to retain an unquestioning *faith* and *belief* in notions that we should surely want to test, understand better, and if they are found wanting, to replace with more adequate conceptualizations. As he put it:

> [We] gain very little, once identities are conceived as complexly articulated collective wills, by referring to them through simple designations such as classes, ethnic groups and so on, which are at best names for transient points of stabilization. The really important task, is to understand the logics of their constitution and dissolution, as well as the formal determinations of the spaces in which they interrelate. (Laclau 2000: 53)

In other words, Laclau's argument is that thinking in terms of 'classes' is to think in terms of 'simple designations'. For him, this can degenerate into the impulse to structure thinking and efforts 'around entities – class, class struggle, capitalism – which are largely fetishes dispossessed of any precise meaning' (2000: 201). In other words, Laclau suggests that, like street-fetishism, to organize one's efforts around 'class' is another kind of fetishism. Of course, as Arditi and Valentine put it, categories like 'class' are still available in cultural and political discourses 'as poles of identification, as positions that could be occupied'. But, as they see it, to organize oneself and one's thinking in this (fetishistic) way is to 'obey one of the most traditional aspirations of Western thought: namely, the desire to condense normative value and empirical existence in a single point' (1999: vii–viii). For, to say 'I am working class' or 'this is working class' is one thing – and problematic enough at that. But to invest this designation with an 'ontological centrality' is very self-aggrandizing. Such a fetishistic tendency exemplifies a desire related to the metaphysics of presence that we have seen throughout.

Nevertheless, class has always been presented as objectively real. This imputed reality is why it has lived such a lively life. The figure of class as something real – something to fight in the name of – has certainly mobilized myriad political struggles. (So have notions like 'God', 'freedom', 'democracy', 'country', etc., of course.) Thus, one might say, its *actual* reality or otherwise is beside the point. Its *apparent* reality is everything, making it available as a pole of identification and a rallying point for political mobilization. Its power derives not from its *objectivity*, but from the rhetorical reserves of its imputed ontological status: that is, from the rhetorico-political force of (the belief in) objectivity. It is an image, phantasm, metaphor: and these are the reserves by which any supposed entity can orientate lives and projects. The recent waning of the affect of 'class interpellations', the dissipation of the force class politics once held, has caused confusion, disappointment and anger among many on the left. For class oriented and enabled so much. If it has now fizzled out, the question would be why, and what is to be made of the apparent demise of something that was so generative for so long?

Some say that those who deconstructed class are complicit in the demise of class politics. Of course, this presumes a lot: it presumes, for instance, a simple relationship between academia and political work, one which is based on a very self-aggrandizing conception of the 'intellectual function'. For to argue that the intellectual deconstruction of class (or anything else) has led to the dissolution of class politics presumes that academics are held in very high regard by 'the masses' – that academics are 'popular'. In psychoanalytic terms, this can be rendered as the supposition that 'the people' regard academics as subjects who are 'supposed to know' (i.e., persons that 'the people' regard as wise), so that when academics speak they are addressing the masses, who are supposed to listen. Furthermore, it presumes that 'they' (the masses) *can* hear, and that they will act upon hearing academics' words, and that one can predict the nature of 'their' response – as if politics *responds to* academic statements in a kind of 'monkey see, monkey do' manner. It also supposes that the wise, listened-to subject is 'us', and that 'we' have 'a' message. And it presumes that our voices are simply audible, intelligible, or even translatable into what are sometimes called 'everyday' or 'normal' languages, contexts, or movements. It presumes simple influence, straightforward and predictable causality, an intellectual function conceived of through the analogy of one speaker with one microphone speaking to one audience who desperately want to hear and believe one univocally communicated message, and act predictably in accordance. There are a lot of presumptions here!

They are all dubious. Surely, Laclau and Mouffe did not deal a death-blow to 'class politics'. Rather, they *demystified the discourse about class*, showing how it has worked as a Marxian ideology. That is to say, Laclau and Mouffe argued that class is not the basic unit of society or of political or cultural theory. Rather, what is more fundamental is the way in which different agencies, groups and identities come to be *articulated* – that is, linked, connected, bound together. They accept that, historically, the main forms of articulation (of linking, grouping, connecting) can be regarded as having been determined by the forces and relations and groupings induced by the economy. Hence, the main forms of politics since the industrial revolution have been class-based. But this, Laclau and Mouffe remind us, is of descriptive rather than analytical significance. That is to say, they argue that the fundamental characteristic of politics is articulation. Different groups can articulate different demands, and these are no less political than working-class politics 'proper'. They add to this that articulations become hegemonic when those involved in one particular struggle tend to identify with those involved in another struggle, and vice versa, such that alliances are built, coalitions are formed through groups identifying with each other and 'relating to' each other. Thus, rather than politics necessarily being class politics, Laclau and Mouffe's deconstruction and reconstruction of politics suggests that all aspects of culture can have a political role to play. But what is that role?

(The) Deconstructing revolution

This kind of line of argumentation has led many 'serious' or 'proper' political thinkers to declare a distaste for deconstruction. For many, deconstructive argumentation seems preposterous. On the one hand, it seems frustrating, slippery, contradictory, producing only undecidability, leading to deferrals of conclusions and displacing the terms of debate. Its main conclusions always seem to involve pointing out aporias and impossibilities. So it can seem indecisive and hence of 'no use' to politics. On the other hand, as we have seen, deconstructive analysis can lead to some fairly revolutionary conclusions. As Hardt and Negri point out at the beginning of *Empire* (2000), the deconstruction 'of the spectral reign of globalized capitalism, reveals the possibility of alternative social organizations'; and this, they remind us, is 'an enormous contribution' to political thinking, on the part of deconstruction (2000: 48).

These different insights into the processes of politics and into the underlying mechanisms of social, cultural and political change are particularly important because, according to Hardt and Negri, nowadays all former political certainties have gone, or have become extremely difficult to establish. For instance, one of the most importance concepts that organized many forms of politics – from working-class to feminist and anti-racist politics – was the notion of 'exploitation'. But, are we being exploited? By whom? This was the question that organized many political projects: workers against their exploitation and oppression by capitalists and capitalism, women against their exploitation and oppression by patriarchs and patriarchy, non-whites against their exploitation and oppression by white imperialists, colonialists, and so on. But, Hardt and Negri observe, in the complexity of contemporary global contexts – contexts which are always difficult to delimit – even this most important of concepts, exploitation, 'can no longer be localized and quantified' (2000: 209). This arguably deals a paralysing blow to left political thought and action. For certainty about exploitation (what, where, how and why it '*is*') formerly set up clear and stable coordinates for establishing what political projects, political practice and agency were. However, as Hardt and Negri put it, the contemporary political problem is now actually one of trying to establish 'how to determine the enemy against which to rebel' (211). And, of course, deciding the answer to this question will also help to work out what forms or strategies of 'political action' we think need to be taken.

According to Hardt and Negri, 'the left', 'the people', 'the workers', etc., have lost a singular, identifiable and determinable enemy because 'we are immersed in a system of power so deep and complex that we can no longer determine specific difference or measure' (2000: 211). Power is everywhere. Power relations are everywhere. Which ones are 'exploitative' or 'exclusionary'? Wendy Brown suggests that the political uncertainty we now *always* appear to face is a problem of how to construct 'politics without banisters' (2001: 91–120). By this she means to suggest that now we've lost all of the fixed certainties that we used to hold onto in order to construct our political convictions: employers don't seem to be so obviously exploitative in ways which 'oppress' workers – indeed, the very distinction between employer and worker has been eroded in many realms; men don't seem to be obviously or always oppressing women; society seems increasingly less racist, and so on. Politically speaking, then, Brown suggests that we have moved into a condition of great indeterminacy.

This is perhaps where deconstructive reflection becomes invaluable: as a means of rethinking, reconsidering, re-reading, reflecting, and reinterpreting. Of course, as we have seen, deconstruction suggests that we should not maintain a simple binary between 'thinking' and 'action'. Reinterpretations themselves can amount to decisive actions. But the point is that acts of *revaluation* are arguably constitutive of change. We might go further and posit that *an event is an event* only to the extent that it forces revaluation. For, if revaluation is *not* required, then has there really been any change at all? Has there really been an event? And an *event* – an event which *changes* things – is arguably the first and last element of politics.

This is why many believe that politics involves partial or gradual changes; small, pragmatic, policy changes, 'progressive' stages of 'improvement'. Indeed, in recent decades, more and more political thinkers have abandoned the idea of 'revolution' as the supposed ideal, and instead of evoking revolution, many thinkers prefer the less utopian-sounding ideal of 'progress'. However, as thinkers from Lyotard to Laclau have argued, the invocation of 'progress' is itself a kind of utopian thinking. Laclau calls it the first of all utopias (2000: 198). This is because the notion of 'progress' implies that we are *already on track*, and that we *know* what the goal is, in advance of any change. But do we really? In this kind of thinking, 'politics' becomes merely the banal implementation of a *predetermined programme*. In other words, *administration*. Indeed, 'partialism', 'gradualism', or 'progress', all presuppose a fundamental stability. This has led thinkers like Slavoj Žižek to argue that those who abandon the ideal of *revolution* have effectively abandoned the ideal of politics or change itself. In this line of thinking, an 'act', a 'revolution', must change *all* coordinates, including those of its own measurement and evaluation (Žižek 2000: 121–2). The necessity of *revaluation* is therefore part and parcel of any significant change, or indeed, revolution.

However, we seem to be living in a period when even hitting on a way to be able to *think* revolution as being something desirable, workable, plausible or realistic would itself amount to a revolutionary achievement. Although, to be sure: things called revolutions do occur, in and as reality, in many places. Actual political agencies still engage in revolutionary struggles around the globe, without doubting the reality of revolution. But the point is that there is a crisis at the heart of the idea of revolution that any attempt to think it cannot easily avoid. This crisis (impasse or aporia) presents itself when one tries to think revolution as meaning radical emancipatory transformation, rather than mere regime change. Indeed, thinking of revolution entirely in terms of regime change reduces it to meaning nothing more than the revolving of different faces, different names, different figures, against the same backdrop. What is revolutionary about that? Thinkers as diametrically opposed as the neoliberal Francis Fukuyama and the revolutionary Marxist Slavoj Žižek would agree that something like this, travelling under the name of revolution, is far from the 'real thing'. For a revolution would be that which utterly changed the rules of the game, and therefore the game itself. Neoliberal Fukuyama once declared that revolution of such an order could no longer occur nowadays, because he believed us to be living at the 'end of history', where things might change a bit, here and there, but where we now have the final world order – the hybrid unity, neoliberalist-capitalism (Fukuyama 1992). On the other side of the same coin, Žižek's revolutionary Marxist position insists that revolution of a 'total' order *must* be its form, otherwise it isn't revolution. Clearly, revolution is a troublesome problematic for political thought. Perhaps it is actually identical to the thought of the possibility of politics itself.

But, if we return to deconstruction, a possibility suggests itself. Namely, this: if even the *very thought* of revolution today so quickly opens out onto complexity, uncertainty, undecidability and aporia, therefore doesn't a mode of thought and engagement that is actually enlivened rather than paralysed by aporia and impossibility seem somewhat *called for*? Yet as some have retorted: isn't capitalism itself a most radical form of deconstruction? In a sense, the answer is yes. But capitalism 'deconstructs' institutions because they are not *profit*. To deconstruct that which is not *just*, not *justice* – either not based in justice or producing injustice – is something else entirely. This kind of deconstruction is an emancipatory and antagonistic process which is not in contradiction with the Marxist revolutionary ideal of revealing and countering the injustice of capitalist relations themselves. The difference between the deconstructive sense of justice and Marxism's is that deconstruction's is a justice which *we can never assume has arrived*. This is because to make such an assumption would be to suppose that one particular state of affairs is already perfectly just, *which is impossible*. The assumption that the present is just, that justice is present, is always an unjust assumption. Any assumption that the just is here is an assumption that will work forcefully for the exclusion of any change.

This is why Protevi (2001) calls deconstruction 'democratic justice': it is the interminable effort to listen and try to address and redress injustice. Deconstruction in this sense is the *revolutionary demand for radical democratic justice*, a demand for the impossible. But, therein lies the objection: Isn't this an *opposition without opposition*? A resigned, negative, pessimistic abdication from fighting for a radical new world view? An impossible and therefore pointless pointing out of something impossible? I would like to suggest why it is not. Indeed, I would like to suggest that there may be a 'forcefulness' to *not* offering explicit revolutionary manifestos, and instead to attempt simply to *redress injustice*.

This may seem like a peculiar position. But there is a sense in which making *strong* demands may be a *weaker* strategy than 'innocently' seeking to 'reasonably' redress justice or inequality. (We will return to this more fully in Chapter 8.) For, when a demand is for something *other*, and when that demand seems to come from some *other* people, some *other* place, or be infused with *other* values, it is more easily *ignorable*. As Thomas Docherty puts it: oppositional speech (such as revolutionary Marxism) is arguably 'always already negated by the structure of the entity which it wishes to oppose', and as such actually amounts to 'nothing more than an inoculation of sorts which allows the dominant political power in a social formation further to strengthen itself' (1993: 322).

But what of utopian calls for otherness, for proposed alternative visions, for a different and better (socialist) world? Isn't it only by forming some completely different model that we might construct a positive politics and political strategy? No. This fantasy about 'otherness to come', when metaphysically construed, is often recruited as an argument against deconstruction – in the claim that deconstruction cannot found or propose a positive alternative or oppositional politics, etc. Well, this is true: deconstruction *can't* propose a 'positive' (metaphysical) politics. However, what deconstruction does is to show the alterity, the impossibility, the *lack* at the heart of *any* positive, empirical arrangement. Alterity does not come from 'over there'. It is produced by the (impossibility of the) here and now. This is important. And it actually suggests a deconstructive political strategy.

One paradoxical slogan of the events in Paris during May 1968 is instructive in this regard. The slogan was, 'Be realistic: demand the impossible'. Of course, this avails itself of many interpretations. All of them suggest fidelity to the promise of an alterity 'to come'. However, I would prefer to manipulate it into 'Be unrealistic: demand the possible'. For what might demanding the *impossible* mean today? Would it mean demanding something thoroughly other, something thoroughly different (as Žižek or revolutionary Marxism demands)? This conception of otherness does seem difficult to demand, at the moment. *But* – and this too is a big 'but' – demanding the impossible might also be shown to be identical to *demanding the possible*: *demanding the explicit letter of what is held to be the case*. For, what are we meant to have already in this day and age? Freedom, accountability, justice, prosperity, equality, security, liberty, and so on. But do we? Demanding the impossible today would actually be to demand these things that are supposedly already present, such as democracy, accountability, transparency, justice, prosperity, emancipation – all those things that we are said to 'have, already'.

The commonsensical and ideological 'truths' of today are double and duplicitous. For, first, it is axiomatic that these things *do not need to be demanded*, as they are already held to be the case, believed present. We are already supposed to have them. Yet, where they are absent, you are not supposed to demand them, and it is impropriety itself to expect them. These 'truths', these 'values' are expected and supposed present. But only to the extent that they are *not* looked for. They are imposed as supposed: seeking or trying to activate them is actively dissuaded. As Baudrillard might say, they are simulated as their own deterrence. Yet, they are also arguably a Derridean *pharmakon*: both medicine and poison: the medicine of capitalism to the extent that they are the poison of all alternatives to it. But they are also the poison of capitalism to the extent that they *consciously* become the medicine of alternatives to it (Derrida 1982: 102–5, 119, 127, 169).

This is to suggest, following a deconstructive impulse within the work of Žižek, that the most subversive thing you could do would be to hold every institution, every claim, to nothing other than the literality of the letter of what they claim. As deconstruction has shown most literally, literality is impossible, and is always only forcefully imposed (Derrida 1982: 207–72; 307–30; Protevi 2001: 63–5). As Žižek might prefer it expressed, every institution is constituted around a denial of its own 'obscenity', its own inherent 'transgression'. He argues:

> ... my notion of 'inherent transgression', far from playing another variation on this theme (resistance reproduces that to which it resists), makes the power edifice even *more* vulnerable: in so far as power relies on its 'inherent transgression', then – sometimes, at least – *overidentifying* with the explicit power discourse – *ignoring* this inherent obscene underside and simply taking the power discourse at its (public) word, acting as if it really means what it explicitly says (and promises) – can be the most effective way of disturbing its smooth functioning. (Žižek 2000: 220)

Derrida also shows how the foundation of law, when appraised in the law's or the legal system's own terms, is unlawful (and 'violent'); and that, for this constitutive unlawfulness and all subsequent contingencies, no law can 'be' just/justice. Both Derrida and Žižek would be equally able to reveal the ways that even any democratic arrangement has something 'obscenely' undemocratic 'at its heart', and so on (Derrida 1992b: 29–30).

So, to demand the literal, the real, the true, could be to subvert any instituted order *in its own terms*, *because of* its own terms, and *towards* its own declared terms. But this 'towards' would amount to a revolutionary transformation of that which only (un)becomes 'itself' in being approached. To expose anything to its own law or claims is already to step outside of what it 'is', and to demand its becoming something entirely other; namely, what it itself says it should be (Godzich 1987: 156). The 'promise' of something other 'to come' does not relate to an alterity that might arrive from elsewhere. So actually proposing something antagonistic or 'thoroughly different' to what is held to be already in existence automatically entails that the proposed alternative cannot but be negated.

Utopias constitutively confound themselves. The neoliberalist-capitalist consensus, masquerading as perfection, must be held to the literality of what it preaches about itself. To the extent that it says, 'utopia is here', one need only ask, 'Where? Show me'. In fact, *we need no other prophet of paradise to come*: we need look no further than the most mainstream of cultural productions, and the most powerful of political declarations, to learn superlative lessons in the justice, liberty, equality, democracy, the power and goodness of the polity, that we are supposed to have already. Ask for them: *they are not given*. Shouldn't this be enough?

Robert Young concludes an analysis of Margaret Thatcher's use of Adam Smith's economic and political theory (Young 1992: 99–122) with the suggestion that perhaps the *worst* thing that one can do, the most politically *useless*, is to *oppose* any system. Young, like Docherty, agrees that opposition, not advocation, is what oils any system's own stability. Paradoxically then, in effect, we reach the sternest Marxist position, in which the best thing one can do is to wholeheartedly, enthusiastically, subscribe to and *support* the system. For this will help it to collapse itself (Young 1992: 120–1). For the only way 'the system' survives is to the extent that it *is not itself*, to the extent that it puts the brakes on itself, lives 'outside itself', parasitically, vampirically, spectrally. So Young teases out one conclusion that is repressed within Adam Smith's logic: 'the system' *cannot be itself* and survive. Hence, Young proposes that the political task of today is not to oppose 'the system', but to find ways of producing a surplus that it cannot comprehend.

A deconstructive political strategy, then, would have certain features. Never propose concrete utopian alternatives, as these cannot but be refuted. Always insist on the *letter* of that which is claimed present. Proposed alternative visions, like Marxism, faltered in the light of the literality of their letters. So now, they say, only the spirit remains. This spirit is wrong. We can no longer put any faith in spirits, even spirits and spectres of Marx, Marxism, or revolution. For spirits too are duplicitous. They help stability: every stability requires not only its letter, but also its spirit. As Wittgenstein put it, every law interminably requires *one more law* to explain how it should be implemented (see Laclau 2000: 77–8). This interminable slippage can only be halted by invoking a *spirit* of the law. So the invocation of the spirit, the ethos, the proper, of any system is an appeal to a constitutive outside that transgresses the letter and law of the system. The spirit must be refused, in the name of preserving the other (of the) spirit of the promise of revolution. Marxist and deconstructive orthodoxy are guilty in claiming spectres and spirits – spectres of Marx, spirits of revolution. No one and nothing should need to invoke its own proper spirit if its letter could do its proper job. The spirit is the most improper, non-revolutionary and non-*revaluationary* entity one could ever invoke. It preserves stability. Spirits justify living in repetition, the creation of fictions, the production of business (as usual), and help to console, help us to endure absence. Instead of thinking through *absence*, I prefer, as Barthes puts it, *frustration*, which 'would have Presence as its figure (I see the other every day, yet I am not satisfied . . .)' (Barthes 1990: 16). The proper spirit of revolution demands perversions of and infidelity to the proper; faithful infidelity to opposition; monstrous fidelity to the letter of every law, just to be just, which is always only to demand the im/possible. 'Our task is to be just. That is, we must only point out and resolve . . . injustices . . . and not posit new parties – and creeds' (Wittgenstein quoted in Owen 2001: 139).

PART II

Displacement

Counter-Culture versus Counter-*Culture*

Let's get retarded

Why be so serious all the time? Surely popular culture is *not serious*. Surely, popular culture is not something that demands seriousness. Surely, in fact, it demands the *opposite* of this. Just look around you! What's all this about 'significance'? A song by The Black Eyed Peas is instructive here. Its title itself is gloriously 'un-PC' ('un-Politically Correct'): 'Let's Get Retarded' (2003). The word 'retard' is nowadays much frowned-upon. For it is often used pejoratively, as an insult. Yet this song does not use the term pejoratively. In fact, the very start of the song takes the form of a long, loud, clear, drawn-out call, sung *a cappella* by the female vocalist, ringing out like a call to prayer – 'Let's get retarded in here!' The ensuing song is a celebration of 'getting retarded'. So, not only is the term *not* being used pejoratively, 'getting retarded' is actually being *advocated*. Immediately after the first words enjoin us to 'get retarded in here', drums fire up, quickly followed by a contagiously catchy bass riff. The first thing the lyrics do is point out what the bass is doing. At the exact moment the bass-line starts, the lyrics start:

> And the bass keeps runnin' runnin', and runnin' runnin', and runnin' runnin', and runnin' runnin', and runnin' runnin', and runnin' runnin', and runnin' runnin', and runnin' runnin', and …

The voices build throughout this intro, starting from one male voice, soon joined by a female voice, and then ever more layers of harmonizing female vocals, until a lead guitar enters and ushers in the transition to the first verse, which proceeds as follows:

> In this context, there's no disrespect,
> So when I bust my rhyme, you break your necks
> We got five minutes for us to disconnect,
> From all intellect, collect the rhythm effect.
> Obstacles are inefficient,
> Follow your intuition,
> Free your inner soul and break away from tradition.
> Coz when we beat out, girl it's pullin' without.
> You wouldn't believe how we wow shit out.
> Burn it till it's burned out. Turn it till it's turned out.
> Act up from north, west, east, south.

From here we move directly into the first chorus:

> Everybody (ye-a!), everybody (ye-a!), let's get into it (Yea!).
> Get stoopid (come on!).
> Get retarded (come on!), get retarded (come on!), get retarded.
> Let's get retarded (ha), let's get retarded in here.
> Let's get retarded (ha), let's get retarded in here.
> Let's get retarded (ha), let's get retarded in here.
> Let's get retarded (ha), let's get retarded in here.
> Yeah.

Obviously, written down like this, it doesn't look like much. The point is, it's designed to be *listened* to, *heard*, *felt*, danced to. Writing the lyrics down, reading them, and thinking about it *obviously* transgresses the spirit, which is all about the *experience* of it. The lyrics are clear on this: right from the beginning they direct us to the fact that this is all about what happens when 'the bass keeps runnin', runnin' '. And, what is it that happens? The first verse explains.

We are told: 'In this context, there's no disrespect'. The normal conventions and protocols of behaviour (for which 'respect' and 'disrespect' might be read as shorthand) do not apply *here*. The reason for this suspension of normal conventions is that 'when I bust my rhyme, you break your necks': when the song starts, bodies will *automatically* respond to the bass and to the rhythm and to the rhymes. When you listen to the music, you will feel the rhythm. This (the lyricist suggests) can *eradicate* social conventions by calling to *everyone* 'in here' *in the same way*. Of course, we have to 'disconnect' in order to 'get into it' – and vice versa: get into it in order to disconnect. This is what it proposes: 'We got five minutes for us to disconnect from all intellect [in order to] collect the rhythm effect'. So, 'Let's Get Retarded' says, let's 'disconnect' from the social 'obstacles' of conventions like protocols of respect and disrespect, and indeed from anything to do with 'intellect'. Such 'obstacles are inefficient'. Instead, one should 'Follow your intuition, free your inner soul and break away from tradition'.

The sentiment expressed here is strongly reminiscent of the injunction in countless popular cultural 'resistance-to-convention' narratives (such as Baz Luhrmann's *Strictly Ballroom*, in which the rebellious young ballroom dancer is re-educated in the ways of a more 'natural' paso doble: 'do not be afraid, listen to the rhythm'; or the Wachowski brothers' *Matrix*, in which Neo is enjoined to believe in his ability to 'just do it'). The idea is that by *getting into* the music our bodies will get the better of us and we will be able to 'free' our 'inner soul and break away from tradition'. These are interesting claims to make. Would it be too much to take such a seriously anti-serious song *seriously*?

Free your inner soul and break away from tradition

Again, there is a question about whether we are 'reading too much into' a text like this. After all, it's only a pop song, and moreover, a pop song which seems to be demanding *less* intellectual activity and *not more*. Nevertheless, 'Let's Get Retarded' does give voice to a very precise sentiment: never mind the mind, respond to the music and thereby 'free your inner soul and break away from tradition'. What seems particularly significant is that this sentiment – this argument – can be linked to a very long history.

Joseph Heath and Andrew Potter (2005) have characterized this tradition as one of 'romantic individualism'. And romantic individualism, they argue, is a key attitude of what they call the *countercultural critique*. Of course, The Black Eyed Peas hardly warrant designation as 'countercultural'. By any conventional measure, they are clearly 'pop'. Nevertheless, it seems worthwhile to examine traces of counterculture in the heart of what appears to be mainstream, if only to problematize the very distinction between 'mainstream' and 'alternative', or culture and counterculture, or indeed culture and subculture. For, as Jeremy Gilbert and Ewan Pearson point out, academics are too often 'obsessed with producing taxonomies of dubious value, sorting and labelling, freezing the cultural continuum for a little while and then moving on' (1999: 23). In other words, the very idea of a clear and sharp distinction between culture and sub- or counterculture may itself be a complete 'red herring': the notion of 'subculture', for example, may merely be one of cultural studies' and sociology's favourite 'seductive rhetorical fictions by which contemporary youth cultures are pressed into service as re-enactments of familiar myths of identity' (22). As Gilbert and Pearson see it, such supposed distinctions between 'groups' may not be as valid a notion as Pierre Bourdieu's proposal that the most active force within identity construction is a desire not for group same-ness but for individual *distinction*: in other words, not a desire to be a homogenous part of a group, but rather a desire for distinction from others. The notion of homogeneous sub- or countercultural 'groups' may merely be academia's fantasy-production.

Nevertheless, what Heath and Potter mean by 'countercultural cri-tique' is a line of thinking that they argue can be traced back hundreds of years (to thinkers like Rousseau), but that really took off in the USA and Europe in the late 1950s and especially the 1960s, and whose legacy persists to this day. According to them, the countercultural attitude is characterized by what might be called a *rage against the machine*: a belief that there is a *system*, a system that is *repressive, intolerant*, and *bad*. Against the system stands any heroic individual who has somehow reached awareness, insight, or awakening – like Neo in *The Matrix*. Of course, there are many other figures for the countercultural opponent of 'the system': the beatnik of the 50s; the hippy or 'New Ager' of the 60s who has opened the doors of perception, reached 'awareness' or 'insight' about the blinkers that 'reality' has drawn over our perceptions, and who believes in the need for a 'psychic revolution'; the anarchic punk of the 70s who hates 'the system' which stultifies and turns peo-ple into mindless zombies, etc. According to Heath and Potter, the USA was the driving force of countercultural thinking after the Second World War. This, they claim, was largely because of the absence in the USA of a socialist tradition. So, whilst in Europe and elsewhere countercultural thinking was normally a supplement to a socialist or communist polit-ical programme, in the USA countercultural thinking *per se* became *the* alternative to 'mainstream' worldviews. This, they argue, is where the problems start to come in.

For, according to their argument, countercultural thinking involves a belief in what they call 'romantic individualism': namely, the belief that if only we could remove the shackles of culture, which repress and control us, we could be truly *free*. Romantic individualism is, then, anti-institutional and against convention. However, Heath and Potter observe, there are two uncannily similar versions of romantic individualism: a left-wing version *and* a right-wing version. For, as they see it, both counterculture *and* capitalist ideology romanticize the notion of the 'free', 'unique' individual. The right-wing spin on this is that individuals, left to themselves, will be 'more competitive' and 'more efficient'. So this line of thinking is used as an argument against the state and the welfare state in particular. Left-wing romantic individualism, on the other hand, differs from right-wing romantic individualism in that it tends to renounce 'property' and the competitive capitalist system; so it has tended to prefer anarchism as its guiding ideology or philosophy. This anarchism was perhaps articulated most clearly in punk, in which a key impulse was to 'smash the system', to end *coercion* and *control*. But, whereas left-wing counterculture has tended to think that coercion and control arise because 'the system' is repressive or 'evil', right-wing ideologues tend to think that coercion and control arise because 'the other' is 'evil', so control over 'us' is necessary in order to prevent some demonized 'other' ('them') taking over. According to Heath and Potter, the fundamental problem with countercultural thinking is that it makes the logical mistake of reasoning that because 'some rules are bad, therefore rules as such are bad'. So, they argue that both left and right countercultural thinking rely on a notion of romantic individualism and mistakenly equate 'rules' with 'repression'.

Disconnect from all intellect, collect the rhythm effect

But what has this got to do with our song, or with popular culture, whether 'mainstream', 'sub-' or 'countercultural'? Well, first, there is the sense in which we might detect traces of this style of thinking, supplementing, structuring or gently guiding the connections and assertions made in 'Let's Get Retarded', even though the song is avowedly a pop song and it would be hard to categorize it as 'countercultural' by any stretch of the imagination. Indeed, 'Let's Get Retarded' has no 'militancy' other than a fervently declared desire to encourage its listeners to 'disconnect' and 'get stoopid'. However, because of this imperative in the song, there is another sense in which the song might be said to contain a kind of 'countercultural' trait, traces of which are characteristic of many realms of 'frivolous', 'enjoyable' or supposedly 'trivial' popular culture. This relates precisely to the encouragement to 'disconnect' the brain and 'get into' the music (with the body).

As Jeremy Gilbert and Ewan Pearson point out, the 'non-verbal aspect of music's effectivity ... has given rise to its [having a] strange status in western thought' (1999: 39). They explain this 'strange status' by making a wide analysis of many influential Western philosophers.

As they remind us, in Plato's *Republic*, Socrates approves only of simple, functional, militaristic music, and definitely not revelry. Furthermore, in Platonic-Socratic thinking more generally, music is regarded as something that must be tied down to and by *words* (40). They note that Rousseau too distinguishes between music as *affect* (involving the body) and music as source of *meaning* (involving the intellect); and they also note that Kant hated what he called '*Tafelmusik*' – table music, music not designed for *contemplation* (41). And even Adorno, who saw the critical potential of music, was opposed to bourgeois *dance* music of his day. Thus, according to Gilbert and Pearson, 'this tradition tends to demand of music that it – as far as possible – *be meaningful*, that even where it does not have words, it should offer itself up as an object of intellectual contemplation' (42).

In this, they identify a distinct Western tradition of *devaluing* the pleasures of the body (such as dance) and an elevation of logocentrism, or meaning. Music designed specifically for dancing, then, might be regarded as *unintentionally* 'countercultural', at least to the extent that 'culture' is to be regarded as logocentric. For the body has been subordinated to the mind and does actually seem counter to the logocentrism of much Western 'culture' and philosophy in this sense. Indeed, quite distinct from the *logocentrism* of Western intellectual orientations, Gilbert and Pearson argue that there is a physicality to sound: music is *felt* by the body, and so 'music – like all sound – is registered on a fundamentally different level to language or modes of visual communication' (44). Thus, they argue, 'music can be said to, as Robert Walser suggests, "hail the body directly"' (46). Yet scholarly work has until recently been neglectful of the relationship between music and dance, and of its significance (47).

From this position, Gilbert and Pearson propose that the physical materiality of music and dance *is* both theoretically (philosophically) and practically (culturally and politically) important. As they argue, the logocentrism of Western intellectual culture has led to the suppression of the materiality and physicality of music (55), as is demonstrated by the tradition's overvaluation of words and meanings. However, they reiterate, dance is a physical experience (60) which does not necessarily have *one* – or indeed *any* – 'meaning'. Hence its denigration by the Western intellectual tradition: 'Much contemporary "popular" music discourse also marginalizes dance as an activity and marginalizes those forms of music associated with it' (60–1). Therefore, as they see it, 'There are reasons why all of this matters ... There are reasons why instrumental popular musics face far greater resistance from powerful institutions than song-based forms' (38). These reasons are related to the metaphysical, logocentric bias of Western culture.

Of course, 'Let's Get Retarded' is far from a marginalized, resisted, non-lyrical or obviously countercultural production. But it certainly has a relationship to the 'dance music' with which Gilbert and Pearson are concerned. And in this respect it is organized by something that might be called a 'countercultural' impulse. But what are we to make of such an impulse? Is it really significant? In what sense, and for whom? Or is it indeed the case that, as Heath and Potter's argument would have it, there is a sense in which not only *counter*cultural practices but actually *all cultural* practices are politically insignificant. According to them:

> The idea of counterculture is ultimately based on a mistake. At best, countercultural rebellion is pseudo-rebellion: a set of dramatic gestures that are devoid of any progressive political or economic consequences and that detract from the urgent task of building a more just society. (Heath and Potter 2006: 69)

Of course, Gilbert and Pearson do not argue that music or dancing is political or consequential *per se*. Indeed, they are unequivocal that experiences and practices are only 'radical' depending on the contexts in which they occur: 'Like all politics, the politics of dance cultures is relational and context-specific, a matter of the relationships between different groups and formations, rather than something inherent in its very nature' (1999: 158). And, as they themselves ask: 'when we get back from the party, have we just left all [the usual social] structures as intact as they were before?' (162) Their answer is that, although in and of itself 'carnival' is no threat to the social order, nevertheless carnival sites *have* worked as points and moments of the initiation of social and political agitation. But they absolutely reject the thesis that all popular culture is apolitical and of no consequence for anything 'important'. As they explain:

> ... we do not give much credence to the idea that dance culture is simply a distraction for the oppressed masses. Apart from anything else, we do not believe that people suffering serious oppression are stupid enough to be 'bought off' with an 'E' and a house beat; if many young people are more interested in the latter than in conventional politics, this is probably because of a realistic assessment on their part of the lack of scope for political intervention at the present time. (Gilbert and Pearson 1999: 163)

In fact, they contend, dance culture has challenged and does challenge hegemony in lots of ways. For one thing, dance culture in the UK in the late 80s and early 90s changed an awful lot to do with British social and cultural life. This was the period of the birth of 24-hour partying, the likes of which had never been seen before. 'These aren't small changes', they point out. 'In 1987, the 17 year old probably had little else to do but get drunk at his/her local pub' (Gilbert and Pearson 1999: 180). Indeed, along with the embryonic encounters and possibilities for new forms of community and social interaction that dance culture precipitated, they propose that 'If Ecstasy and house music have even slightly displaced drunkenness and violence as the common culture of young men in Britain, then Britain can only be a better place for it' (182).

But Heath and Potter's position implies that such deconstructive insights as those offered by Gilbert and Pearson may merely be pointless. Of course, this is a position which implicitly regards culture itself – never mind popular culture or counterculture – to be of no political consequence. The case that Heath and Potter make is effectively a version of an accusation that is often levelled against both deconstructive evocations of 'the political' dimensions of this or that, as well as against the kind of attention given to popular culture within fields such as cultural studies. So, the question is: are both deconstruction and cultural studies pointless and misguided? Is considering popular culture to be 'important' in any respect simply a case of barking up the wrong tree?

Rage against the machine

For Heath and Potter, the fundamental problem with investing any political or wider significance in popular culture is that 'the idea of counterculture ... has become the conceptual template for all contemporary leftist politics [having] almost completely replaced socialism as the basis of radical political thought' (2005: 17). To make their case, *The Rebel Sell* consists of chapters which aim to debunk the myths of different manifestations of countercultural orientations: from 'culture-jamming' activities, such as the way Adbusters construct ironic and satirical versions of adverts, to hippy, punk and grunge attitudes towards 'authenticity' in the face of 'selling out', and so on. Taking Adbusters as their prime example, Heath and Potter argue that although the goal of culture-jammers is quite literally to 'jam' the culture, by subverting the messages and blocking the channels through which capitalist ideology is propagated, they note the irony of the birth of *an Adbusters range of products*, such as footwear designed to compete with Niké. As they see it, this development is *not* 'counter' anything at all. It is not in any sense *alternative*, *political* or *consequential*. Rather, it exemplifies the very essence of capitalism: entrepreneurial niche-marketing.

They make an equivalent argument about the drive for 'authenticity' that can be seen in all manner of movements, such as in musical 'sub-cultures' (their prime example here being Kurt Cobain of Nirvana), but particularly in the travel ideology represented in the novel and film, *The Beach*. In both cases, what they isolate are the myths and fantasies of the drive for the ultimate 'authentic' experience. But a word like 'authenticity' should set alarm bells ringing. For, what is *'authenticity'*? A first response might be to suggest that *authenticity* is something good that is to be opposed to all things *fake*. Hence, 'authenticity' might be the opposite of 'selling out'. In the field of music, 'selling out' might involve any form of supposed compromise with 'the system'. But, Heath and Potter point out, musicians do not become commodified when they reach a certain *level* of success. Rather, as soon as they produce a track for sale – indeed, as soon as they play a gig or a venue with an entry price or a pay-bar – they are already involved in an economic circuit. As the comedian Rob Newman once ironically put it, saying that you used to be into a band before they 'sold out' is a bit like saying you used to support a football team until they sold out by moving to the top of the league or winning trophies. In other words, the notion of authenticity versus inauthenticity (such as, say, 'selling out'), is based on a misunderstanding of the nature of culture. There is no authenticity as such. But belief in 'authenticity' persists and can be tragically ironic. According to Heath and Potter:

> Some myths die hard. One can see the cycle [of 'authenticity'] repeating itself in hip hop. The countercultural idea here takes the form of a romantic view of ghetto life and gang culture. Successful rappers must fight hard to retain their street cred, to 'keep it real'. They'll pack guns, do time, even get shot up, just to prove they're not just 'studio gangstas'. So instead of punks and hippies, we now have a steadily growing pantheon of dead rappers. People talk about the 'assassination' of Tupac Shakur, as though he actually posed a threat to the system. Eminem claims his arrest for possession of a concealed weapon was 'all political', designed to get him off the streets. It's the same thing all over again. (Heath and Potter 2005: 17)

The desire for the elusive notion of 'authenticity' has dogged countercultural musicians in particular since the 70s. The cultural theorist Fredric Jameson once observed the apparent plight of punk bands such as The Clash, who made politically charged 'angry' protest music, but inadvertently produced only more commodities – records, cassettes and other merchandise, and subsequently, of course, videos, CDs, DVDs, etc.. This is often presented as the 'Catch-22' situation of inevitably being 'co-opted' by 'the system'. Namely, you want to oppose 'the system', you want to 'smash the system', but you become part of it. This perceived problem and the 'rage against the machine' that it leads to was dramatized wonderfully by the stand-up comedian Bill Hicks:

> By the way if anyone here is in advertising or marketing . . . kill yourself. . . . There's no rationalisation for what you do and you are Satan's little helpers. Okay? Kill yourself. Seriously. You are the ruiner of all things good. Seriously. . . . . Planting seeds. I know all the marketing people are going, 'he's doing a joke'. There's no joke here whatsoever. Suck a tail-pipe, fucking hang yourself, borrow a gun from a Yank friend: I don't care how you do it. Rid the world of your evil fucking machinations. 'Machinations'? Whatever. You know what I mean.
>
> I know what all the marketing people are thinking right now, too: 'Oh, you know what Bill's doing? He's going for that anti-marketing dollar. That's a good market, he's very smart'.
>
> Oh man, I am not doing that, you fucking evil scumbags!
>
> 'Ooh! You know what Bill's doing now? He's going for the righteous indignation dollar. That's a big dollar. A lot of people are feeling that indignation. We've done research – huge market. He's doing a good thing'.
>
> God damn it, I'm not doing that, you scumbags! Quit putting a god damn dollar sign on every fucking thing on this planet!
>
> 'Ooh, the anger dollar! Huge. Huge in times of recession. Giant market. Bill's very bright to do that'.
>
> God, I'm just caught in a fucking web.
>
> 'Ooh the trapped dollar! Big dollar, huge dollar. Good market – look at our research. We see that many people feel trapped. If we play to them and separate them into the trapped dollar . . . .' (Hicks 2005: 134–5)

How might one respond to such a countercultural characterization of the 'system' of commodification? Heath and Potter suggest that the answer given by today's countercultural thinkers is that we should try to 'subvert' or 'jam' it. Their preferred example with which to illustrate the countercultural critique is the film *The Matrix*. In this film, humans are represented as working ignorantly for 'the system'. In *The Matrix*, humans are *literally the batteries* powering the inhuman system, but they don't know it because they are fed what Marxist theory would once have called 'false consciousness'. A few exceptional souls have been able to perceive the artifice of the system and its ideology, and have been able to free themselves and to begin to free others – those whose minds are 'ready', such as Neo (Keanu Reeves). Indeed, it is only possible to rescue those who are 'ready', willing *and able* to have the blinkers of false consciousness lifted. As Heath and Potter see it, this exemplifies the countercultural world view. (It also has close affinities with what is now called 'crude' or 'vulgar' Marxism, especially in its proposition that 'the masses' are subject to the 'false consciousness' of ideology, while only an avant-garde of (Marxist) intellectuals can perceive the truth.) In this view, the 'enemy' is the 'system' which disseminates 'false consciousness', while the masses are exploited, fed images, and kept docile, placid and in a state of ignorance, with no political consciousness. Heath and Potter point out that this is the view developed by Guy Debord, in his influential book, *The Society of the Spectacle*; a perspective later developed by Jean Baudrillard, with his theory of the contemporary world being dominated by hyperreality and simulation.

For Heath and Potter, the fundamental problem with this countercultural theory is the belief that the veil of illusion is to be pierced by 'cognitive dissonance' – by drawing people's attention to the falsity of capitalist ideology. However, in the long term, they argue, this has had the politically debilitating effect of redirecting people's energies from *political* projects with socialist aims and towards counter*cultural* projects with all sorts of varying – often individualistic – aims. Heath and Potter construe such countercultural efforts as simply barking up the wrong tree. If one has a problem with, say, the activities of multinational corporations, they suggest that defacing some of their adverts is not necessarily going to change anything. If one has a problem with capitalist commodification, then consuming or producing different commodities is certainly not going to be a solution to the problem. Ultimately, in fact, not only do Heath and Potter reject the *countercultural* critique, they reject any notion of cultural politics at all. Their position is not only *counter*-countercultural, then. It is also counter*cultural*. For they reject the possibility that anything other than parliamentary or state-directed politics might change things.

Resistance is useless

The question, then, is: is the notion of *cultural politics* – of the political significance of *culture* (if not countercultural politics) – based on a myth, or a mistake? Must politics be addressed to the state? This is a well-worn topic that introduces a set of questions which regularly arise in the face of the question of the significance of popular culture and of whether or not it is legitimate to take it seriously as a topic of study. Despite their writing an entire book on different versions of countercultural projects, Heath and Potter's position is actually representative of a version of thinking which argues that there is no real political significance to popular culture. The logical conclusion to be drawn from this is that the academic study of popular culture is also of no political significance.

Such a view has been offered most clearly in recent years by the prolific and vociferous Slovenian philosopher and political and cultural critic, Slavoj Žižek, who has had an increasing amount to say about cultural studies in this regard, too. Cultural studies is a field which often studies popular culture and in which his work has had a marked impact since the explosive arrival of his first book in English, *The Sublime Object of Ideology* (1989). In fact, as Michael Walsh observes, even though Žižek was unpublished in English as recently as 1988, since then he has published 'an average of more than one monograph a year, not to speak of a [growing] number of edited collections', works which have proved so influential that today 'a speaker giving a presentation at a scholarly conference may now find that s/he is giving the second or third Žižekian talk in a row. For full-blown appearance on the intellectual scene, then, Žižek has few rivals' (Walsh 2002: 390). There are perhaps two glaring reasons for Žižek's phenomenally successful arrival. The first is suggested by Catherine Belsey, who observes that 'when Žižek slips easily and wittily between Kantian philosophy and demotic jokes, Hegel and Hitchcock, the effect is exhilarating' (Belsey 2003: 27). So, firstly (at least for an academic readership used to very dry scholarship), Žižek is *fun*, a lively and enthralling read, combining philosophy with popular culture in novel and interesting ways. The second reason is suggested by Terry Eagleton, whose now-famous description of Žižek as 'the most formidably brilliant exponent of psychoanalysis, indeed of cultural theory in general, to have emerged from Europe in some decades' now graces the covers of many of Žižek's rapidly expanding list of publications. Indeed, as these enthusiastic endorsements (from academics associated with cultural studies) suggest, Žižek's theoretically lucid and radically politicized cultural criticism seems tailor-made for cultural studies. Given this, the fact that most of what Žižek has to say about cultural studies and the investment in (popular) culture is often scathingly critical may seem surprising.

Tony Myers notes the irony: Žižek's work is increasingly 'a staple on cultural studies programmes' at the same time as his work is becoming more and more clearly marked by a growing 'disavowal of cultural studies' (Myers 2003: 124). However, this chapter will go on to argue that Žižek's disavowal of cultural studies is *deliberate* and *strategic* (whilst the knee-jerk adoption or rejection of his work within cultural studies is not always so well considered), and that Žižek's strategic and apparently belligerent relation to cultural studies' arguments about the political dimensions of popular culture actually offers something of a 'royal road' to approaching and understanding his work. Indeed, making sense of this peculiar relation offers the most important insights into his entire orientation. So, let's examine Žižek's polemics against cultural studies, and assess the grounds and value of this often downplayed aspect of his work for the study of popular culture. This will help us to question – as Žižek regularly does – the place, role, responsibilities and significance of cultural studies and popular culture in the contemporary world.

Slavoj Žižek's counter-countercultural critique

Interestingly, Žižek actually contends that cultural studies exists and operates right at the heart – indeed, on the 'radical' side – of a dispute that divides and structures the entire contemporary academic world. That is, he takes cultural studies to be the exemplary case of a strand of scholarship that he characterizes (variously) as postmodernist, deconstructionist, relativist, historicist, or postcolonialist, which he then opposes to an entity that he calls the 'standard' or 'naïve cognitivist approach' of most other contemporary scholarship (Žižek 2001a: 223). Many may baulk at such a schema, and at what may well be taken as a reductive or unjustly simplifying representation of, we must remember, *the entire academic world*. But this is typical Žižek: his work is saturated with and organized by sweeping statements, stark oppositions and binary schemas – binaries that ultimately become tripartite, once Žižek's own position is added to the mix. Here, for instance, with a strand of scholarship embodied by cultural studies on the one hand, and another embodied by the 'cognitivist popularizers of the "hard" sciences' (Žižek, 2001a: 210) on the other, Žižek ultimately merely uses them to argue for his own position, which 'transcends' – or at least trumps – them both. So, quite distinct from scholars like Jacques Derrida (of whose cultural studies 'acolytes' Žižek is most critical), whose main strategy involves 'microscopic' readings of the minutiae of specific texts (often in order thereupon to comment on wider issues, problems, institutions, or phenomena (Derrida 1998a: 40), Žižek's approach is chiefly one of quickly conjuring up (through allusion and assertion) wider issues, problems, institutions, or phenomena, in order to diagnose them in terms of his own preferred categories (Laclau 2004: 327). This is quite problematic, and we will return to this aspect of Žižek's approach in due course. At this stage it is sufficient to note that when Žižek bandies around

terms like 'cultural studies', he is not interested in trying to demonstrate, justify or prove any of his points or assertions. Rather, he simply
wishes to set the scene quickly for his diagnosing and philosophizing on
issues he treats as if already self-evident, widely known and in general
circulation.

Žižek's primary claim in relation to cultural studies is that his work
has nothing in common with it. This is because he views himself as an
'authentic philosopher' (Žižek 2001b: 125). He views cultural studies
as 'ersatz philosophy' (2001a: 224). In fact, it is always clear that Žižek
himself values and identifies with Philosophy overall. But this leads
him to project his own values onto other objects (here, cultural studies
is represented as if merely wanting to be philosophy), and to interpret
them entirely in his own terms. So, cultural studies is simply 'ersatz
philosophy', while the rest of the university is allegedly dogged by
the shackling anti-philosophical animus of the aforementioned 'naïve
cognitivist approach' (2001a: 223). As he puts it, characteristically
polemically, he sees his position *vis-à-vis* these alternatives as neither
that of 'today's twin brothers of deconstructionist sophistry and New
Age obscurantism' (1998: 1007), nor the 'capitulation itself' of most other
social and political thinking, such as that of the 'Third Way' ideologues
like Anthony Giddens or Ulrich Beck, whom he regards as the lapdogs
of neoliberalist ideology (Žižek 2001b: 32–3; 2002: 308). This pejorative
view makes more sense when it is understood that by 'capitulation'
Žižek means the 'the acceptance of capitalism as "the only game in
town", [and hence] the renunciation of any real attempt to overcome
the existing capitalist liberal regime' (2000a: 95). This 'resignation' to
capitalism is something that he sees and decries everywhere: in the
positions of all 'standard' social and political thinkers, in all political
and cultural movements that are not explicitly anti-capitalist (and even,
it seems, most that are), as well as, in a different way, in what he calls
'naïve cognitivism', or 'the standard functioning of academic knowledge – "professional", rational, empirical, problem-solving' scholarship
(2001a: 226). For even scholarship that is allegedly neutral, objective
and supposedly non-political *is* political precisely because it is that of
the status quo (which is a political formation).

Against simple 'capitulation', cultural studies, deconstruction and
postmodernism are – according to Žižek – 'sophistry' because (like
New Age mysticism) they do not properly engage with the 'truth', nor
with 'material reality' (Žižek 2001b: 1–2). The only saving grace that
deconstructionism and postmodernism (but never New Ageism) can
sometimes have, in his eyes, is that they do not *completely* capitulate to
the status quo of today's 'capitalism'. In fact, as we will see, Žižek does

think that there is something fundamentally intellectually and politically radical and *potentially* transformative about cultural studies. This is because integral to the differences he sees between cultural studies and cognitivism is the 'deconstructionist' and otherwise *theoretical* character of cultural studies versus the philosophical naïveté of 'standard' scholarship. For Žižek's contention is that most scholarship clings to the naïve operating assumption that humans can simply, immediately and directly access the truth of reality in unbiased, unmediated and untheoretical ways. Thus, argues Žižek, there is 'a dimension that simply eludes its grasp'; a dimension 'properly visible only from the standpoint of Cultural Studies' (Žižek 2001a: 223). This dimension is the insight that *all* knowledge, even 'objective' knowledge, is constitutively and inescapably 'part of the social relations of power' (225). Despite this insight, despite the grain of truth that it holds as its starting point (that we are barred access to the truth, because we are limited, partisan, and flung into a world made up of different discourses and ideologies), the problem with cultural studies is said to be that it does not engage with material reality properly, and contents itself with the 'cognitive suspension' of refusing to ask direct ontological questions about reality in favour of discussing 'different discursive formations evaluated not with regard to their inherent truth-value, but with regard to their sociopolitical status and impact' (2001a: 219). This, for Žižek, is a cop-out. Thus, he complains, the cultural studies-style scholarship of incessantly 'historicizing' and 'contextualizing' in terms of politics and power actually *avoids* the hard questions of truth and reality – questions which to its credit cognitivism takes on, albeit naively.

The inauthentic relative

So, Žižek sees mushy, wishy-washy relativists to the left of him and diligent knaves to the right. We might critique Žižek on the basis of this simplifying schema – as Ernesto Laclau does when he says that Žižek's style often reminds him of the parable of a 'village priest ... who in his sermons imagined a stupid Manichean to be able to more easily refute Manicheanism' (Laclau 2004: 327). And this tendency in Žižek is problematic. Yet there is a sense in which to criticize Žižek for this without taking on board *why* he proceeds in this manner is to miss something important. For his target is the anti-theoretical, anti-philosophical, intellectually 'naïve' character of much scholarship, on the one hand, and the over-theoretical but misguided intellectual 'sophistry' of cultural studies in its 'postmodernist, deconstructionist, historicizing' forms, on the other. (Žižek is entirely uninterested in any version of cultural studies other than its 'high theory' incarnations, consigning all empirical work to the status (quo) of 'the standard functioning of knowledge'.) In other words, cognitivism is a non-starter while cultural studies stumbles at the first hurdle because of an unfortunate tendency to *relativism*:

> Why is [cultural studies-style] radical historicizing false, despite the obvious moment of truth it contains? Because *today's (late capitalist global market) social reality itself is dominated by what Marx referred to as the power of 'real abstraction'*: the circulation of Capital is the force of radical 'deterritorialization' (to use Deleuze's term) which, in its very functioning, actively ignores specific conditions and cannot be 'rooted' in them. It is no longer, as in the standard ideology, the universality that occludes the twist of its partiality, of its privileging a particular content; rather, it is the very attempt to locate particular roots that ideologically occludes the social reality of the reign of 'real abstraction'. (Žižek 2001a: 1–2)

Thus, the postmodern claim of the value of context and contingency *would* be true were it not for the objective and universal truth of capitalism, which behaves predictably (it commodifies, it exploits, subjecting all to the logic of the market) and obscures its simple actions by blinding us all with a chimerical sense of the all-consuming complexity, disconnectedness or *unmasterableness* of it all. Žižek claims to be able to cut through this misunderstanding by way of his 'authentic' tripartite paradigm consisting of a combination of the insights of Hegel, Marx, and Lacan. Firstly, Hegel provides a universally applicable (meta-transcendental) way of understanding the logic of historical development (not to mention a proto-Lacanian account of the fundamental human condition in the master-and-slave dialectic (Hegel 1977), a dialectic which renders human identity as always inextricably bound up in complex identifications with significant others, and which Žižek maps onto Freud's Oedipus Complex and onto Lacanian theory). Secondly, Žižek marries this to the ('crude') Marxian claim that the truth of today's material reality is governed by the logic of capitalism. And thirdly, the problems of the limited, biased contextuality of all viewpoints Žižek 'resolves' through appeal to a series of Lacanian psychoanalytic insights, wherein, for example, because any viewer's 'gaze is inscribed into the "objective" features' of material reality (Žižek 2001a: 150), therefore what is required, to step out of the deadlock between naïveté and relativism, is for cognitivist science (and everyone else, for that matter) to retheorize objectivity in line with the lessons of Lacanian psychoanalysis. Accordingly, science and other forms of scholarship both need to be psychoanalysed and need to psychoanalyse, and indeed to be contextualized and historicized. But *not* 'relativized'. This is because, for Žižek, there *is* an objective truth and a determinant reality that governs human society: it is the 'material reality', 'objective conditions' and 'logic' of capitalism into which we psychoanalysable subjects find ourselves thrown. Thus, as can be seen from the passage quoted above, relativism may be *relatively* true, but the objective reality of the universality of capitalism has circled around to undercut relativism, by simultaneously *using* relativism's apparent truth (mushy relativism becoming the ideology of capitalism) and *thereby* invalidating it (for in reality, there is no relativism: capitalism is 'universal').

These are the key coordinates of Žižek's claim of 'authenticity'. It is a more radical rejection of culture than even Heath and Potter's. His Hegel offers a transcendental philosophy of the logical (dialectical) processes of history. This is completed by Marxist knowledge of the 'logic' of capitalism plus Lacanian psychoanalytic insights into the human condition. The person whom Žižek thinks best managed to '*act*' most successfully against the systemic stranglehold of capitalism is Lenin, and Žižek's ultimate ambition is that of 'repeating Lenin' (Žižek 2001c; 2002). In other words, as Žižek sees it, 'For an authentic philosopher, *everything has always-already happened*; what is difficult to grasp is how this notion not only does *not* prevent engaged activity, but effectively *sustains* it' (2001b: 125). Žižek sees his theoretical responsibilities to be those of 'holding the place' (2000b), of repeating the 'truth' of his insights into capitalism, ideology and subjectivity (namely, that although ideology 'goes all the way down' (Walsh 2002: 393) and the 'fundamental level of ideology . . . is not that of an illusion masking the real state of things but that of an (unconscious) fantasy structuring our social reality itself' (Žižek 1989: 33), this is set against the real backdrop of capitalism). Žižek's approach is to insist upon these truths until such a time as . . . as . . . well . . . until such a time as *someone* will 'act' decisively. In other words, in Žižek's political theory there is the universal 'system', on the one hand, and on the other the individual (exemplified by Lenin) who has the potential to 'act' in a revolutionary manner, to change this system.

This position harbours more than a few difficulties and limitations, and it has some highly problematic consequences. One is apparent superciliousness. As Michael Walsh explains, 'there's no arguing with a thoroughgoing Hegelian; theirs is a position that always-already anticipates (or sometimes just "implies") anything of value that is subsequently voiced' (2002: 391). Another is with this very *combination* of a meta-transcendentalist position claiming to know the universal truth of history (Hegel), with a putatively materialist economico-political position claiming to know the truth of contemporary reality (Marxism), and a psychoanalytical position claiming access to the fundamental truth of the human condition (Lacan). In Žižek, they are all presented as if *simply* overlaying, consolidating and unproblematically reinforcing each other, such that Žižek can 'dialectic' his way out of any corner and make pronouncements and diagnoses on apparently *any* subject. This leads to the serious problem of the formulaic repetition that one often finds in Žižek, and the wreaking of a kind of 'violence' over all other forensic, argumentative and methodological considerations. In Žižek, that is, one rarely finds detailed textual analysis (for what's the point when you already know what you will find?), no real genealogical, archival or historiographical examination (there is no need when a Marxian and/or psychoanalytic explanatory matrix is already to hand), nor indeed any contextual analysis, whether of his own position or of whatever is under discussion. This is because, from a position always confident that it *already* knows and speaks the truth, there is no need to contextualize one's own 'position' (it *is* the correct one).

So, one might say, Žižek's is a very peculiar 'philosophy' or 'theory' – one that does not really *think* (or *read* or *study*) as such. Indeed, Žižek views with suspicion any intellectual position, work or methodological considerations other than those he discerns in Hegel, Marx and Lacan – unless he can represent it as somehow being Hegelian/Marxian/ Lacanian. In particular, as we have seen, Žižek is suspicious of cultural studies, because in its historicizing, contextualizing, relativizing, 'positioning', 'politically correct' impulses, it seems to both corrupt his 'authentic' position and to repackage it in an ideologically acceptable form. Indeed he claims that in contemporary cultural studies, erstwhile radical 'notions of "European" critical theory are imperceptibly translated into the benign universe of Cultural Studies chic':

> At a certain point, this chic becomes indistinguishable from the famous Citibank commercial in which East Asian, European, Black and American children playing is accompanied by the voice-over: 'People once divided by a continent . . . are now united by an economy' – at this concluding highpoint, of course, the children are replaced by the Citibank logo. (Žižek 2002: 171)

In other words, for Žižek, despite all appearances, *it's always the economy, dummy!* And, to Žižek as to Marx and Engels, capitalism is a vampire.

So, when it comes to cultural studies, Žižek's critique is based on the claim that any move towards retheorizing or rethinking either politics or the obligations of an engaged intellectual (Gary Hall 2002) necessarily entails a 'silent suspension of class analysis' (Žižek 2000: 96) and hence a regressive move away from 'authentic' (Marxist, class-based) political engagement. As he theorizes it, the 'postmodern Leftist narrative of the passage [of cultural studies-type scholarship] from "essentialist" Marxism, [which viewed] the proletariat as the unique Historical Subject, [and entailed] the privileging of economic class struggle, and so on, to the postmodern [argument about the] irreducible plurality of struggles ... leave[s] out the resignation at its heart – the acceptance of capitalism as "the only game in town", the renunciation of any real attempt to overcome the existing capitalist liberal regime' (2000: 95). Thus, not only does Žižek view all of the 'posts-' associated with cultural studies as being politically 'resigned and cynical', he ultimately contends that *if* cultural studies is at the radical, challenging, cutting edge of anything at all, then that thing is quite simply the advancement of the ideology of contemporary capitalism. In other words, although cultural studies may perhaps tout as radical its preoccupations with such subjects as democracy, emancipation, egalitarianism, identity-formation, multiculturalism, postmodernism, feminism, queer studies, anti-racism, postcolonialism, marginality, hybridity, and so on, in actual fact these are simply struggles at the cutting edge of the 'politically correct' ideology of capitalist expansion. So, for Žižek, cultural studies is a trail-blazer of neoliberal ideology, which pushes 'political correctness' in order to ensure that everyone is invested chiefly in their own 'individuality' and 'difference'. This is unfortunate because it precludes effective political struggle, solidarity and agency. For, of course, individuality and difference are construed by Žižek as chiefly manifesting in different, pseudo-individual forms of consumption and leisure activities.

This, for Žižek, is an exemplary travesty, and a corruption of what cultural studies could and therefore should be. Rather than working towards 'true' emancipation (anti-capitalist revolution), cultural studies' investment in the notion of 'cultural politics' merely furthers 'politically correct' tolerant consumer multiculturalist relativism. It may *seem* 'radical', but, he counters, 'in the generalized perversion of late capitalism, transgression itself is solicited' (2001b: 20); 'transgression itself is appropriated – even encouraged – by the dominant institutions, the predominant doxa as a rule presents itself as a subversive transgression' (2001a: 141); or, 'To put it in Hegel's terms, the "truth" of [any] transgressive revolt against the Establishment is the emergence

of a new establishment in which transgression is part of the game'
(2001b: 31). Needless to say, to Žižek's mind, this rings true even for
such supposedly radical, emancipatory or otherwise transformative
intellectual efforts as the 'progressive' cultural studies impulse towards
inter-, post- and anti-disciplinarity that developed 'to overthrow the
Eurocentrist curriculum' (Žižek 2001a: 215; Stuart Hall 1992). To him,
it is merely another facet of the 'deconstructive' or 'deterritorializing'
logic of capital.

Of course, Žižek was not the first and will surely not be the last
to regard the international proliferation of cultural studies within and
at the limits of capitalism with some suspicion (Lyotard 1984; Readings 1996; Rutherford 2005). In a recent issue of the journal *Cultural
Studies* (itself only one more instalment in the long-running engagement of cultural studies with the question of cultural studies within
economic, political and other 'social relations of power'), for instance,
Jonathan Rutherford begins his reflection on 'Cultural studies in the corporate university' by recalling the memorable edict from his superiors
that, even as an academic, his 'priority should be costs' (2005: 297).
This prompts the following observations, in a narrative that will be
representative of many others from those working within cultural
studies:

> When I got my first permanent, full-time lecturing post ten years ago, my
> ideal of an academic was modelled on Gramsci's organic intellectual: 'The
> mode of being of the new intellectual can no longer consist in eloquence ...
> but in active participation in practical life, as constructor, organiser,
> "permanent persuader" and not just a simple orator' (Gramsci 1988). Cul-
> tural Studies was about the world beyond the university. I saw the institution
> itself as a benign presence, the neutral, depoliticised element in the equa-
> tion. This rather naïve view failed to survive the market-based reforms of
> the subsequent decade. I found myself increasingly preoccupied with the
> university itself, and my relationship with it. The site of political change was
> no longer 'out there', but right here in the practice of being an academic and
> a university employee. I can't recall what it was I lectured about when I first
> began, but it undoubtedly reflected my own recent struggles in the library,
> studying postcolonialist texts by Gayatri Spivak or Homi Bhabha. There is
> an irony in the resurgence of neo-colonialism because Media and Cultural
> Studies' modules that might incorporate these ideas are sold to institutions
> in China, India and East Asia. Our universities pursue business in coun-
> tries with governments who have scant regard for academic freedom and
> where academics are locked up for writing the wrong kinds of history. This
> is not the realisation of the dream of international exchange and dialogue.

The university is a global business and Media and Cultural Studies finds itself a commodity at the heart of it. (Rutherford 2005: 298)

Stuart Hall, too, once confessed to being 'completely dumfounded' by the 'rapid professionalization and institutionalization' of cultural studies in the USA (1992: 285), and he too suggested that this 'professionalization and institutionalization' could 'formalize out of existence the critical questions of power, history, and politics' (286). Žižek regularly returns to the 'professionalization' of cultural studies, even remarking anecdotally and with a certain incredulity that he has heard of American cultural studies professors who play the stock market (2002: 171–2). This is why he suggests that perhaps 'the field of Cultural Studies, far from actually threatening today's global relations of domination, fits their framework perfectly' (2001a: 225–6). What cultural studies needs to do, he asserts, is to take a dose of its own medicine, take stock of itself, and remember its roots:

> Academically recognized 'radical thought' in the liberal West does not operate in a void, but is part of the social relations of power. Apropos of Cultural Studies, one has again to ask the old Benjaminian question: not how do they explicitly *relate to* power, but how are they themselves *situated within* the predominant power relations? Do not Cultural Studies also function as a discourse which pretends to be critically self-reflexive, revealing predominant power relations, while in reality it obfuscates its own mode of participating in them? So it would be productive to apply to Cultural Studies themselves the Foucauldian notion of productive 'bio-power' as opposed to 'repressive'/prohibitory legal power: what if the field of Cultural Studies, far from actually threatening today's global relations of domination, fits their framework perfectly, just as sexuality and the 'repressive' discourse that regulates it are fully complementary? What if the criticism of patriarchal/identitarian ideology betrays an ambiguous fascination with it, rather than an actual will to undermine it? Crucial here is the shift from English to American Cultural Studies: even if we find in both the same themes, notions, and so on, the socio-ideological functioning is completely different: we shift from an engagement with real working-class culture to academic radical chic.
>
> Despite such critical remarks, however, the very fact of *resistance* against Cultural Studies proves that they remain a foreign body unable to fit fully into existing academia . . . . (Žižek 2001a: 225–6)

Now, despite the appearances caused by the crescendo of *ad hominem* insinuations here, this is not simply an entirely untenable argument about sincerity versus pretence, nor a facile anti-American argument. It is certainly problematically phrased, particularly in the claim that cultural studies no longer engages properly 'with real working-class culture' (whatever this might ever be taken to mean – and it might be taken to mean lots of different things), having become instead mere 'academic radical chic' in 'the shift from English to American Cultural Studies'. But, as a Lawrence Grossberg essay title puts it, 'Where Is the "America" in American Cultural Studies?' (Grossberg 1997). That is, key to cultural studies is the questioning of such distinctions as this one, between 'English' and 'American' cultural studies. Of course, as we have seen, this is a tendency that Žižek thinks exacts a cost on 'an engagement with real working-class culture'. Either way, it should perhaps be assumed that Žižek is simply using the distinction as shorthand, in much the same way that Stuart Hall uses this same schematic in order to discuss the palpably different institutional contexts of cultural studies' reception, development, 'professionalization and institutionalization' (Hall 1992: 285). For Žižek wants basically to challenge cultural studies to apply some of its own stock insights *to itself*. This is not a new idea, of course. (Indeed, the fluency and fluidity with which Žižek poses the question could itself be taken as a sign of cultural questions having been formalized 'out of existence', or of the main thing that Stuart Hall cautions against in this essay, namely easy 'theoretical fluency', which indicates institutional comfort and political complacency. In Hall's terms, then, *Žižek himself* could be taken as an exemplary case of the institutionally comfortable theoretical formalist.) Similarly, the 'bastard child of capitalist ideology' argument is not a new argument against cultural studies: thinkers like Readings (1996), Bourdieu (1998) and Mowitt (2003), for instance, have variously argued that cultural studies is unable to comprehend or 'grasp its own condition of possibility' precisely because 'the concepts at its disposal ... are forged out of a structural mis-recognition of their corporate and ultimately US corporate derivation' (Mowitt 2003: 178). In other words: cultural studies fetishizes 'resistance', but the theme of 'resistance' is equally *de rigueur* in the marketing and advertising of brands of jeans, meaning that resistance really is useless.

Specifically, Žižek's argument is actually to do with the vicissitudes of time, place and (yes) capitalism: 'even if we find in both the same themes, notions, and so on, the socio-ideological functioning is completely different'. So, the crux of his argument is that when cultural studies first began, its engagement with working-class culture was an involvement with an active and potentially transformative form of politics (working-class, socialist). But subsequently, as socialist class politics were increasingly discredited by mainstream culture, politics and ideology, cultural studies began to prefer 'difference', 'individuality', 'consumption', 'identity politics', and so on. So the extent to which the growth of cultural studies in Western universities is marked by an increasing 'celebration' of such things signifies to Žižek that cultural studies is coming more and more into line with mainstream ideological discourse – whilst still claiming to be somehow radical.

So, *is* cultural studies really a hapless dupe, or an ignorant, unknowing, unaware pawn of 'capitalism'? Is 'deconstructionism' really a political and theoretical mistake? Is the move from 'essentialist' studies of 'class' to the broadening of the theoretical, ethical and political agenda to embrace questions of ethnicity, gender, sexuality, place, and so on, really a costly wrong move, to the benefit only of 'capitalism'? As Derrida once stated of deconstruction *vis-à-vis* questions of politics:

> All that a deconstructive point of view tries to show is that since convention, institutions and consensus are stabilizations (sometimes stabilizations of great duration, sometimes micro-stabilizations), this means that they are stabilizations of something essentially unstable and chaotic. Thus it becomes necessary to stabilize precisely because stability is not natural; it is because there is instability that stabilization becomes necessary; it is because there is chaos that there is a need for stability. Now, this chaos and instability, which is fundamental, founding and irreducible, is at once naturally the worst against which we struggle with laws, rules, conventions, politics and provisional hegemony, but at the same time it is a chance, a chance to change, to destabilize. If there were continual stability, there would be no need for politics, and it is to the extent that stability is not natural, essential or substantial, that politics exists and ethics is possible. Chaos is at once a risk and a chance, and it is here that the possible and the impossible cross each other. (Derrida 1996: 84)

Far from relativism, such deconstruction is an impetus to responsible politicization – a claim of the political character of all institutions, interpretations and establishments. This Žižek would not dispute. But, on the basis of the political character of interpretation (reading/rewriting), Derridean deconstruction asserts the importance of 'microscopic' readings/rewritings of texts (Derrida 1998a: 40). Žižek has no patience with this; evidently worrying that there is a mutually exclusive *choice*, an *either-or*: it is *either* deconstruction (and endless questions about interpretation and textuality) *or* Marxism and politics; *either* theorizing *or* action; *either* scholarship *or* politics; *either* theory *or* practice.

Now, neither Derridean deconstruction (Derrida 1992b; Protevi 2001) nor cultural studies (Stuart Hall 1992), nor indeed 'deconstructive cultural studies' (Mowitt 1992; Gary Hall 2002; Mowitt 2002) – *nor even Žižekian theory itself* – could be satisfied with such a simple opposition between theory and practice, theory and politics. As Žižek has noted with approval, cultural studies is aware of its ensnarement within the social relations of power and the political consequentiality of the biases of such key social institutions as the university and its disciplines. However, his strategic polemic in defence of 'pure' revolutionary politics leads him to refuse to theorize politics any further than supposedly free, individual, totalizing, voluntarist 'revolutionary acts'. This has the consequence that his theory of political change is somewhat limited. According to Simon Critchley, his rigid 'theoretical grid' leads him 'to a complete ultra-leftist cul-de-sac' (Critchley 2003: 65–6). Moreover, as scholarship, this 'type of analysis sacrifices the texture of any particular production for a pre-emptory political evaluation' (Mowitt 1992: 17). This synthesizes into problematic and limiting dogmatism and refusals. His core assertion is that all everyone needs to do is to begin 'finally, again conceiving of capitalism neither as a solution nor as one of the problems, but as *the* problem itself' (Žižek 2002: 308). Thus, laments Laclau, Žižek 'transforms "the economy" into a self-defined homogeneous instance operating as the ground of society – ... that is, he reduces it to a Hegelian explanatory model' (Laclau 2005: 237). This has the peculiar double consequence of causing Žižek to refuse apparently *all* political efforts and, paradoxically, all *study of* capitalism. Thus, he even claims that activities 'like *Médecins Sans Frontières*, Greenpeace, feminist and anti-racist campaigns' provide a 'perfect example of interpassivity: of doing things not in order to achieve something, but to prevent something from really happening, really changing. All this frenetic humanitarian, Politically Correct, etc., activity fits the formula of "Let's go on changing something all the time so that, globally, things will remain the same!"' (Žižek 2002: 170). As Laclau observes: Žižek refuses 'to accept the aims of all contestatory movements in the name of pure anti-capitalist struggle, [so] one is left wondering: who for him are the agents of a historical transformation? Martians, perhaps?' (Laclau 2004: 327). Simon Critchley goes further: 'What he is unable to think, in my view, is *politics*. That's because he's thinking politics on the basis of the wrong categories, namely psychoanalytic categories. I remain doubtful as to whether Lacanian psychoanalytic categories are going to be able to bring you any understanding of politics, certainly in the way Žižek uses them' (Critchley 2003: 65–6).

Of politics and/of popular culture

In a study of cultural studies, Gary Hall observed that, often,

> ... the last thing that is raised in all this talk about the importance of politics for cultural studies *is* the question of politics ... Politics is the one thing it is vital to understand, as it is that by which everything else is judged. But politics is at the same time the one thing that *cannot* be understood; for the one thing that cannot be judged by the transcendentally raised criteria of politics is politics itself. (Hall 2002: 6)

In Žižek, the things that it is vital to understand are not only 'politics' but also 'capitalism'. Yet it seems that these are the very things upon which Žižek can shed no strategic light. 'Capitalism' is simply the 'empty signifier' of pure negativity that organizes Žižek's entire orientation. It is the tautological start and end-point of his whole thinking. This is a problem, both theoretically and politically; one that Žižek and Žižekian scholars, theorists and activists (whatever a Žižekian activist might be) must address. Cultural studies could be of assistance here – although without pretending to know the answers already. For cultural studies, countercultural movements of all kinds, and indeed even Slavoj Žižek, all share an incomplete project, which hinges on the theory and practice of how to make effective ethical and political interventions. Reciprocally, if cultural studies is indeed 'a politically committed questioning of culture/power relations which at the same time theoretically interrogates its own relation to politics and to power' (Hall 2002: 10), then Žižek's demand that it address the political and ideological ramifications of its orientations should constitute the rest of the grounds of an ongoing dialogue between cultural studies and Slavoj Žižek. The gauntlet he throws down for cultural studies and for any interested in cultural politics is merely the 'difficult question: how are we to remain faithful to the Old in the new conditions? *Only* in this way can we generate something effectively New' (Žižek 2001b: 32–3).

Other-Wise Popular

Above, not a tile to cover the head;
Below, not an inch of ground for the foot.

Zenrin Poem

All that is solid melts into air, all that is sacred is profaned.

Karl Marx and Friedrich Engels

The Taoist ethic and the spirit of global capitalism

Slavoj Žižek suggests that the 'difficult question' facing cultural activity and political thought today is, 'How are we to remain faithful to the Old in the new conditions?' He suggests that the question must be posed in this way because '*Only* in this way can we generate something effectively New' (Žižek 2001b: 32–3). What might Žižek mean by this? It may seem like a peculiar question, one that you may not have considered in any form at all. To broach it, and to make sense of it, we could consider one popular manifestation of many people's attempt to 'remain faithful to the Old in the new conditions': the case of what Žižek calls 'Western Buddhism', or 'Western Taoism'. This is a particularly interesting example not only because it is one of Žižek's particular bugbears, but also because the list of contemporary books whose titles begin with the phrase *The Tao of...* is extensive, and growing, and perhaps therefore testifies to some kind of significant cultural 'movement'. These books range from scholarly works to business manuals, via all kinds of self-help and pop psychology to clearly New Age publications. In fact, the list of topics that allegedly have a Tao of their own now encompasses virtually every mainstream and marginal academic discipline as well as multiple (and – apparently – multiplying) cultural practices. There are Taos on topics that extend from the predictable to the preposterous, from the esoteric to the exoteric, and from the sublime to the ridiculous.

Apparently everything can be made into a book propounding this or that Tao: from the nooks of philosophy to the crannies of science (Siu 1957; Watts 1995), and from individual subsets of science to the relationships between 'modern physics and eastern mysticism' (Capra 1975), and beyond. Prominent are books on the Taos of this or that kind of human selfhood: from the Tao of the psychological subject (Bolen 1982) to the Taos of the genders (Metz and Tobin 1996); from the Taos of competitive subjects (Landsberg 1996) to those of getting motivated (Landsberg 2000); from the Tao of the health-focused subject (Blate 1978) to the Taos of work: there are Taos of business (Autry and Mitchell 1998), management (Messing 1989), and sales (Behr and Lao 1997). There are Taos of icons like Bruce Lee (Miller 2000) as well as Taos *by* them (selections from Bruce Lee's notebooks have been posthumously published under the titles *The Tao of Jeet Kune Do* (Lee 1975) and *The Tao of Gung Fu* (Lee and Little 1997)). There is also a *Tao of Muhammad Ali* (Miller 1997), and even a *Tao of Islam* (Murata 1992). There is also, of course, a *Tao of Pooh* (Hoff 1982).

As J. J. Clarke points out, the original and central text of Taoism, the *Tao te Ching* (a title that is usually taken to mean 'The Way of Virtue') has recently become 'one of the most frequently translated of all the world's classic texts, with over two hundred versions in seventeen different languages' (Clarke 2000: 56). As the *Tao te Ching* itself might say, from this original Tao 'the ten thousand things have sprung': myriad translations, offshoots, books, manuals, practices and worldviews each characterized by some relation to Taoism have emerged. What is more, this does not even scratch the surface of the vast and immeasurable sea of publications and practices that entail strong Taoist-sounding orientations and pretensions yet without explicitly shouting 'Tao' in their titles. Once more, prominent among these is the veritable torrent of management self-help books all heavily reliant on pseudo-Taoist tropes, of which (as we saw in Chapter 1) *Who Moved My Cheese?: An Amazing Way to Deal With Change in Your Work and In Your Life* (Johnson 1998) is but one exemplary case.

Quite why there is such a contemporary proliferation both of the 'original' *Tao* and of new Taos is debatable. (According to Clarke, 'There are various possible reasons for its wide appeal. One is the protean quality of the text, namely its readiness, as one writer puts it somewhat cynically, to "furnish whatever the reader needs", a factor which gives it "an immense advantage over books written so clearly that they have only one meaning" ' (Clarke 2000: 56).) Of course, *no* text will ever 'have only one meaning'. The endless proliferation of translations of the *Tao te Ching* may merely testify to the fact that the Tao that can and will be translated is never going to be the final translation, because 'translation' is one version of the question of 'interpretation', and every interpretation of any text is never going to be the final interpretation. Texts are read in contexts, and contexts cannot be exactly the same twice. Pragmatic problems of *translation* can themselves be referred back to the fundamental problem of *interpretation* (Derrida 1992; Mowitt 1992; Zhang 1992). But Slavoj Žižek's interpretation is unequivocal: the emergence of Taoist and Buddhist worldviews is, he contends, a 'spontaneous ideology' (Žižek 2001a: 216), an ideological response to the 'new conditions', in two crucial realms: that of *science* and that of *the economy*. That is, Žižek regards 'Western Buddhism' chiefly as *a non-scientific response to science* (a 'supplement'), and 'Western Taoism' chiefly as a straightforwardly ideological response to the chaos caused by contemporary economic processes. This is the root of Žižek's very obvious disdain for all things 'New Age' (Žižek 2000, 2001a, 2001b, 2005).

In fact, it is crucial to note that Žižek's disdain for all things 'New Age' is much more than a '*mere*' distaste. It is not any old distaste. Rather, to Žižek, *this* taste – the taste for all things 'New Age' – is exemplarily ideological, in the most pejorative sense. Indeed, Žižek actually argues that the contemporary Western interest in and turn to 'New Age "Asiatic" thought . . . in its different guises, from "Western Buddhism" . . . to different "Taos", is establishing itself as the hegemonic ideology of global capitalism' (2001b: 12). In other words, for Žižek, the contemporary 'Western' engagement with the 'mystical Oriental Other' is far from an innocuous or insignificant matter. Rather, *it is the exemplary ideological – and therefore fundamentally intellectual and political – problem of our time and place*. This is because, to Žižek's mind, the contemporary 'Western' recourse to Buddhism and Taoism is simply the perfect way to *avoid* intellectual, political and economic problems, by having recourse to a fetishistic supplement:

> 'Western Buddhism' is such a fetish: it enables you to fully participate in the frantic pace of the capitalist game while sustaining the belief that you are not really in it, that you are well aware of how worthless the spectacle is – what really matters is the peace of the inner Self to which you know you can always withdraw . . . as in the case of a Western Buddhist unaware that the 'truth' of his existence is the social involvement which he tends to dismiss as a mere game. (Žižek 2001b: 15)

Žižek offers this image of a meditating yuppie in order to claim that there is a widespread cultural growth of a vaguely Taoist-sounding 'acceptance of change' as the dominant 'ideological attitude'. To Žižek's mind, this arises because the contemporary experience of global capitalism tends to be that of 'being thrown around by market forces' (2001b: 116). He takes this to be definitive of the form of life under contemporary capitalism, owing to the turbulent effects of deregulated markets and chaotic international flows of capital. Because of this, Žižek argues that there is now a growing ideological injunction not to 'cling' to old forms and values. In these conditions, he suggests, other than a retreat into defensive fundamentalisms, a Taoist ethic presents itself as an ideal ideological option. However, Žižek's point is that this 'Western Taoist' attitude is no *solution* to the problems of capitalism. In fact, for Žižek, this 'celebration' or resigned acceptance of unfixity, flow, and non-clinging, is *nothing but the problem itself in inverted form, masquerading as (if) the solution*. It is an active misrecognition of a problem as (if) a solution, one that presumably, to Žižek's mind (although this is never really spelt out), facilitates the intensification of everyone's exploitation.

The very high incidence of business management or performative-capitalist titles in the list of books entitled *The Tao of . . .* (management, sales, motivation, competition, performance: *results!*), as well as the immediately palpable sense in which Taoism is very often taken to mean *individualist laissez-faire passivity* passed off as enlightened empowerment, certainly bolsters the Žižekian position (see Chapter 3). As such, Žižek's argument recasts contemporary interest in all things 'New Age' and 'Oriental' in a provocative new light. But what is the source of that light? And what are the implications of this particular perspective?

The answer is simple. Žižek's entire argument is specifically designed to refute every other contemporary approach to understanding culture, society, politics and ideology than his own. The argument about New Age Taoism as ideology is primarily a key part in Žižek's ongoing critique of 'postmodernist relativism', 'deconstructionism', identity politics, multiculturalism and cultural studies (among others, as we will see). For, in recasting something so *apparently* innocuous, gentle, naturalistic, sweet and innocent as Taoism as *ideological*, Žižek seeks reciprocally to implicate any approach that might regard it as an interesting or beneficial 'multicultural' development or 'encounter'. For Žižek, both the practice and any intellectual interest in it or approval of it are *strictly ideological* (Žižek 2001a). Against this, rather than running with the multiculturalists, postmodernists or post-Marxists who might

view the contemporary articulation of East and West as truly new, Žižek
sees himself as remaining courageously faithful to the truth of Marxism
(2001b: 33, 2002: 308). Thus, he begins his argument about Western
Buddhism and Taoism by finding a precedent in the work of Max Weber.

For Weber, Žižek reminds us, Protestantism was a necessary ideology of industrial-stage capitalism. By the same token, proposes Žižek,
Taoism, Buddhism and New Age mysticism are to be regarded as the
necessary ideology of contemporary 'postmodern' capitalism. This is
because, for Žižek, it's like this: according to Weber, during the 'industrial stage', the religiously informed work ethic of Protestantism ('suffer
now for rewards in the hereafter') guaranteed the discipline and active
participation of the workforce. So, Žižek argues, Taoism and mysticism
function in a similar way today: 'If Max Weber were alive today', he
declares, 'he would definitely write a second, supplementary volume
to his *Protestant Ethic*, entitled *The Taoist Ethic and the Spirit of Global Capitalism*' (2001b: 13). What defines the new spirit of capitalism is no longer
the former need to embrace frugality, moderation, hardship and a sedulous work ethic as virtues (as was the case during the 'industrial stage').
Rather, today sees the new 'need' to actively embrace ceaseless change
and rootlessness, because 'being thrown around by market forces' (116)
is definitive of the contemporary era. Thus, not clinging to stable forms
becomes a 'virtue', because it is the current way of capitalism. The way
of ideology is the emergence of value systems produced to enable us to
cope with – *by in some sense 'avoiding' the truth of* – real conditions.

For Žižek, the embracing of Taoism is the recourse to an ideological 'supplement'. It becomes a kind of fetish. Thus, in his signature
psychoanalytic idiom, Žižek classes 'Western Buddhism' as a perfect
example of a *'fetishist* mode of ideology', in which the fetishistic attachment functions as 'the embodiment of the Lie which enables us to sustain
the unbearable truth'. It remains a kind of avoidance of the truth even
though 'fetishists are not dreamers lost in their private worlds, they
are thoroughly "realists", able to accept the way things effectively are –
since they have their fetish to which they can cling in order to cancel
the full impact of reality' (2001b: 13–14).

Of course, there may be no 'problem' with such a crutch in itself.
Surely, finding ways to cope with the contexts into which one is flung
and within which one finds oneself is not only a necessary but also
a good thing. But, implicitly at least, Žižek is concerned that in this
ideological attitude the problem itself returns as (if) both virtue and
solution. Also, it is expressed through the sentiments of it being a 'good
thing' not to cling, and instead to move with the times, go with the
flow, not expect stability, and just change with changes. Ultimately,

'clinging' itself is couched as a *personal* failing, a shortcoming, a psychological problem, and is rearticulated as if irrational (Johnson 1998; see Chapter 1). As Žižek formulates this: when 'you can no longer rely on the standard health insurance and retirement plan, so that you have to opt for additional coverage for which you have to pay', the ideological injunction has become one in which you must 'perceive it as an additional opportunity to choose: either better life now or long-term security? And if this predicament causes you anxiety', he concludes, you are likely to be accused 'of being unable to assume full freedom, . . . of the immature sticking to old stable forms' (2001b: 116). So, Žižek implies, 'Taoist' tropes help facilitate the re-presentation of what are in truth collective socio-economic and political problems as if they are individual and subjective matters.

In this regard, 'Taoism' could be said to facilitate the ethically and politically debilitating ideology of *individualism*. For, overall, Žižek's argument is that the contemporary logic of capitalism demands that change become a virtue. (And, as we saw, *Tao te Ching* is mostly translated as 'The Way of Virtue'.) The necessary ideology is one that valorizes change, makes it a virtue. But crucial here is that this is not *active* change. An ideology of the value of *active* change could lead to group action and fundamental socio-political change. Rather, *passive* change is what is demanded: passivity in the face of unquestioned change; rudderless change. (Again, Johnson 1998 is an exemplary case.) As Žižek concludes, when this is combined with 'the ideology of the subject as the psychological individual pregnant with natural abilities and tendencies', then everyone will tend to 'automatically interpret all these changes as the result of my personality, not as the result of me being thrown around by market forces' (2001b: 116). (Hence the utility of so many Taos about this or that essence of human selfhood. The ultimate Tao book 'to come' would surely be best entitled *The Tao of Sacking and Being Sacked*.)

That is, Taoism becomes the order of the day not because it is true but simply because the virtually global advocation of free-market capitalism means, as Marx and Engels prophesied, that:

All fixed, fast-frozen relations, with their train of ancient and venerable prejudices and opinions are swept away, [that] all new-formed ones become antiquated before they can ossify [and that] All that is solid melts into air, all that is sacred is profaned. (Marx and Engels 1967: 83)

In contexts 'outside' of working life – and ironically particularly in contexts specifically intended to offer ways of escaping the stresses of working life – this New Age mysticism and spirituality arises as offering a very effective way of appearing to cope with working life. One may engage in t'ai chi-ch'üan, chi-gung, yoga or meditative practices as escape, release, or respite. But, says Žižek, 'the "Western Buddhist" meditative stance is arguably the most efficient way, for us, to fully participate in the capitalist dynamic while retaining the appearance of mental sanity' (2001b: 13). So, even though '"Western Buddhism" presents itself as the remedy against the stressful tension of the capitalist dynamic, allowing us to uncouple and retain inner peace and *Gelassenheit*, it actually functions as its perfect ideological supplement' (12). For Žižek, the way of capitalist ideology is the way of the fetishistic and mystificatory ideological supplement, which closes down the possibility for sustained thought and collective political action.

The way of the supplement

As Žižek sees it, this mystificatory supplement springs up everywhere – even where one would expect it least, and where it should be least welcome: namely, in putatively rational intellectual and academic contexts, contexts that explicitly champion *science*. In the scientific realm, he contends, such radical developments as quantum physics and astrophysics introduce a deeply disturbing ontological complexity and undecidability into traditional notions of reality. This is so much so that what he calls the 'dominant', 'traditional', 'positivist' and 'cognitivist' approaches *cannot* grasp contemporary science's transformed notions of reality. Thus, he claims, vaguely Buddhist 'spiritualist' interpretations have sprung up to supplement conventional rationality's lack of ability to interpret current scientific theory, practice, and findings.

Žižek claims that the problem is that 'the moment one wants to provide an ontological account of quantum physics (what notion of reality fits its results), paradoxes emerge which undermine standard common-sense scientistic objectivism' (2001a: 217). As a consequence, 'contemporary cognitivism often produce[s] formulations that sound uncannily familiar to those who are acquainted with different versions of ancient and modern philosophy, from the Buddhist notion of the Void, and the German Idealist notion of "being-in-the-world", [to] the deconstructionist notion of *différance*' (2001a: 200), and ultimately to the situation wherein:

> from David Bohm to Fritjof Capra, examples abound of different versions of 'dancing Wu Li masters', teaching us about the Tao of physics, the 'end of the Cartesian paradigm', the significance of the anthropic principle and

the holistic approach, and so on. To avoid any misunderstanding: as an old fashioned dialectical materialist, I am opposed as ferociously as possible to these obscurantist appropriations of quantum physics and astronomy; all I claim is that these obscurantist shoots are not simply imposed from outside, but function as what Louis Althusser would have called a 'spontaneous ideology' of scientists themselves, as a kind of spiritualist supplement to the predominant reductionist-proceduralist attitude of 'only what can be precisely measured counts'. (Žižek 2001a: 216)

So, Žižek claims that the 'standard common-sense scientistic objectivism' of mainstream scholarship resists acknowledging the fact that its own central ontological premises and tenets about reality are 'naïve', and have been demonstrably undermined by science itself. Because such developments as quantum mechanics *cannot* be translated into the 'dominant' ways of understanding what counts as reality, Žižek's argument is that 'obscurantist', 'spiritualist' interpretations spring up to supplement them at their points of failure and inadequacy. These supplements are attempts to plug the holes in a dominant paradigm that really should be rejected *tout court*. But the 'spiritualist supplement' supports – maintains – the dominant view by fudging over or obscuring its limitations, its failures. Žižek's claim, then, is that because *the spiritual* is of an entirely different order to *the rational* or *scientific*, and indeed to *knowledge per se*, then recourse to the 'spiritualist supplement' is utterly at odds with knowledge as such. Any recourse to 'spiritualist' accounts of ontology by avowedly 'rational' thinkers is, for Žižek, deeply self-contradictory. It has happened because common-sense rationality *cannot* comprehend the truth approached by science, so it hides its inability by making a pathetic recourse to a spiritualist mumbo-jumbo. This is why he contends that 'obscurantist New Age ideology is *an immanent outgrowth of modern science itself*' (Žižek 2001a: 216).

So, Žižek regards any unscientific supplement to science to be evidence of a (dominant) form of rationality transgressing its own central (Enlightenment) premises. Recourse to a 'spiritualist supplement' means, for Žižek, that any 'interpretations' made on the strength of this supplement are actually *anti*-intellectual *non*-interpretations. The spiritualist supplement not only *answers nothing*, it actually works to close down rigorous ontological inquiry. It is also, once again, the return of the problem as (if) a solution. Accordingly, as Žižek implies, any such supplement that operates like this, to close down thinking and analysis, is to be identified *and rejected*. (His ultimate argument, of course, is that 'standard common-sense scientistic objectivism' needs to be replaced, because it is intellectually naïve and ideologically unsound – because it cannot handle 'the real'. To his mind, his own Lacanian paradigm is the answer, the solution, the best candidate for the job of understanding all realms and registers of reality: from the 'impossible Real' which cannot be directly apprehended, to the failed attempts to approach it in the 'symbolic order'; to, in fact, *all* other aspects of the human condition.)

For, to Žižek, the supplement is that which *seems* to stabilize something, *seems* to answer a question, *seems* to fix a problem, fill a hole, etc.; but which *actually* subverts the entire system that it initially seemed to support. In this, Žižek *directly* appropriates and form(ulaic)ally applies Derrida's trail-blazing analysis and account of the work of *supplements* (Derrida 1974). Here, Žižek identifies the 'Western Buddhist' ideological supplement in the realm of academia as a 'red herring' that actually operates to *close down* thinking and analysis and the vaguely 'Taoist' stance as the general contemporary ideological supplement, which operates to close down thinking and anti-capitalist politics. Because of this, Žižek claims to be explicitly opposed to anything that functions as a '*denkverbot*' or implicit or explicit 'prohibition' against thought (Žižek 2001a: 3). Indeed, Žižek claims to be opposed to *any and all* 'obscurantism'. So it must also be asked whether Žižek is exempt from doing anything as suspect as operating in a way that might close down thinking and analysis, or from any obscurantist supplements.

The Tao of hegemony

One obvious way to broach this question is merely to ask: is Žižek's argument *coherent*? At times it seems persuasive, but on what model of causality is it premised, and is this model or paradigm *sound*? Does it *think* and *analyse* everything, or does it rely on any unthought (unacknowledged, unanalysed, un-thought-through) or even obscurantist supplements?

The first thing that must be made clear is that Žižek's account hinges on a very particular conception of ideology. It also bundles heterogeneous practices together, claims that they constitute a coherent entity or collection of equivalent entities, and claims that this object or field *is* the 'hegemonic ideology of global capitalism'. Already there may be much to doubt here. One might merely ask, for instance, what grounds there are for accepting that there *is* 'ideology', or that 'it' is what Žižek says it is, or that 'this' is 'it'. But we are not all at sea here. These are not 'abstract' questions to be subjected to supposedly context-free, value-free interrogation. For Žižek speaks of 'hegemonic ideology', and makes reference and appeal to some ostensibly legitimating truth of Marxism. Now, it is unquestionably the case that *any* academic or intellectual usage of the term 'hegemonic' necessarily evokes Antonio Gramsci's seminal theorization of culture and society (Gramsci 1971). This is never more so than when the term 'hegemonic' arises in a Marxist text. Indeed, here, the passage through Gramsci is overdetermined. Thus, we ought to tarry a while, and unpack Žižek's phrase 'hegemonic ideology'.

In the wake of Gramsci, whatever is called hegemonic (from the Greek *hegemon*, meaning prince, leader or guide) is to be regarded as being of both ethical and political significance and consequence. This is because, in Gramsci's paradigm, the discourses and practices that permeate and constitute society, culture and politics are involved in 'discursive' (i.e., open-ended, contingent, quasi-'conversational', institutional) processes, wherein parties and ideologies

> come into confrontation and conflict, until one of them or at least a combination of them tends to prevail, to gain the upper hand, to propagate itself throughout society – bringing about not only a unison of economic and political aims, but also intellectual and moral unity, a 'universal' plane, and thus creating the hegemony of a fundamental group over a series of subordinate groups. (Gramsci 1971: 181–2)

This does not sit entirely comfortably with Žižek's use of the term 'hegemonic ideology'. For a key point that the avowedly Gramscian theorists Laclau and Mouffe (1985) extracted from Gramsci's perspective is the insight that *therefore* culture and society are thoroughly contingent and *political achievements* in and of themselves. They are not passive expressions of the 'economic infrastructure' or indeed the 'economic base' (which is what Žižek's theory of Taoism-as-ideology implies). Indeed, in Gramsci and in Laclau and Mouffe (and beyond), 'hegemony' is clearly at odds with the paradigm that Žižek uses to make his claim about 'ideology'. This is because Žižek uses a paradigm that is now often termed 'crude' or 'vulgar' Marxism. Its central claim is that the 'economic base' (capitalism) *determines* the 'ideological superstructure' (the beliefs and practices of culture and society). The problematic difference between Žižek's and the Gramscian (and Laclauian) understandings of hegemony is that, for Žižek, hegemony is something that *is simply ideological*, in the sense that it all 'grows out from' and sits 'on top of' the economic base, which is the driving force of everything.

In contrast to Žižek's usage, Laclau and Mouffe argue that the *economic cannot be divorced from the political*. What this means becomes apparent when one translates Laclau and Mouffe's terms back into those of the crude Marxism that they reject. In this retranslation, any transformation in the 'ideological superstructure' may well have effects on the 'economic base', because base and superstructure are no longer conceived of as separable, but rather as contingent political establishments and constellations in the larger discursive movements of history. In other words, the notion of hegemony *subverts* the 'ideology' (and) paradigm of crude Marxism, in which the superstructure is regarded as distinct from yet determined by the economic base. In the post-Marxist theory of hegemony, in fact, there is no fundamentally distinct base and superstructure, only contingent political establishments, which will take the form of different forms of socio-political arrangements. Human life is not a passive reflection of economic dictates. It can and does intervene decisively in 'the economic system'. As Laclau puts it, in response to Žižek's criticisms of poststructuralism and post-Marxism:

> Nobody seriously denies [the centrality of economic processes in capitalist societies]. The difficulties come when [Žižek] transforms 'the economy' into a self-defined homogeneous instance operating as the ground of society – when, that is, he reduces it to a Hegelian explanatory model. The truth of the economy is, like anything else in society, the locus of an overdetermination of social logics, and its centrality is the result of the obvious fact that the material reproduction of society has more repercussions for social processes than do other instances. This does not mean that capitalist reproduction can be reduced to a single, self-defining mechanism. (Laclau 2005: 237)

The way of changeless change: Žižek's limit problem

But Žižek does not accept the Laclauian argument about hegemony, nor does he accept the efficacy or even the reality of politics construed as changes in legislation, inter-institutional organization, or anything 'pragmatic' like that. Indeed, he refers to every such kind of non-revolutionary politics as proof of 'the sad predicament of today's Left'. This he says is characterized by 'the acceptance of the Cultural Wars (feminist, gay, anti-racist, etc., multiculturalist struggles) as the dominant terrain of emancipatory politics; [and] the purely defensive stance of protecting the achievements of the Welfare State' (Žižek 2002: 308). To this impulse in Žižek's work, Laclau replies: because Žižek 'refuses to accept the aims of all contestatory movements in the name of pure anti-capitalist struggle, one is left wondering: who for him are the agents of a historical transformation? Martians, perhaps?' (Laclau 2004: 327).

The point here is that the theory of hegemony construes society (including the economy) as consisting of contingent political constructs which can be intervened in and altered to effect significant alteration. Žižek, on the contrary, regards such change as 'intra-systemic', as obscuring and preserving 'a certain limit' (Žižek 2002: 170; Laclau 2000: 205). Thus, he argues, even efforts 'like *Médecins Sans Frontières*, Greenpeace, feminist and anti-racist campaigns ... are all not only tolerated but even supported by the media, even if they seemingly encroach on economic territory (for example, denouncing and boycotting companies which do not respect ecological conditions, or use child labour) – they are tolerated and supported as long as they do not get too close to a certain limit' (Žižek 2002: 170). What is this 'limit'? Žižek explains:

> This kind of activity provides the perfect example of interpassivity: of doing things not in order to achieve something, but to prevent something from really happening, really changing. All this frenetic humanitarian, Politically Correct, etc., activity fits the formula of 'Let's go on changing something all the time so that, globally, things will remain the same!' (Žižek 2002: 170)

This 'formula' is Žižek's interpretation of politics under capitalism. Thus, what 'invisibly' remains the same is *the way of capital per se*. Žižek calls this the unseen 'backdrop', the unacknowledged 'horizon', the unapproachable 'limit'. He has even argued that there is a 'silent prohibition' against *even talking about* anti-capitalism or undertaking class analysis in the contemporary university. (The fact that this is *demonstrably* false, especially for UK universities, does not stop him from regularly making this polemical claim. He makes it mainly to try to provoke American intellectuals to start to construe 'capitalism' as 'the problem itself'.) In other words, quite against Laclau who exemplifies the tendency to regard the organization of culture and society as the result of fundamentally consequential socio-political 'battles', Žižek regards all of this as the simple *imposition* of a particular ideology determined by an agenda set by the requirements of 'global capitalism', in an automatic process. This is what leads him to regard all politics (other than globally revolutionary anti-capitalist 'class' politics) as blind to their own 'context' – what he calls the 'backdrop' or 'horizon': The Capitalist System. For 'backdrop' and 'horizon' one cannot but read 'economic base' (Laclau 2005: 205).

Thus, ultimately, Žižek's vision of Taoism as/and ideology has been produced by a crude base/superstructure model of the world. In this, the *hegemon* that guides ideology is not a prince but a straightforward *henchman*; not a leader or guide in any sense, but a collaborator, in the service of the capitalist 'economic infrastructure' (Žižek 2001b: 12).

That being said, what nevertheless makes Žižek's rejection of politics strangely consistent and apparently (paradoxically) 'valid' is the fact that he does *not* actually think that the majority of the population *are* subjugated and controlled by *actual* groups or classes. Or, that is: even if people *are* subjugated by other people, by *particular* groups, the buck does not stop there. On the contrary, for Žižek, the problem is strictly 'systemic'. The problem with capitalism is not *capitalists*. The true problem is the *system*. His conviction is that what is leading and guiding and controlling all of us today is the invisible hand of the capitalist *system* itself. So, for Žižek, the universal/class enemy is not some actual or fixed class or group of *people* 'in control'. Rather, what Žižek deems to be 'in control' is a machinic *system* (Žižek 2001a: 1–2). This is why Žižek can claim simultaneously that 'the fundamental antagonism' is 'the class antagonism' *and* that there is no 'authentic working class' (2002: 308). That is, because the problem is systemic or structural, then every actual instance of its realisation is asymptotic to the real of the structure that it (never quite) exemplifies.

This 'system' or 'structure', construed through an ultra-formalist perspective, is the problem, for Žižek (2002: 308). It is also the problem *of* Žižek, in the sense that his hyperbolically 'consistent' ultra-political stance must paradoxically reject all forms of politics other than something he conceives of as complete 'systemic' global anti-capitalist revolution (2002: 170). His polemical target is a perceived contemporary 'consensus' (that he regards as 'resigned and cynical') that capitalism is 'the only game in town' (2000a: 95). From this perspective, all non-revolutionary or non-anti-capitalist theory and practice cannot see the changeless 'backdrop' to its own activity: capitalism, the horizon within which all actually existing politics drone on, but always avoiding '*the* problem itself'. This is why Žižek accuses contemporary cultural, intellectual and political life of having fallen all but entirely under the sway of capitalism. He portrays 'capitalism' and its liberal or neoliberal ideology as the total and universal backdrop against or within which things *appear* to change but fundamentally remain the same.

But, just to be clear, the basic problem here remains that this very position arises only through the optic of what Laclau calls a very 'crude version of the base/superstructure model' (Laclau 2000: 205). Adopted in the name of furthering *radical* politics, it paradoxically *rejects* all politics, because none could possibly hope to measure up to the impossibly total demands generated by such a caricatural and hyperbolic paradigm. It 'totalizes' everything ('*the* global capitalist system'), and so precludes the value of specific action. In insisting on inferred fundamental ('ontological' or 'Real') structures it refuses even to look at any significant aspect of actually existing ('ontic') reality. In insisting on radical politics, it even prohibits working out *what* valid political action might be. (It merely evokes some enigmatic kind of universal spontaneous political combustion.) In fact, Žižek's totalizing leads to a *prohibition of any analysis*.

This is because Žižek's polemical gestures levy a very heavy rhetorical and analytical toll. In order to make them, Žižek cannot analyse or question his own central categories (the notions he champions or denounces). This is so much the case that, rather than treating 'neoliberalism' (for example) as a complex, historically real, deliberately implemented geopolitical economic 'experiment' of ongoing, piecemeal, pragmatic, legislative violence (Kingsnorth 2003), Žižek merely picks up some familiar emotive terms – 'capitalism', 'the system' – and deploys them *as if they are already fully understood* and as if they simply *must* be taken to be millenarian signifiers of pure evil. In short, 'capitalism', 'liberalism', etc., function within Žižek's discourse *purely as emotive rhetorical devices*, whilst being analytically empty (not to mention often categorically dubious). That is, on the one hand, these terms are *irreducible, central* to his discourse: they actually overdetermine, constitute, and orientate the shape and form of his intellectual production through and through. But, on the other hand (and unfortunately for anyone concerned with knowledge, analysis, or politics), they also signal the *limit* of his thought. 'Capitalism' is the central, fundamental point beyond which Žižek cannot or will not go; something that a Rortyan perspective might regard as Žižek's 'final vocabulary': the tautological start and end-point of his discourse; as if the entire political dimension of the work of Žižek consists in the repetition of the following mantra or koan: '*What is the problem? Capitalism. What is capitalism? The problem*'.

The Tao of holding the place

The reasons for Žižek's refusal to analyse are certainly multiple. But they hinge on his avowed aim of 'holding the place' (Žižek 2000). He sees it as his intellectual responsibility to keep 'radical' theoretical and political themes on the table of public intellectual debate. As we have seen, in the cultural and political dimension, for Žižek this basically means maintaining a crude Marxian mantra. This is because, as he sees it, he is actually being courageous by *resolutely not losing his nerve*, 'in a time of continuous rapid changes' when 'the retreat of old social forms' means that 'thought is more than ever exposed to the temptation of "losing its nerve"', of precociously abandoning the old conceptual coordinates' (2001b: 32). As he rather surprisingly alleges, even 'The media constantly bombards us with the need to abandon the "old paradigms"' (32). (Quite *which* media it is that 'constantly bombards' Žižek with such intellectually stimulating provocations is – regrettably – left unsaid. If he had named them, I for one would be tuning in!) But, he counters: 'Against this temptation, one should rather follow the unsurpassed model of Pascal and ask the difficult question: how are we to remain faithful to the Old in the new conditions? *Only* in this way can we generate something effectively New' (2001b: 33). *This* is Žižek's wager, Žižek's act: rejection of the way of capitalism; holding the place of the old against 'today's twin brothers of deconstructionist sophistry and New Age obscurantism' (1998: 1007), and against 'capitulation itself' (2002: 308), the position of 'Third Way' ideologues, like Giddens or Beck, and all who do not vociferously oppose capitalism.

What is particularly striking, however, is the way that the rhetorical *'points de capiton'* that structure Žižek's texts – signifiers like 'capitalism', 'the system', 'anti-capitalism', 'revolution' – are *entirely hypostatized place-holders*. That is, they are never specified further. Indeed, one might say, within Žižek's discourse, his key categories are *supplements*, in an almost exemplary sense. (Indeed, more than Žižek's *use* of the deconstructive notion of the supplement, his fundamental *reliance on* it should be noted. For, he both *relies on* the supplement in many of his arguments, and yet *disavows deconstruction*. This means that, here, *deconstruction is literally Žižek's own supplement*. In Derrida's analyses, this is *precisely* what a supplement is: that which is simultaneously central *and* excluded; something apparently only 'added on' but actually fundamental, constitutive; something disavowed yet relied upon. What becomes apparent in reading Žižek is that deconstruction is subordinated or even excluded by his own avowed position, yet nevertheless central to it. Furthermore, the very fact that he always deploys the notion of the supplement so *formalistically* and *formulaically* (and without any actual 'reading') actually means that Žižek himself seems to be the best example of a 'deconstructionist' – or the sort of proponent of *formulaic* deconstruction that he regularly denounces – to be found.) And these hypostatized place-holders do exactly the same kind of work as the recourse to spiritualism that he criticizes in his object of critique. His key categories are uninterrogated 'pegs'; 'pins', whose removal would cause his text to unravel entirely. But, furthermore, these place-holders are actually elevated to something very like the status of the figure of the 'the eternal Tao' in the *Tao te Ching*. In deconstructive terms, this means that the central categories of Žižek's system are actually radically external to it, strangely excluded from it. They are there on full show, yet concealed from inspection. Placing them on full show is actually the way Žižek conceals them from inspection. To echo Žižek's 'formula' of the nonpolitics of politics, his approach is thus: 'Let's go on talking about something all the time so as to avoid talking about it' (see Žižek 2002: 170, quoted above). This rhetorical (anti-)analytical strategy puts Žižek's entire approach on a par with the very style of mystificatory (non-)engagement and intellectual failure that he critiques as being *the* move of the 'hegemonic ideology of global capitalism'.

Does this mean that the way of Žižek is somehow a manifestation of the hegemonic ideology of global capitalism? This would be the deepest irony, given Žižek's explicit declaration to try to 'remain faithful to the Old in the new conditions'. The problem is that his (e)very effort to move involves tying his laces together. Every possible theoretical or political move meets one of his own unnecessary self-imposed puritanical 'prohibitions' (2001a: 204–5, 220). The most striking is perhaps the refusal to question the supposedly 'old' *paradigm itself*, in the name of 'remaining faithful' to it. This amounts to the advocation of an anti-theoretical and straightforwardly anti-intellectual, quasi-religious or spiritualist *'denkverbot'* or 'prohibition against thinking' (2001a: 3).

Of course, such a strangely paranoid defensive reaction *might –possibly* – but only tentatively, and forever only tenuously – *sometimes* – be *strategically* justifiable in the context of Žižek's claim that he sees his role and intellectual contribution to be that of 'holding the place', of keeping traditional radical political questions and perspectives on the agenda, so to speak, *lest we forget*. But there are many other, more honest, intellectually open ways to do this than simply *refusing* to think, theorize, and analyse. But, *even if* as an intellectual, philosopher, theorist or academic one could possibly decide something like 'it's not how crude it is but what you do with it that counts', the problem remains that Žižek refuses to do *anything* with his crude paradigm. He refuses to question, interrogate or analyse anything to do with the supposedly determinant 'base' at all. This refusal begs a question of the *point* of analysing *anything*, especially anything in or of the superstructure. In other words, Žižek does not do with the paradigm the very thing that the paradigm is supposedly set up to do, the very thing it seems to demand and that he implicitly most advocates. That is, as 'the economy' is placed in a determinant position, one might expect some analysis of it – perhaps of consequential moments, movements, acts, interventions or events that have taken place in the determinant realm. But this never appears. This is because any attempt at such analysis would reveal the economic system to be contingently and politically instituted and modifiable, thus revealing the inadequacy and untenability of his paradigm and his entire position (Laclau and Mouffe 1985; Laclau 2004). (Žižek's argument in his analysis of Lenin is a case in point (Žižek 2002). Here Žižek effectively argues for the primacy of the *political* intervention over the 'economic system'.)

Thus, Žižek's own position is strictly fetishistic. According to his own argument, this makes Žižek entirely consistent with the logic of contemporary capitalism. As a 'position', Žižek's work straightforwardly relies upon the logic of the supplement. It falls apart according to that same logic too. But Žižek does not care, because although he relies upon the deconstructive supplement, his work proceeds according to the psychoanalytic logic of the fetish. Thus, his mantras enable him to 'fully participate in the frantic pace of the capitalist game while sustaining the belief that [he is] not really in it, that [he is] well aware of how worthless the spectacle is . . . unaware that the "truth" of his existence is the social involvement which he tends to dismiss as a mere game' (Žižek 2001b: 15).

For Žižek, the name of the game is 'holding the place'. This relies on 'place-holders': repeated evocations of the *names* of problematics as if naming them is everything. Naming is both to gesture at and yet *thereby* bracket off, silence, close down analysis, *in the same gesture*. This is a structure of foreclosure and denial in which what *apparently* holds the structure in place *actually* lacks any possible content. Were the supplements – the place-holders – engaged, fleshed out, the structure would collapse. Žižek joyously ignores this untenable incoherence because he obeys his fetish: '*I know very well* [that what I am saying is untenable and empty], *but nevertheless* [I will continue to say it – because I enjoy it/it enables me to 'face' things] . . .'. *So what? Who cares?* The issue here, as Žižek so completely demonstrates, is that this gesture is *anti*-theoretical, *anti*-intellectual, *anti*-philosophical, *anti*-analytical and *anti*-political – indeed, arguably exemplifying the very ideological, intellectual and political problem of our time and place.

McDeconstruction, the Popular: Deconstructing 'Deconstructing'

7

> I am not for the destruction of the universitas or the disappearance of the guardians, but precisely one has to make a certain war against them when obscurantism, vulgarity above all, becomes ensconced, as is inevitable.
>
> Jacques Derrida (1987: 88)

The popular response to the death of the guardian

Jacques Derrida died on 8 October 2004. The journalistic responses to his death were many but unfortunately not all that varied. They were overwhelmingly hostile to Derrida, even on the morning after his death. The question is why. Although some of these responses appeared hostile to the *man*, the individual, what drove these attacks was hostility to his *work*: deconstruction. Regrettable as they were, these hostile responses might teach us a lot – but *only* if we deconstruct them. Only then can we perceive what Derrida called the kind of 'violence' involved in all 'metaphysical' institutions. Let me explain.

When I heard and read the public announcements of Derrida's death, I wanted Derrida to be wrong. This was not simply the usual want; namely, what Derrida called the 'irresistible' metaphysical 'desire to restrict play' (Derrida 1974: 59), to police people's interpretations, to try to correct what *I* might perceive as *their* misreading, *their* misunderstanding and misrepresentation. Of course, I did want to be able to do this: surely, everyone does; everyone wants *their* interpretation to be accepted as the correct interpretation. But it was not just this. Rather, what I wanted was for Derrida to *come to be* wrong – so that, in the future, what Derrida's texts focused on and revealed would be no longer the case. So, I did not want Derrida *to have been wrong*; but rather *to come to be wrong*. For, *we ought to want him to come to be wrong*. For this is to hope

147

for an otherness 'to come' – namely, the ethical and political change demanded by deconstruction. Unfortunately, though, Derrida remains only too right. Thus, with the announcement of his death, what arrived with crushing, programmatic predictability were the denunciations, defamations and misrepresentations of Derrida and deconstruction: Derrida, they said, was *unintelligible, nonsensical, meaningless, postmodernist, relativist, 'deconstruction-ist'*, confusing and 'therefore' confused, too serious, too trivial, too difficult, too silly, too much, too little, too French. All of which merely reconfirms precisely *how* right Derrida remains, *and* how wrong this situation is.

But what do I mean by 'right' and 'wrong', and referring to what? I am referring to Derridean deconstruction's primary 'target': the hostility, violence, and resistance of institution – both noun and verb: *institutions*, and *institution*. As Derrida put it, *'Deconstruction is an institutional practice for which the concept of the institution remains a problem'* (Derrida 2002: 53). Given this, you might say, hostility to deconstruction is hardly surprising. But what does the hostility come as a response *to*? Of the widespread hostility and resistance to deconstruction, Derrida once argued:

> If it were only a question of 'my' work, of the particular or isolated research of one individual, this wouldn't happen. Indeed, the violence of these denunciations derives from the fact that the work accused is part of a whole ongoing process. What is unfolding here, like the resistance it necessarily arouses, can't be limited to a personal 'oeuvre', nor to a discipline, nor even to the academic institution. Nor in particular to a generation: it's often the active involvement of students and younger teachers which makes certain of our colleagues nervous to the point that they lose their sense of moderation and of the academic rules they invoke when they attack me and my work. If this work seems so threatening to them, this is because it isn't eccentric or strange, incomprehensible or exotic (which would allow them to dispose of it easily), but as I myself hope, and as they believe more than they admit, competent, rigorously argued, and carrying conviction in its re-examination of the fundamental norms and premises of a number of dominant discourses, the principles underlying many of their evaluations, the structures of academic institutions, and the research that goes on within them. What this kind of questioning does is to modify the rules of the dominant discourse, it tries to politicize and democratize the university scene . . . . (Derrida 1995: 409–10)

In this sense, it is clear that if deconstruction arouses resistance, hostility, or even 'wrath', this is not simply because of its *difference*, but rather because of its uncanny *excess* of propriety, its 'properly improper (uncanny, *unheimlich*)' (Derrida 1998a: 29) character. Accordingly, if we were (reductively) to represent deconstruction as if it were some simply hostile, tendentious or polemical activity (like a straightforwardly political project), then, as we have seen (in Chapter 4), it could be said to proceed according to a strategy described by Slavoj Žižek as:

> *overidentifying* with the explicit power discourse – *ignoring* [its] inherent obscene underside and simply taking the power discourse at its (public) word, acting as if it really means what it explicitly says (and promises) – [as an] effective way of disturbing its smooth functioning. (Žižek 2000: 220)

Viewed like this, then, in its close readings of texts (or any constructions), and in its quasi-transcendental mode of questioning, deconstruction reveals any institution's difference from 'itself', from all that it could or should or might otherwise be, from the thought or promise of its better, less violent, realisation. In this sense, deconstruction is to be regarded as the exposure of any institution or establishment to the enabling limitation that *is* its own contingency and constitutive, contradictory bias. Thus, what deconstruction 'does' is draw attention to the violence of institution, in the hope of inciting acts of re-institution with a view to what Derrida called the 'lesser violence'.

It is because of this hyper-ethico-politicizing movement that perhaps *all* institutions will inevitably *resist* deconstruction. Every 'institute', every instituted institution will try to preserve its present form and resist any transformations. However, as Derrida put it: '*différance* instigates the subversion of every kingdom. Which makes it obviously threatening and infallibly dreaded by everything within us that desires a kingdom' (Derrida 1982: 22). That is, we all want stability, certainty, univocality. However, meanings and readings will slide over time; so stability and fixity are permanently deferred. To the extent to which we have something 'within us that desires a kingdom' everyone therefore wants deconstruction to be wrong. Everyone: those who reject and those who embrace deconstruction. Or rather, everyone wants deconstruction to be wrong *about them*, about *their* institution. No one *wants* (let alone is able) to have to ceaselessly and interminably subject themselves and what they do to the harrowing ordeal of the undecidable. This is as true for those who reject deconstruction and trade in what Derrida called 'clear-conscience certainty' as it is for those who claim to ceaselessly and interminably subject themselves and what they do to the harrowing ordeal of the undecidable. For the whole point here is that *anything* constituted/instituted/established, *resists* (Derrida 1987: 88). Those who are in it or of it or are what they are thanks to it have a vested interest in keeping things as they are.

Yet, for deconstruction, the point is to change it. The question is: to what, and which way? Derrida held that 'the best liberation from violence is a certain putting into question, which makes the search for an *archia* tremble' (Derrida 1978: 141); but also that every obligation activates contradictory and reciprocally subversive injunctions. Thus, even though it seems certain that 'clear-conscience certainty' must be exposed to the ordeal of undeciding, the problem is that so too must the certainty of uncertainty, as well as the certainty that *this* way, my way, our way, is *the* right and most responsible way to do it. Ultimately, then, this remains all about institution – all institution and all institutions. The *object* of deconstruction is *institution* and *the* institution, *establishment* and *the* establishment.

This can be illustrated by looking at the *Guardian* newspaper's collection of largely crass quotes about Derrida shortly after he died, ludicrously entitled 'Deconstructing Jacques'. In it, Julian Baggini, editor of the *Philosophers' Magazine*, made this perhaps inadvertently illuminating observation: 'British-trained philosophers like myself don't know much about Derrida, though that doesn't stop some of them dismissing him. I don't dismiss him, but nor do I know enough to be able to sum him up' (Baggini 2004). With this, Baggini apparently unintentionally strikes a couple of key points. The first might be called the role of *cultural training*. 'British-trained' refers, of course, to a particular type of *institutionalization*. This leads to the second point – although it is really only a more refined version of the first. It is that everything devolves on the force and consequences of contingently instituted reading practices.

As John Protevi puts it, 'the reading of marks is institutionally enforced. Reading strategies outside the institutionally enforced reading code make no sense, as anyone who reads the bewildered responses to deconstructive readings can tell you' (Protevi 2001: 64). Hence, if deconstruction seems 'complicated', 'difficult', or 'unintelligible' it is because it is doing something unusual in looking for the work of *bias* in the textual constructions it is reading. What Protevi calls the dominant 'metaphysical reading code' ('normal' reading) looks only for 'pure meaning', or signification. Deconstruction looks for 'the interweaving of force *and* signification' (64), insisting that all 'contexts' are only established in and 'structured by force': by contingently instituted ways of *making* sense. In other words, *'sense' is always*

made – forcefully, contingently, politically, consequentially. As Protevi
sees it, therefore:

> Deconstruction is political physics, the diagnosis of the metaphysical lifting
> of opposites from the reserved field or general text as a skewing of them into
> new hierarchies, a twisting of them on the basis of previous hierarchies. Any
> hegemonic formation of meaningful force and forceful meaning is, however,
> never total, but has held in reserve the possibility of reinforcing its elements
> in different, disseminative, formation and contexts. (Protevi 2001: 65)

In such a rendering, deconstruction construes the world as a 'general
text of force and signification'. As such, it is far from simply 'about language (or something)'. It is rather a revelation of the imbrication of force
and signification constitutive of what Laclau and Mouffe (1985) present
as the iterative structure of hegemonies. In one respect, this is precisely
what Derrida is about. But, Derrida is even more radical than Laclau
and Mouffe's reconstructed Marxism, because deconstruction (unlike
the disciplines of political theory or philosophy) – ('philosophy (this
will be my hypothesis) *clings to the privilege it exposes*' (Derrida 2002:
1–2)) – is always intimately involved with the question of *how* legitimacy and illegitimacy, intelligibility and unintelligibility are instituted,
established and imposed.

Deconstruction is not about telling stories or painting pictures.
Deconstruction is not just about diagnosing 'conditions of possibility
and impossibility'. It is much more *'about'* and involved with *challenging* 'conditions of *pose-ability* and *impose-ability'*. It is, then, *like*
Laclau and Mouffe's deconstructive post-Gramscian discourse theory, not only emphatically and irreducibly political and politicizing,
construing relations as textual relations of contingent and forceful articulation throughout and constitutive of a rivalrous and non-homogenous
institutional discursive 'terrain'; but also – *unlike*, or *more* (*and 'less'*)
than Laclau and Mouffe – an insistent engagement with the problematic matter and double binds of all, including its *own*, institution.
As Derrida commented, when reflecting on the history of his own
publications:

> it is necessary to begin by publishing works which reassure the univer-
> sity [because] this is also a question of politics and editorial legitimation.
> This is true, but it is not only that. I believe that my first texts, let's call
> them more academic or philosophically more reassuring, were already well
> beyond the editorial field of social legitimation, and were also a discursive

and theoretical (I do not say fundamental or foundational) condition, an irreversibly necessary condition of what came later. (Derrida 1996: 79)

This is why Derridean deconstruction is also *not* a theory of discourse, and why Laclau and Mouffe's appropriation or translation of deconstruction into political theory does not exhaust it. It is not a 'theory' because deconstruction cannot, with a clear conscience, leap out of aporia and undecidability. Moreover, aporia and undecidability are not theoretical constructs within or of a deconstructive theory. These are just terms for what deconstructive readings keep bumping into when reading texts attentively. This is why Derrida suggested that he read so as to be a 'monster of fidelity, the most perverse infidel' (1987: 24). In other words, 'and [here] I am citing, but as always rearranging a little' (1987: 89), deconstruction *is and is not* 'theoretical'. It is 'a program that cannot be formalized' but 'for reasons that *can* be formalized' (1997: 52). As we have already seen, Derrida himself stated it bluntly, simply, and unequivocally: '*Deconstruction is an institutional practice for which the concept of the institution remains a problem*' (2002: 53).

Popular hate objects, and their hate objects

Nevertheless, Derridean deconstruction still established many apparent institutional friendships, allegiances, partnerships, collaborations, and so on. Indeed, as Derrida reminded on many occasions, deconstruction is always only ever only *part* of a process: constitutively; always a *supplement*:

> ... one never does 'keep to deconstruction'. Deconstruction is never concluded because it is never nihilistic, contrary to what they say in *Newsweek*, but rather affirmative and generative. And it is difficult to imagine seriously, without laughing, what 'keeping to deconstruction' could possibly mean! (Derrida 1992b: 211)

As it is a *supplement*, deconstruction is also therefore '*pharmakon*': it can be either medicine or poison for whatever it supplements. In one regard, deconstruction may be helpful to a particular project or institution. But in another, it may also be a false friend: it can come to deconstruct the underpinnings, values, investments and orientations of any particular project. So, it must both 'be' and 'have' its own *faux amis*: false friends; apparent affiliations but deep differences. So, the question, 'Who are Derridean deconstruction's friends?', will have no simple answer, especially given that, deconstructively speaking, friendship is *never* neutral, simple or innocent. There are always political ramifications to friend-ship (Derrida 1997). Tony Blair and George W. Bush were said to be 'friends'. The UK and the USA are said to have a 'special relation-ship'. Friendship cannot be separated from rivalry, nor indeed from corruption. Friends can become oligarchs, structured in relations of dominance and subservience. Friendships become institutions. So, *vis-à-vis* deconstruction, who or what are the friendships, and what are the politics?

For Derrida, in one trope, the *political* moment or event arises when 'telecommunication' or regular relations and distributions and communications are 'derailed', 'jammed' and warped (Derrida 1987: 20). This is basically (to reiterate) why deconstruction places such great emphasis on 'merely' *reading* – on working interminably and vigilantly at reading, listening, being attentive and sensitive, and not presuming in advance that something is already simply understood. Reading is never 'mere', *if it is reading*: it is the possibility of freeing from sedimented practices, presumptions, strictures, institutions and establishments; and re-deciding, re-establishing, re-instituting. As such, any who engage in such work might be numbered among deconstruction's ethico-political 'friends'. Derridean deconstruction's 'friends', then, will obviously not be limited to literal or explicit friends of Derrida. Nor need one be Machiavelli to comprehend that even avowed or intentional 'friends' may actually be *faux amis*. 'Friendship' is of undecidable ethical and political status.

We can see this by considering the way that in Derrida's work, both *deconstruction* and *writing* are deemed to be (among other things) *democratic* (1997: 144). Because of deconstruction's commitment to *reading*, Protevi concludes that: 'Deconstruction is democratic justice, responding to the calls from all others' (2001: 70). On this note, we might conclude that all those who affiliate themselves with 'radi-cal democratic politics' might *seem* to qualify as friends of Derridean deconstruction. However, as John Mowitt reminds us, there's more to radicalizing democracy than saying 'radical democracy'. What is vital to such a commitment, he argues, is 'inscribing within one's own position the possibility and necessity of a position which is obscured by what one opposes. Radical democracy ought to involve listening to those whose voices have been drowned out by the very voice of advocacy' (Mowitt 1992: 221). And not everyone wants to do this.

The specific character of deconstruction is trying to be open *to* alter-ity by *reading*, and by *looking for the bias* in all interpretations. This is a kind of reading which, as Derrida phrases it in *Dissemination*, will attract the 'wrath' of whichever God or King (or institution) supervenes.

In *Dissemination*, Derrida reads Socrates-Plato's rendition of the myth of Theuth's invention of writing. Right from the outset, the god-king begins by 'pointing out not only its uselessness but its menace and its mischief' (1982: 76). Being 'useless', a 'menace', a 'mischief'-maker, or all at once; being excessive, or inadequate, or multiply improper; being sophistry, simulation, equivocation; introducing triviality or over-seriousness; digressiveness or tendentiousness; pointlessness or bias; playfulness or murderous intent; anarchy, demonic democracy or totalitarian conservatism; elitism or iconoclasm; from being terrible and destructive to being trivial and gratuitously additive – and *always* being that which 'doesn't come from around here' (1997: 104): these are the key coordinates of the attacks made against what Derrida calls 'writing', 'supplement', 'pharmakon', 'parasite', throughout the canonical institutional history of the West (Derrida 1997: 149). These accusations are the same as those made against deconstruction itself. They are also, of course, identical to those made against cultural studies.

Does this mean that deconstruction and cultural studies are identical, related, or equivalent; or friends? From what viewpoint? According to whom? Representation is never neutral. We would have to enquire into the perspective that would want to construe any '*x*' and '*y*' as the same or equivalent. For instance, someone with a critical or hostile view from elsewhere might not be the best judge of something like deconstruction's and cultural studies' similarities or differences. But who *could* be the best possible judge? Derrida? Someone '*in*' deconstruction? Someone '*in*' cultural studies? Someone '*in*' deconstructive cultural studies? Someone from somewhere else entirely? This is the problem of all articulation or representation: it's never neutral, never certain, and always working for certain (or uncertain) interests.

Take this friendly representation, for instance: Following the first wave of insulting obituaries to Derrida, Terry Eagleton emphasized the importance of what Derrida 'opened up' for and 'introduced into' responsible political and ethical thinking. Eagleton insisted that Derrida 'remained a staunch member of the political left' who 'aimed to prise open classical leftist ideas such as Marxism to the marginal, the aberrant' and that 'in this sense his project had affinities with the work of Raymond Williams, E. P. Thompson, Stuart Hall and the 1970s feminists in Britain' (Eagleton 2004). This seems like a very friendly gesture: affiliative, supportive; emphasizing the 'proper' politicality of deconstruction, asserting its fundamental left-ness, its likeness to proper feminism, Derrida's affinity to properly politically responsible intellectuals, like those in cultural studies. Eagleton says: Derrida was one of the good guys, one of us, not one of them: *Derrida was with (proper) cultural studies*. But was he? Speaking of the future of the humanities, Derrida actually once asserted that:

> ... the deconstructive task of the Humanities to come will not let itself be contained within the traditional limits of the departments that today belong, by their very status, to the Humanities. These Humanities to come will cross disciplinary borders without, all the same, dissolving the specificity of each discipline into what is called, often in a very confused way, interdisciplinarity or into what is lumped with another good-for-everything concept, 'cultural studies'. (Derrida 2001: 50)

Now, neither the predicative instability nor the immense interpretive reserves of these formulations (for *who* actually does the lumping and *who* actually is confused?) can eradicate the *negative* marking of cultural studies here (not to mention 'interdisciplinarity' – whatever that is supposed to refer to). What remains clear is that *the deconstructive 'Humanities to come' will not be cultural studies*. Why might Derrida have a problem with cultural studies? Why *won't* the deconstructive Humanities to come be – or even be *like* – cultural studies? He doesn't say. But one of his closest collaborators, Geoffrey Bennington (1998), was once keen to offer a – if not 'deconstructive' (for that would be misrepresentative), certainly 'deconstruction*ist*' – case against cultural studies.

For him, the *problem* with cultural studies relates precisely to the 'legacy' of 'Raymond Williams', 'Stuart Hall', 'Tony Bennett', and indeed 'Terry Eagleton' (Bennington 1998: 105). And, for Bennington, it is their ' "interminable self-confident and self-righteous political-cum-cultural-studies-speak" which lacks the necessary "theoretical sophistication" and self-awareness to even understand its own political and cultural situation, let alone set about changing it' (quoted in Gary Hall 2002: 66). Cultural studies is nothing more than a pseudo-intellectual, 'clear-conscience' soap-box pontificating kind of ' "Late-Show" journalism', waffling on about politics as its *raison d'être* without stopping even for a moment even to think about *what* politics and the political might be. The problem with cultural studies, for Bennington, then, is simply that it doesn't *question* enough, *think* enough or *read* enough. His argument is the following: cultural studies sees itself as a political project. Political responsibility and intervention is its *raison d'être*. It bangs on about politics all the time. But it doesn't actually think about the political. Rather, it presumes it *knows* what politics *is*. Thus, says Bennington, 'politics' – the *heart* of cultural studies – is placed in a 'transcendental position' (*everything* is judged in terms of 'politics') – but it is also absolutely *excluded from* cultural studies. For, in believing it knows what politics is, cultural studies never questions what politics is. The question of politics is excluded from cultural studies, and it labours under the misapprehension and disorientating fantasy that holding forth about the politics of this or that *is* to carry out one's political and intellectual responsibilities. In short, Bennington's problem with cultural studies is expressed in his perception that – *unlike deconstruction* – cultural studies believes it *knows*. Hence it *abandons* reading and thinking (see also Wolfreys 2003: 164–5). This sounds like an impeccably intellectually and politically responsible concern – indeed so much so that it has been picked up by many of the deconstructively inclined within cultural studies with an almost masochistic glee. Surely we can all agree: reading and thinking must *never* be abandoned!

But, according to deconstruction's own values, this begs the question of precisely *what* or *which* particular texts of cultural studies Bennington and Derrida are *reading and thinking about* in order to make or imply their generalizing, pejorative, denunciations. (Who is 'confused', and who is doing the 'lumping'?) Why do first Bennington and then Derrida evoke 'the proper' by way of discriminating *against* cultural studies? Why is there no *reading* in either case? Why is there the very same reductive flattening and homogenizing that is simultaneously said to be anathema to deconstruction? Why scapegoat cultural studies in order to specify deconstruction 'proper'? Moreover, what ultimately is the difference between these write-offs and, say, Slavoj Žižek's relentless 'straw-manning' of a cultural studies of his own invention? For that matter, what is the difference between these and the Richard Dawkins style of scapegoating cultural studies? For Dawkins, cultural studies exemplifies the 'debased', the irresponsible, the trivial, the 'fun' (Dawkins quoted in Zylinska 2001: 175). What are the differences between these constructions of cultural studies as a 'hate object' (Young 1999: 3)?

There is one apparent difference. With Dawkins and the rest of anglophone academia and media, 'cultural-studies-bashing' can joyously go much further than the 'deconstructionist' version. This is because Dawkins & Co can take the extra satisfying step of diagnosing cultural studies as being a *consequence of* (to quote Dawkins) 'the meaningless wordplays of modish francophone *savants*', whose activity 'seems to have no other function than to "impress the gullible"' (Dawkins quoted in Zylinska 2001: 175). Thus, for the mainstream of anglophone academia, cultural studies is merely an errant child infected, seduced, intoxicated by foreign, alien ('French') sophistry. Here, the problem is *French*. For the 'francophone *savants*', on the other hand, cultural studies is surely the bastard child of *them*, from *over there*: unthinking 'British'

PC 'leftism' and/or hyper-ideological 'American' 'multiculturalism'. As Žižek once suggested, the problem with cultural studies is that in it:

> ...notions of 'European' critical theory are imperceptibly translated into the benign universe of Cultural Studies chic. At a certain point, this chic becomes indistinguishable from the famous Citibank commercial in which East Asian, European, Black and American children playing is accompanied by the voice-over: 'People once divided by a continent...are now united by an economy' – at this concluding highpoint, of course, the children are replaced by the Citibank logo. (Žižek 2002: 171)

But, in cultural-studies-bashing, what actually is being bashed? Of the Dawkins variety, Joanna Zylinska argues:

> What is most significant about these attacks is the insubstantiality of the target they both adopt and rely on.... [T]his method works 'by fixing an indeterminate target, to give an illusion that something...concrete and ridiculous...is under attack'. For this purpose, the identity of cultural studies has to be both pre-decided and excluded from investigation...: indeed, the vehemence of such arguments depends on the refusal to engage with, or perhaps the misunderstanding of, the debates *within* cultural studies concerning its legitimacy, its disciplinary boundaries and its political commitment. (Zylinska 2001: 175–6)

Given the fantasy aspect of the non-object of the 'straw-manning', then, maybe we need not worry too much about such attacks. But, as others have argued, such attacks must be 'understood in the context of conflicts between the sciences and the humanities in conjunction with anti-liberalism, anti-intellectualism and conflicts among the left over what constitutes a legitimate politics' (Jennifer Daryl Slack and M. Mehdi Semati, quoted in Zylinska 2001: 175). So, as Derrida advised, we ought to 'stay sensitive both to the comedy and to the seriousness, [to] never give up either the laughter or the seriousness of intellectual and ethico-political responsibility' (1995: 404). Accordingly, we should ask: what is comical about this, and what is serious? In the case of Bennington, perhaps we might merely smile at the fact that he simply 'repeats without knowing' the very crime he accuses cultural studies of committing: for him, as for Dawkins, 'the identity of cultural studies has to be both pre-decided and excluded from investigation'. His is precisely the sort of excluding inclusion that he says is a problem with too much (unspecified) left criticism. He is in fact no different from the very thing he invents and imagines he is responsibly correcting. But what is never-theless serious about such a comedy? The fact that it might be mistaken for deconstruction; taken to be of or for deconstruction; conflated by association; deemed to be in any sense related to anything like the interrogative ethico-political quest for the lesser violence. In fact, such moments seem rather more simply hostile than deconstructive.

Which leads to the question: But what about *this*; what about *myself*? What about my own implication and imbrication in this? Am I so bloody pure, less violent, and holier than thou? Of course not. Which is *precisely* why what is necessary is to inscribe oneself *within* the circle of write-offs, put-downs, ridiculous simplifications and violent reductions that it is always possible to see and denounce and diagnose in others. For, surely, seeing ourselves and our closest acquaintances, most contiguous neigh-bours, and diametrical disputants *within* this very reflex metaphysical schema ought to oblige and authorize a different step, different respon-sibilities, a different engagement . . . Or shall we just enjoy writing off the others, polemically, *again, and again*? This kind of activity is pre-cisely what Marcuse called 'scholarshit': intellectual work 'built upon the model of war and unconditional surrender, designed primarily to eliminate one's opponent' (Giroux 2000: 14), which proceeds by 'mis-taking polemic for its own sake for resistance as such' (Spivak 1999: 337). But this is 'repeating without knowing' (Derrida 1997: 75), 'submission to a law' (123) of 'disciplinarity'; the power of correction, of policing, of the institutional production, regulation, distribution and spacing of 'docile' and 'disciplined' subjects (Mowitt 1992). Quite other than this, fidelity to Derridean deconstruction demands working to make Derridean rectitude be wrong. Otherwise, *deconstruction* risks becoming *McDeconstruction*.

McDeconstruction, embarrassment and studying popular culture

The neologism 'McDeconstruction' makes a clear play on the notorious term 'McDonaldization', of course. So, it takes on a pejorative colour-ing, smacking of globalization, homogenization, standardization, and so on. And 'Mc' is also a Celtic prefix, meaning 'son of'. So, McDecon-struction could be regarded as a 'McDonaldized' son of deconstruction: mass-produced, formalized, standardized, corporate, driven by profit. *The Oxford English Dictionary* adds that it takes the prefix 'Mc' to denote, firstly, 'a person who . . . is considered an exemplar or personification'. (So, immediately, the question becomes: exemplar of *what*? Of decon-struction? or of McDeconstruction?) The second use the *OED* gives for

'Mc' is: as a 'chiefly . . . *depreciative*' prefix 'to form nouns with the sense of "something that is of mass appeal, a standardized or bland variety of or alternative to"'. (It then cites the colloquial American term 'McMansion': 'a modern house built on a large and imposing scale, but regarded as ostentatious and lacking architectural integrity'.) So, clearly, despite appearances, this 'Mc' harbours *doubleness* and *undecidability*; double movements, movements in contrary directions at the same time. (For here we have: either exemplary in the sense of unique, or exemplary in the sense of typical, or indeed *bad*. Moreover: either good or bad son, or simulacrum of a son.)

The oldest record that a Google search can find for the term 'McDeconstruction' is in an academic journal article published in 2001. (As it turns out, the author of that article was myself. Anyway . . . .) This is how the term McDeconstruction was first used:

> The problem though, is that in so loving it, I am abusing it, in fetishizing 'deconstruction(s)' I am reproducing a convention that I keep avowedly attacking. I am torn. It seems that to love deconstruction I should kill it, in using deconstruction I am abusing it, and adding to the 'deluge' of McDeconstruction that is already becoming boring and predictable. [To this, a footnote is attached, which reads: 'Whilst the idea of a creeping 'deconstructionism' is allegedly anathema to 'deconstruction's' 'own' statements about 'itself', it does seem striking that one can now 'explain' what one otherwise 'means' by translating things *into* deconstructive terms. A deconstructive orthodoxy? What *should* that look like?'] (Bowman 2001b: 61, 63, note 93)

So, the issues here again condense around the theme of *institutionalization*. In Derrida's account, deconstruction is something that constitutively, fundamentally, has a *problem* with institutions. So, how are we to assess its own institutionalization? We should not be simplistic about this. For, if deconstruction has taught us nothing else, it is surely a lesson about *doubleness*, about movements in contrary directions. And these are what I want to consider, here. To do so we will need an example. And, in the spirit of double movements, a good example would also be one that related as much to the question of cultural studies' institution as to deconstruction's. One such example can be found in the case of Martin McQuillan. Now, many may not actually associate McQuillan with cultural studies. His work is far more connected to the term 'deconstruction'. But McQuillan does have a relationship with cultural studies, although for some reason it is almost systematically subordinated or downplayed in his work. McQuillan far prefers his ties to 'deconstruction'. But, on the matter of downplaying a relation to cultural studies, one may ask: '*So what*, big deal, who cares? What does it matter what it's called? What's in a name?' I hope to suggest why the relation is important.

In 2003, in an essay/interview entitled 'The Projection of Cultural Studies' (McQuillan 2003b), for a book called *Interrogating Cultural Studies*, McQuillan wrote: 'I was for a long time completely unaware that I did cultural studies. Indeed I did not know that I did cultural studies until you [Paul] told me that I did'. I had suggested to him that he did cultural studies in about 1999 or 2000 – not very long after the publication of his jointly authored book *Deconstructing Disney* (Byrne and McQuillan 1999). And *Deconstructing Disney* is a work categorized on its cover and in the catalogues as 'cultural studies'. Yet McQuillan claimed, in 2003: 'My first response, as you will recall, was "I don't do Cultural Studies"' (McQuillan 2003b). (So, in 2003, McQuillan claimed not to have known that he did cultural studies in 2000, even though the cover of *Deconstructing Disney* (published in 1998 and 1999) announces unequivocally that this is a book of and for cultural studies. This may be a case of publishers saying whatever they think will sell books. But, surely the authors 'signed off' on this designation?)

This may seem to be inconsequential, an 'inconsequentiality', or a forgivable oversight, signifying nothing. But, to use McQuillan own words: 'against such seeming inconsequentialities we have been taught to read' (McQuillan 2003a: 303). So, to be clear, my initial point of leverage is merely this: that McQuillan produces books and journals categorized as cultural studies; he is executive editor of an international cultural studies journal produced by a centre for cultural studies; and he holds a very important position 'in Cultural Theory and Analysis' in that centre for cultural studies. Admittedly, *Deconstructing Disney* came out before he got his job in cultural studies; but it surely played a notable part in him securing that position.

So, my question is: what does his 'amnesia' signify? For Derrida: 'amnesia is never accidental. It signifies something'. It is indicative of a 'hierarchizing operation' that 'organizes ['even produces' an] inheritance' (Derrida 1992b: 200). So, again, to be clear: my first simple claim is that McQuillan *is* associated with cultural studies. My second, less simple claim is that he is *indebted to* cultural studies. By 'indebted' I mean to evoke an argument (one that has also been voiced by McQuillan himself) about 'the becoming-cultural-studies of English' – indeed, what he calls 'the becoming-cultural-studies of the humanities in general' – in which cultural studies could be regarded as something of a 'sublation' of the humanities (Mowitt 2003). (I myself do not agree with this view. As we will see in the next chapter, whilst the humanities may have come to look like cultural studies, and whilst reciprocally cultural studies may therefore have lost a lot of its apparent uniqueness, what the humanities still lack is what I take to be the defining problematic of cultural studies, a problematic shared with deconstruction, namely, the problem of (the) *institution*.) In other words, McQuillan's 'amnesia' could reflect not acknowledging the debt as his own while still drawing interest upon it (see Godzich 1987: 162). So I am going to make a big deal of it.

I do so in full awareness of two possible responses. The first is 'Yeah? Big deal! So what?' The second is McQuillan's own deconstructive problematization of his relation to cultural studies.

Of the 'So what?' response, what has to be pointed out is that if there is what Kant called a 'conflict of the faculties' in British universities, then its name and locus is neither 'Philosophy' (as it was for Kant) nor 'Theory' (as others have suggested), but Cultural Studies. Cultural Studies has attracted a degree and a range of criticism, hostility, and outright attacks that are as fascinating and potentially edifying as they are serious. So, if the question is 'So, cultural studies, so what?', the answer is: it's only 'so what' if one does not acknowledge what Stuart Hall calls the 'stakes' deriving from its *history* and *contingent institution*.

Which brings us to McQuillan's deconstructive problematization of his relation to cultural studies. On the one hand, his problematization of this relation has taken the form of a version of the 'What's in a name?' response. My answer is, again, in this context – however it is characterized – *everything*. On the other hand, though, and stated plainly, what McQuillan simply cannot face is, in his words, ' "coming out" as "doing" cultural studies'. This is because he suffers from what he calls the 'embarrassment of affiliation with an under theorised and "anoraky" version of cultural studies' (McQuillan 2003b: 47). ('Anoraky', of course, is being used to mean 'nerdy'.) Yet, elsewhere, away from all of this mucky, embarrassing cultural studies business, McQuillan is more than prepared to 'come out' as 'a deconstructionist'. One article he wrote (in a cultural studies journal – indeed, in a themed issue of a cultural studies journal, entitled 'Polemics: Against Cultural Studies') – an article that has become the first chapter of his new book – begins with his own version of the gay rights chant, 'We're here, we're queer, get used to it!' Namely, the first words of the article and the book are the proud declaration: 'I am a deconstructionist!'

This is nowhere supplemented/completed with: 'I am a deconstructionist, enabled by cultural studies, get used to it!' In fact, there is a *contrary* movement: an *intellectual* movement that virtually *disavows* cultural studies in tandem with (and riding on) an *institutional* movement *into* it. Again: So what? Let's recall the ill-advised comment that Derrida once made about cultural studies:

> ... the deconstructive task of the Humanities to come will not let itself be contained within the traditional limits of the departments that today belong, by their very status, to the Humanities. These Humanities to come will cross disciplinary borders without, all the same, dissolving the specificity of each discipline into what is called, often in a very confused way, interdisciplinarity or into what is lumped with another good-for-everything concept, 'cultural studies'. (Derrida 2001: 50)

In response to this comment, McQuillan once wrote something of a defence of cultural studies – or rather, something of a critique of the 'very confused way' that Derrida sloppily bandies around the terms 'interdisciplinarity' and 'cultural studies': 'Perhaps I am being too sensitive here', wrote McQuillan, 'a bit like defending a slightly embarrassing relative simply because s/he happens to "belong" to you, but against such seeming inconsequentialities we have been taught to read' (McQuillan 2003a: 303). And McQuillan's point is correct. *Seeming* inconsequentialities are not *necessarily* inconsequential.

This is why I want to read some 'seeming inconsequentialities' in McQuillan own work. I will read *against* them, in the name of the 'mission' (or the transmission, or the transmission of the mission) of *both* deconstruction *and* cultural studies. In a first sense, I view this as the effort to try, in Derrida's words, 'to modify the rules of the dominant discourse, ... to politicize and democratize the university scene' (Derrida 1995: 410). In a second, supplementary, but crucial sense, however, what this relies on is what the likes of Derrida, Stuart Hall, Sam Weber, Wlad Godzich, John Mowitt, and many more have called the constitutive character of *institution*. Without what I have been calling the institutional focus, this mission – the transmission of the mission of deconstruction and cultural studies – becomes impossible. For my argument is that they are both contingently instituted institutional practices, and that there is nothing outside of institution. Accordingly, subordinating, downplaying or overlooking them *qua* particular institutional achievements as if in the name of some (spurious) universal project would be a mistake. Rather, preferences, decisions and orientations are *institutional, instituting*. There is nothing outside of institution. So, to 'para-cite' Derrida: this little point about cultural studies 'joins the great questions of canonization'. It's about the determination of how we 'decide what corpus to study, what research to authorize, what money to distribute, and so on' (Derrida

1992b: 197, 199). It relates to *teleiopoesis*, or the fact that, as John Mowitt puts it:

> ... what we believe to have happened to us bears concretely on what we are prepared to do with ourselves both now and in the future, [and that] the formation of such a memory is inseparable from historical, and ultimately political, practice. (Mowitt 1992: 2)

There is a relationship between memory and orientation. In an interview entitled 'Canons and Metonymies' (Derrida 1992a), Derrida argues, firstly, that there is 'violence marking every procedure of legitimation or canonization' (198). Secondly, that 'deconstruction answers to a greater desire for memory, intelligibility and responsibility in the face of tradition'. Thirdly, that 'a redistribution of canonical values in fact leads, concretely, to difficult choices in the organizing of study and research' (198–9). And fourthly, that 'amnesia is never accidental. It signifies something; its phenomenon is not just negative. It is not just a loss of memory. A selective hierarchizing operation organizes the inheritance. It even produces it' (200). So, the question here is: what does privileging 'deconstruction' over and at the expense of cultural studies 'do'? What is the violence of this choice? What is the redistribution? What amnesia arrives? With what consequences?

Now, although McQuillan is embarrassed by cultural studies and sometimes inexplicably forgets to mention it, he never *rejects* cultural studies. Indeed, McQuillan actually expresses an affiliative relationship to it – or rather to something in it greater than itself (a 'spirit'). (As we saw at the end of Chapter 4, this evocation of a spirit is in many ways a problematic move.) This is because, as he characterizes it, cultural studies might be regarded as 'a transformative critique of the institution'; and something that is what it is 'not because it ... only read[s] popular forms but because it ... neither preclude[s] any object of analysis nor retreat[s] from any theoretical limits' (McQuillan 2003b: 51). In saying this, McQuillan actually sounds a lot like Stuart Hall. He continues:

> ... the whole point of cultural studies is to open the proper to the scrutiny of the improper. This includes the theoretical limits of cultural studies as well as its object of analysis. Transformative critique must also be auto-critique, which not only asks what is proper to cultural studies but what is proper to the impropriety of questioning the proper. ... [W]ithout theory as a certain spirit of auto-critique, cultural studies is in constant danger of becoming just another disciplinary endeavour – the term 'Studies' gives the game away here – with a naff object of analysis. The point would be that

one cannot 'do' cultural studies simply by borrowing its thematics. Any act of cultural analysis (a term I would now prefer to cultural studies) must be interventionist and transformative, theoretical and inaugural, performative of the idiom in which it operates, and 'material' in its attention to what is resistant (both singular and other) in the object it analyses. (McQuillan 2003b: 50)

I totally agree with this. Cultural studies was never supposed to be *just* '*studies*'. As Stuart Hall saw it, something is '*at stake* in cultural studies' (1992: 278), and what that *is* is *consequential ethical and political institutional intervention*. Quite how one measures 'consequentiality' may be in question, but McQuillan, like Stuart Hall, is clear that, as he puts it, one 'cannot "do" [it] simply by borrowing its thematics' (McQuillan 2003b: 50), and 'the endless articles on Foucault and football are not "doing" cultural studies anymore' (49), either. Indeed, such work, he states, can be a decidedly 'conservative force' – or, so to speak, *Mc*Cultural Studies.

But this very argument – that *cultural studies is not just Studies* – is what makes McQuillan's proposed abandonment of the *name* and its replacement with 'cultural analysis' doubly troubling. In fact, it opens the door to the abandonment of its entire constitutive problematic: if cultural studies is *not* just meant to be *studies*, then in what way is renaming it *analysis* a solution? I would suggest that this proposed name change signals a move away from the *institutional problematic* that is constitutive and definitive of cultural studies. Moreover, with this, something uniquely political to do with (at least) the British institutionalization of 'deconstruction' is also lost. Such a claim might seem controversial. However, to reiterate: following the likes of Stuart Hall, this formative problematic is that of working out *how* intellectual work might possibly make a difference that could count in the wider institutional-political field (Hall 1992). For Derrida, this takes the form of construing one's effort as '*an institutional practice for which the concept of the institution remains a problem*' (Derrida 2002: 53). As Godzich puts it, *the* 'target' here is *institution* (1987: 162). And Mowitt points out that what is most politically valuable about deconstruction is the way that its focus obliges one to 'pose questions that bear on the institutional maintenance of the hermeneutical field as such – questions which quickly center upon the political problems of how institutions are constituted, reproduced, and transformed' (Mowitt 1992: 214–15).

What is clear (both theoretically and empirically or observably) is that such a problematic does not just magically *happen*. Rather it relies entirely on '*teleiopoesis*' or 'the formation of . . . a memory [that] is inseparable from historical, and ultimately political, practice' (Mowitt

1992: 2). Substituting 'analysis' for 'studies' will obviously *not* stop academic work from being mere study. If anything, it will *guarantee* it. In Hall's Gramscian words, there is a vast difference between academic work and intellectual intervention. (Or, in our terms, a vast difference between cultural studies and McCultural Studies.)

To be fair, though, McQuillan mainly proposes the switch to 'analysis' to solve the problem of his 'embarrassment of affiliation with [an] under theorised and "anoraky" version of cultural studies', or what he rightly calls 'little more than a reversed Leavisitism, [which] construct[s] alternative canons of culture, [and] prais[es] them for the exercise of differing units of value within equally restricted economies' (McQuillan 2003b: 47), by which he means work that is nerdy, hobbyist, anthropological, taxonomical, and panoptical. Such un-self-reflexive and ultimately conservative 'nerdy' studies are chiefly what provoke his argument that 'Where cultural studies is "going", if I had my way, would be to become departments of Reading or even departments of Reading and Writing, although these "departments" would soon have to evolve into something else' (51). Evolve into what? He explains:

> ...cultural studies – or perhaps now we ought to speak of the spirit of cultural studies, the ways in which the ghost of cultural studies haunts the academic castle – if it is to continue its work, may need to abandon its name. As long as the work gets done one might as well call it comparative literature, or, reading and writing, or whatever. The same goes for Theory, call it philosophy, call it thinking, such sobriquets can only have ever been strategic. There can be no systematic pronouncements on cultural studies (and/or theory). Cultural studies will – if it is to be true to itself – always be half inside, half outside the academy, crossing borders from exile to exile. (McQuillan 2003b: 52)

Now, most of this I do not agree with. Moreover, since *Specters of Marx* (Derrida 1994), this sort of thing has become 'Deconstruction 101'. What is unfortunate about it is that, in this formulaic form, it overlooks the very thing one might expect and want a 'deconstructionist' to pay attention to, namely the contingency of the constitutive institutional supplement. That is, it surely makes a *big* difference where and in what way this supposed 'spirit' is instituted. Is there some transcendent 'spirit' of cultural studies (or deconstruction or Marx) *outside* of its institution? Of course not. Nor does it simply reside 'in' its texts. It consists in and as its or their contingent instituted form. I rather think that to 'haunt the academic castle', and to do 'comparative literature, or, reading and writing, or whatever' is quite different from doing cultural studies too. The name is indeed 'strategic'. It comes to *matter*.

Nerds Я Us

Of course, I agree that actually existing cultural studies is often embarrassingly nerdy and, worse, shoddy. But I think that this is true of *most* scholarship. Indeed, I think that the demand – *justify your anorakiness!* – should be generalized to *all* scholarship (Bahti 1992: 72–3): work *should* be supplemented with an account of the *point* of doing it, an explanation of *why* it supposedly matters, to *what*, and, importantly, *how*.[1] Until we can answer these questions, we are *all* naff and nerdy here. We may never cease being nerds. But the 'force' proper to both cultural studies and deconstruction relates to the extent to which such difficult questions are inscribed, institutionally, as constitutive.

This brings us back to Derrida's claim to try 'to politicize and democratize the university scene' (1995: 410). A strong part of this process is certainly quasi-transcendental deconstructive questioning. Yet we must still be hospitable to the *other* nerds in their anoraks, no matter how embarrassing. (For nerds are us.) But when *either* 'transcendentalizing' or some *other* version of 'train-spotting' or 'stamp-collecting' threatens to lead to the effective disavowal of the contingent constitutive formation which enabled this institutionalization of deconstruction in the first place, then the claim of some universality of 'rigour' becomes spurious. This move does *not* guarantee the interventional, political, or politicizing impetus: if anything, it gets you 'off the hook' (Hall, Morley and Chen 1996: 146). Worse, it leads to the institution of tightly policed strictures.

For what is rigour? It is clear that the way McQuillan conceptualizes the 'good reading' that he advocates has (as Slavoj Žižek might put it) been 'hegemonized' by deconstruction. By 'good reading', McQuillan clearly means deconstruction. Ironically, or paradoxically, however, this 'hegemonizing' gesture institutes a problematic relation to *difference*. This can be seen in his claim that there is a need for cultural studies to become 'more study, less culture'. He continues: 'If you really wonder where cultural studies "should" go then I think it needs to redress the imbalance between "culture" and "study" which has marked its formation up till now' (McQuillan 2003b: 52). However, this itself supposes that there is no *culture* in study, that *study* is not cultural. His polemical point is against shabby, shoddy scholarship. And I do agree with it. But the problem lies with the presumption that 'good reading' will *solve* this. My suggestion is that, if anything, the injunction to 'good reading' could lead to the most radically conservative enclaving imposition of propriety in exactly the realm where it should not be: i.e., *reading*. There is no 'one' good reading.

So, my argument is that the 'classical protocols' evoked by McQuillan's teleiopoetic gesture of 'evolving' cultural studies into Departments of Reading and Writing does *not* constitute an evolution but rather a *regression from* deconstruction *and* cultural studies. This is because it relies on a *pre*-cultural-studies and *un*deconstructive conception of political intervention. This can be seen in McQuillan's declared pedagogical and institutional aim: at Leeds University, he says, their declared departmental aim is 'to produce good readers'.[2] He regards this as 'a modest enough claim', yet one 'from which everything else flows, including [he proposes] all the political and institutional claims made for cultural studies .... What matters [he continues] is that the messy business of education is done and everything else (the victory of the proletariat, if there are any left, or the democracy to come, if it ever gets here) will follow from this' (McQuillan 2003b: 54).

Unfortunately, this supposed 'causal relation' (*from* reading *to* revolution) is not one. Rather, it is an *aporia*. *Nothing necessarily follows* – either in theory or (very evidently) in practice from reading. And 'critique', whether good or bad, will not necessarily change a thing, even if you call it 'transformative critique'. This is important, because McQuillan bases his whole account of the 'force', 'agency' or 'interventionality' of institutional academia in the most traditional, 'arboreal', phonocentric and subject-centred notion of 'critique'.

This is significant because McQuillan also invaluably reminds us that *calls* for change *do not necessarily change anything*; and that it is a mistake to conflate calling for change with *making* an effective intervention *in* anything (McQuillan 2001). Thus, McQuillan invaluably cautions us against believing in a kind of 'soap-box' conception of politics (namely: as if politics consists of one speaker holding forth to one assembled and enthralled audience who are willing and able to react in a predictable and programmatic manner to whatever the preacher preaches or teacher teaches). McQuillan importantly reminds us that things are not so simple.

This important insight, however, makes his *own* elevation of the value of *critique* particularly problematic. For not only is the belief in the necessary transformative value of critique both phonocentric and subject-centred, it basically *forgets* not only the theory of hegemony but also deconstruction: it overlooks the institutional complexity and heterogeneity of discourse and hegemony. As John Mowitt has observed of this tendency: 'why should we reconceive the social as discourse' – or indeed, why should we bother with deconstruction at all – 'if, in the final analysis, we are only really interested in the consciousness motivating agents?' (Mowitt 1992: 17). For, if we do think that 'transformation' primarily involves something like speaking (or critiquing) to a public – or if the focus on *'contingency'* is replaced by vague evocations of 'chance', as it appears to sometimes in many deconstructionists' work – then *one does not need deconstruction.* In fact, *one abandons deconstruction.*[3]

Critique of the institution is one thing; *transformation* of it is another. So, this ethico-political matter demands attention and interventions that are perhaps other than critique. My suggestion is that the construal of the *work* or *missions* of deconstruction or cultural studies as if merely 'critique' is a reduction in purview and remit of both.

In his forgotten work of cultural studies, McQuillan tells us, 'critique' has 'long since lost any power to surprise let alone illuminate' (Byrne and McQuillan 1999: 1). I think he may be right. If, as he rightly says he is, McQuillan remains 'keen to retain the spirit of cultural studies as a transformative lever able to enact shifts within the powerfully inertial hierarchies of the institution' (McQuillan 2003b: 53), the question is: What institutes a 'spirit' as a 'lever'? Moreover, as Derrida asks: 'what is technique in this case? Is there a lever? Is there a better lever?' (1992: 205). The final chapter will offer an answer to this question.

Alterdisciplinarity: Deconstructing Popular Cultural Studies

Against the urgency of people dying in the streets, what in God's name is the point of cultural studies?

Stuart Hall (1996: 272)

...if there is polemos, and irreducible polemos, this cannot, in the final analysis, be accounted for by a taste for war, and still less for polemics.

Jacques Derrida (2003: 12)

The critique of critique

A cartoon drawing by the disconcerting British artist David Shrigley depicts a list of random activities on a peculiar calendar of events. In the middle of the list, there is one particularly arresting entry: the announcement of a forthcoming conference, entitled 'How are we supposed to know that what we are doing is right?' This title is striking not just because of its incongruity; but also because it actually seems to offer an uncanny insight or revelation – perhaps even a definitive 'meta'- statement – of what *all* academic conferences are basically 'about'. Most conferences implicitly or explicitly ask: Why are we doing what we are doing? Is what we are doing right? How can we 'know' this?

Let's have one final look at these important questions, by considering the ways that they have been answered – or not – within the realms of politicized critical and cultural theory, and particularly those informed by deconstruction. I want to do this in order to draw attention to and take issue with the most prevalent yet rather untheoretical and uncritical form of response which has taken hold in putatively theoretical and critical circles; a response which I argue is now working to *close down* thinking on these critical questions. So, I will proceed by sketching out the most influential theorization that has underpinned and guided

169

the work of some exemplary politically engaged cultural theorists and activists. Basically, this is the widely accepted belief in the political value of *critique*. Critique is held to be somehow politically consequential. This chapter seeks to interrogate this hazy 'somehow', by asking: *precisely how* is critique consequential?

But before we get into the critique of the theory that critique has political value, we should first clarify for whom this is important, and for what reason. My starting point is the observation that central to the formation and orientation of ethical and politicized academic subjects is the notion of *intervention*. In other words, the tacit agreement in critical theory, poststructuralism, post-Marxism, cultural studies, and so on, is that *the point* of our intellectual, theoretical, critical and analytical efforts is always '*to change it*'. In other words, the aim is ethical political intervention (alteration). And this aim is fundamental to the orientation of a diverse range of figures and fields, particularly those of cultural studies. Indeed, the stated aim of achieving effective, reorientating, consequential intervention is shared in common by academics of all orders, whether humanist or structuralist, whether Marxist or postmodernist, as well as by Derridean deconstruction, leftist liberal humanism, and beyond. It is also, of course, an aim with which I, too, strongly identify. It is what prompts my intervention here.

There have been many attempts to intervene, to make a difference, by applying the insights of cultural theory. My discussion will begin from one exemplary case: Stuart Hall's influential theorization of cultural studies as a 'project'. By looking at this theorization, we can grasp one prevailing conception of *what* academic intervention is deemed to be, and the ways it has been deemed able to 'carry out its worldly responsibilities'. As I say, my argument is that for a long time and with a very widespread regularity in dispersal the answer has been: critique. This is so much so that today this answer has allowed something of a hiatus to arise in politicized theory: on the one hand, it reflects an inability to come up with any answer other than 'critique'; yet on the other hand it maintains a degree of vagueness about *precisely how* our critiques might actually intervene in anything in particular. In other words, my argument is that the prevailing notion of how academics and intellectuals can intervene effectively relies on a rather vague, under-theorized and nebulous faith in the value of critique.

This should make us pause for thought. For the possibility that there may be an untheorized or under-theorized blind spot at the heart of avowedly intervention-orientated (politicized) theory would surely be surprising. That this blind spot in theory might be on the very issue that should be most central to it – namely, *how this theory itself theorizes itself as or in relation to intervention* – would surely be scandalous. My suggestion is that 'theory' is indeed currently in an under-theorized hiatus, and that what has caused this is precisely an unquestioned faith in the political value of critique. My suggestion is that this investment (or liberal hope) in the power of critique both *regresses from* and *contradicts* the theoretical insights of the (poststructuralist and post-Marxist) theory that otherwise orientates these academic and theoretical interventional efforts. In short, my argument is that recourse to (and) faith in critique is undertheoretical, broadly metaphysical, subject-centred, and an ultimately anti-intellectual regression from poststructuralist-informed theories of the political.

By revisiting the implications of deconstruction for an answer to the question of precisely *how* academic work relates or amounts to political intervention, my proposal is that what is required is more thoroughgoing attention to the place and character of *disciplinarity* in the pragmatic mechanics of culture and society's institutions, discourses and hegemonies. The theoretical contention here is that the conditions of possibility for intervention are indissociable from the institutional and disciplinary character of (post)modernity. That is, they relate to the 'academic condition', which is one of unavoidably heterogeneous language games in a web of disciplinary differences wherein what has arisen is *disciplinary enclaving, mutual unintelligibility* and *disarticulation*. In this situation, it often appears that the only possible form of ethical and political intervention is critique – either within one's own discipline or 'in public', journalistically. However, against this, my polemical argument is that currently the interventional effectiveness of any critique should be regarded as dubious at best. Although critique may be necessary, it is insufficient. So, in the wake of this critique of critique, I propose that attention be turned to a theory and practice of what I call *alterdisciplinarity*.

This is not a new theory or practice, although it may be a new term. But what it demands is a new theorization of academic practice, a retheorization of politicized theoretical practice. For a basic premise here is that no style of intervention can use the same strategy and tactics or stay the same for very long. So, my proposal for a new alterdisciplinary practice remains grounded in poststructuralism and deconstructive discourse theory, but rather than living in repetition by repeating the gestures of a former style, the aim is to alter *other* disciplinary discourses and their productions (knowledges) not by critiquing them (from afar) but by intervening in the disciplinary spaces of their production and legitimation – that is: getting *inside knowledge* and *undoing other methodologies* as an alternative practice of consequential intervention.

The alterdisciplinary theory of theory

To flesh out the claim that current politicized academic practice is living in an ineffectual repetition of repeating the gestures of the past, we need a clear picture of why and how the gestures we are repeating may once have worked, and why they may do so no longer. Now, without necessarily claiming it to be the sole parent of the present, it is well worth considering the case of the alterdisciplinary theory and practice that can be seen in the project of cultural studies, as theorized by Stuart Hall, particularly in his influential 1992 retrospective, entitled 'Cultural Studies and Its Theoretical Legacies'. Here, Hall defines cultural studies as an intellectual practice dominated by a strong 'will to connect' (Hall 1992: 278). For Hall, this 'will to connect' means that *by definition* cultural studies 'tries to make a difference in the institutional world in which it is located' (285). Accordingly – and despite the embarrassing vagueness of the name cultural studies (that we discussed in the Introduction) – this is a definition which means that cultural studies *cannot* simply be just 'whatever people [choose to] do' (277). Indeed, says Hall:

> It can't be just any old thing which chooses to march under a particular banner. It is a serious enterprise, or project, and that is inscribed in what is sometimes called the 'political' aspect of cultural studies. Not that there's one politics already inscribed in it. But there is something *at stake* in cultural studies, in a way that I think, and hope, is not exactly true of many other very important intellectual and critical practices. (Hall 1992: 278)

In Hall's account, cultural studies was formed in 'a discursive formation, in Foucault's sense' (Hall 1992: 278), emerging within the 'milieu' of the New Left in the UK (Rojek 2003: 23). It was a university institution that was explicitly ethico-politically motivated: open to alterity, intent on pushing exclusionary limits, borders, conventions, boundaries, orientations, hierarchies, and so on. In short, as Hall makes clear: cultural studies was intent on *intervening*, on *altering*. It was never 'merely academic', either in the literal or the pejorative sense of this term. Rather, to (re-)employ one of Derrida's definitions of deconstruction, although located within the university institution, cultural studies was always *'an institutional practice for which . . . the institution remains a problem'* (Derrida 2002: 53) – and hence institution is one of its central and defining problematics.

It seems important to reiterate that this focus on the university institution was not selected as an avoidance of 'real' political issues 'out there' in the 'real world'. It was never (as many critics and commentators still maintain) a *retreat* from 'the real world' or a regression into narcissistic and 'politically correct' nit-picking about merely academic issues. Rather, the institutional focus of cultural studies (and indeed of deconstruction) always rested on the theory that culture and society are *contingent, changeable, consequential,* and hence *political* formations. This interpretation asserts that the character of culture and society is irreducibly *institutional* (i.e., *instituted*), and that therefore there are *political* implications to everything that is instituted (Derrida 1992; Hall 1992). In such an interpretation, an inestimably important 'political' significance cannot but be attached to the matter of *knowledge*: of *how* knowledge is established, of *what* passes for knowledge, and *why* (Peters 2001: 27–33).

Thus, the basic orientation of cultural studies (and, equally, deconstruction) is alterdisciplinary. The aim is to alter the 'business as usual' production of knowledge – in Derrida's words, 'to politicize and democratize the university scene', in order, ultimately, to 'modify' dominant discourses (Derrida 1995: 409–10; see also Mowitt 1992: 27). Such an orientation undercuts and recasts the terms that organize many other notions of intervention, such as those which tend to distinguish 'academic work' from 'political work' (or 'theory' from 'practice') and the 'university' from 'the real world' (see, for example, Rorty (1996); discussed in Bowman (2007)). Of course, valid distinctions and differences between certain forms of 'academic work' and 'political practice' *can* be made; but once one construes culture, society, politics and history as contingent, discursive, and mutable, then academic work *cannot* be divorced or disentangled from the political field. Work may be 'conservative' and hence not obviously politicized, but this still amounts to *a* political bias, however tacit. The original alterdisciplinary strategy of cultural studies was to unmask this partiality, *through critique.*

This alterdisciplinary critique was successful (although not without its vicissitudes, as we shall see). Mieke Bal explains:

> ... [along with] women's studies, cultural studies [was] responsible for the absolutely indispensable opening up of the disciplinary structure of the humanities. By challenging methodological dogma, and elitist prejudice and value judgement, it has been uniquely instrumental in at least making the academic community aware of the conservative nature of its endeavours, if not everywhere forcing it to change. It has, if nothing else, forced the academy to realise its collusion with an elitist white-male politics of exclusion and its subsequent intellectual closure. (Bal 2003: 30)

Alterdisciplinary critique, often in the form of polemic, was the primary form of cultural studies' original intervention: the 'knock-on effect' of its ethically and politically inflected critiques was the alteration of other disciplines. Although 'merely academic', this was regarded in cultural studies as political, because the theory was that culture and society are contingent and hence political, so to change what is produced and legitimated as knowledge will be 'discursively' (ethico-politically) consequential. The 'method' or pragmatics of this intervention takes the form of revealing what Derrida called the bias and even the 'violence' of the 'nonconceptual orders' upon which different conceptual orders (i.e., 'knowledges') are articulated (Derrida 1982: 329). In cultural studies this process of political revelation largely took the form of *directly* pointing out political biases such as Eurocentrism, heteronormativity, and so on. The deconstructive strategy, on the other hand, took the form of evoking what Derrida (teleiopoetically) called 'classical protocols' – namely, privileging above all else rigorous, rational, reasonable, incisive questioning and 'reading' – in order to demonstrate the biases underpinning this or that accepted 'truth'.[1] In Derrida, the expression 'classical protocols' functions as a *teleiopoetic* term that he regularly conjures up in order to engender what it would seem to evoke or promise – namely, *more* analytical 'rigour' through *more* 'sensitivity' in reading; *more* 'listening' for the voices that have been drowned out, *more* questioning of the political implications of interpretive decisions, and so on (see, for instance, Derrida 1992b: 11.) This is why John Protevi proposes that 'deconstruction is democratic justice, responding to the calls from all others' (2001: 70). And this is also why many things other than what Derrida and friends did can be called 'deconstructive'.

From this perspective, the politicized alterdisciplinary strategy may sound very grand. But Hall is keen that we do not get too carried away with the lofty significance we may wish to attribute to our own efforts. Rather, despite any theoretically imputed self-importance, Hall emphasizes the fundamental obscenity of deluding oneself that one's obligations have been carried out merely by studying, theorizing, or otherwise holding forth on urgent political issues. He apostrophizes: 'Against the urgency of people dying in the streets, what in God's name is the point of cultural studies?' (1996: 272). But, rather than writing off the worth of academic and intellectual work in the face of the urgency and enormity of culture and politics, Hall reiterates rather the 'deadly seriousness of intellectual work. It is a deadly serious matter', he insists (287). It is important to add that this is so whether one's preferred style or idiom of discourse is 'theoretical', 'academic', 'journalistic' or 'commonsense'. For *no* style of critique *necessarily* 'connects', intervenes, or makes a difference. And, if one risk of theoretical discourse is that we end up content with 'dwelling in profundity' (as Butler puts it in a criticism of Žižek: 'it will not do simply to say that all these concrete struggles exemplify something more profound, and that our task is to dwell in that profundity' (Butler 2000: 161)), the symmetrical risk of 'common-sense' and 'journalistic' discourse is that the refusal of theorization leads us to become 'fatally mortgaged to the phenomenality of the nightly news' (McQuillan 2001: 117). As Martin McQuillan reminds us, in either orientation, to *call* for change is certainly not necessarily to go any way towards *actually precipitating* a change (120). The problematic to be emphasized here is: *how* are we to intervene *responsibly, effectively*? In what ways (and to what) does what we do make any difference?

This is hard to know. In fact, it is undecidable – particularly in advance. And the intangibility – the deferred, displaced, delayed, indecisive character (*différance*) – of academic work easily leads to *frustration* with the political 'effectiveness' of intellectual work in relation to politics and the political. This can lead to a repudiation of the argument that theoretical or academic work might possibly ever constitute a significant ethico-political intervention. For, because writing arguments, analyses or critiques does not easily seem like direct action, this can lead to the rationalization: 'Action has value and is therefore knowable as true politics, while thought is a self-indulgent "preoccupation" which is worth nothing because it prevents "participation" in politics' (McQuillan 2001: 120). In the extreme, this can lead 'activists' to entirely dismiss 'thought' on the ground that it 'impedes action'. (As McQuillan argues, even Naomi Klein 'similarly dismisses thought because it impedes action' (121).) Judith Butler points out that this is deeply problematic because therefore 'those who fear the retarding effects of theory do not want to think too hard about what it is they are doing, what kind of discourse they are using'; presumably because they suspect that 'if they think too hard about what it is they are doing, they fear that they will no longer do it' (Butler 2000: 265). In other words: 'Paradoxically, such positions require the paralysis of critical reflection in order to avoid the prospect of paralysis on the level of action' (Butler 2000: 265).

Of course, such a rationale is untenable, self-contradictory, and self-refuting. All 'direct action', however 'anti-theoretical' it may be, is based on a theory (see Derrida 1978: 152; Godzich 1987: 163; Gilbert 2003: 151). But the *frustration* it signals remains valid. Hall concurs:

> I think anybody who is into cultural studies seriously as an intellectual practice, must feel, on their pulse, its ephemerality, its insubstantiality, how little it registers, how little we've been able to change anything or get anybody to do anything. [Indeed] If you don't feel that as one tension in the work you are doing, theory has let you off the hook. (Hall 1992: 286)

So, impatience or perceived urgency in no way justifies a refutation of the value of thinking and theorizing. Indeed, for Hall, 'there are no theoretical limits from which cultural studies can turn back', and not only because 'if you are in the game of hegemony you have to be smarter than "them"' (Hall 1992: 282), but also because 'unless we operate in this tension, we don't know what cultural studies can do, can't, can never do; but also, what it has to do, what it alone has a privileged capacity to do' (286). So, unless we theorize, think, analyse, engage, and do not retreat from *any* theoretical limits, we cannot really establish that we even think we know what 'directly doing politics' might mean or entail in this or that context (see also Gary Hall 2002). This or that form of action – 'direct' or 'indirect' – may be nothing more than the reiteration of empty or ineffectual gestures.

Thus, what seems required at this point is an assessment, audit or evaluation of what I am calling the alterdisciplinary strategy of the basic cultural studies intervention. For, if what it sought to *alter* was *disciplinarity*, then the most important question to ask is: *Did it work*? If so, *how* and *why* did it work? With what consequences? Moreover: Does it *still* work? Can we still intervene – consequentially – in the same way? If not, why not? And what theoretical and practical strategies of intellectual intervention might remain viable and politically effective today?

The vanishing intervener

There are many possible evaluations of the cultural studies intervention. The fact that there are so many of these, and that they so often veer off into febrile condemnations of cultural studies, actually helps to strengthen the claim that, *whatever else* may be said about it, there is a widespread and virtually universal agreement that cultural studies *did* intervene 'alter-disciplinarily', and that it had significant effects on *other* disciplines and *other* cultural discourses. Its significance is perhaps nowhere better demonstrated than in the existence of the bitter denial of its significance by some critics. Žižek's polemical tirades against cultural studies (as being a discourse that is at the forefront of 'politically correct postmodernist deconstructionist liberal ideology') typify many of the reactions to cultural studies; and of course demonstrate that cultural studies did have 'wider effects', however *simultaneously denounced and denied* they may be. Indeed, the ensemble of Žižek's diverse sweeping statements reveals a kind of 'kettle logic' at play in reactions to cultural studies: a *simultaneous* admission *and* denial (plus an accusation) of its achievements (Bowman 2001b). Put

differently: there is a sense in which the alterdisciplinary intervention was *so* successful that, retrospectively, it no longer looks like it
ever intervened in anything at all; that it worked so well that it now
looks like it was never even needed and that nothing happened. In
this argument, cultural studies is something of a 'vanishing mediator':
an agency that blazed a trail; a trail which has now become a standard thoroughfare, a required route. (The term is Fredric Jameson's and
refers to 'an element essential to a historical and/or intellectual transition that disappears when its work is done' (Walsh 2002: 396).) In other
words, what cultural studies once did (almost) alone, everyone does
now. So, the problematics first thoroughly instituted, disseminated and
(shall we say) 'popularized' by cultural studies are now the stock-in-
trade of the vast majority of arts and humanities academic-intellectual
production.

However, this trail-blazing was obviously far from a smooth transition (or 'sublation'). Inevitably, the generalization or 'popularization' of
cultural studies-type problematics moved hand in hand with its simultaneous *unpopularity*. Lola Young once accounted for the twin forces of
attraction and repulsion attached to cultural studies like this: cultural
studies is 'vilified along with media studies, amongst others, as being a
"Mickey Mouse" subject'; yet 'it is somewhat ironic . . . that there have
been repeated attacks on the subject in the media' because 'ideas and
analyses which are now firmly embedded in media discourses have
increasingly come to resemble closely the kind of cultural textual analysis that has been nurtured through cultural studies'. At the same time,
'critical and theoretical paradigms derived from, and influenced by
cultural studies, have seeped into the study of a wide range of disciplines: History, English Literature, Geography, Sociology and so on'.
Thus, cultural studies was 'a key element in the movement of disciplinary boundaries, and . . . of wider shifts in political and intellectual
sensibilities' (Young 1999: 5).

Ironically, then, John Mowitt suggests that 'just as it has established
itself as something like a new paradigm, it has begun to vanish into
the very effects this paradigm is generating in cognate fields within
the humanities and social sciences' (2003: 184). Or, to the extent that it
was a trail-blazer, cultural studies 'will come to have been' a vanishing
mediator in the sublation of the humanities by the new paradigm or,
in Robert Young's words, the new 'architectonic of knowledge' that it
exemplifies: namely, 'the contemporary assertion of political truth as the
most comprehensive metalanguage' (1992: 111–12). Thus, the logic of
its intervention means, in effect, that 'cultural studies can only succeed
by failing'.[2] The greater its success in disseminating, circulating and
instituting its problematics, the more its work, as *intervention*, is done.

Of course, cultural studies *the institution* will remain as long as there are enough students applying to do it to protect departments from the axe. But, if so many other fields and disciplines now appear to do what once only cultural studies did, then surely its work is done. So, is this the end of the cultural studies intervention?

The end of the intervention

In one sense, I think, yes. This is the end of that intervention. It 'worked' because the questions posed by cultural studies precipitated crises in established disciplines. And this is where we began – with the deconstructive effects of sets of politicized questions that seek to lever at the fault lines, contradictions, biases and values of other disciplines (see Bahti 1992: 72–3). But, that was then. This is now. And surely one must historicize – at least often, if not always. Indeed, one need only historicize in a very formalist and rather trans-contextualist manner to grasp that – *inevitably* – the interruptive and disruptive power of such a strategy of intervention *will* dissipate. Politicized critiques will cease to shock. They will cease to interrupt, cease to disrupt, cease to alter anything.

However, it is ironic that the end of the alterdisciplinary intervention took the form of a generalized 'theoretical fluency': what Hall calls 'a mere repetition, a sort of mimicry or deconstructive ventriloquism' which, paradoxically, actually 'formalize[s] out of existence the critical questions of power, history, and politics' that it seems nevertheless 'extensively and without end, to theorize' (Hall 1992: 287). Or, as Martin McQuillan puts it: 'one cannot "do" cultural studies simply by borrowing its thematics' (2003: 50). One *may well* be studying, theorizing, or diagnosing 'the political' in this or that aspect of culture, but one is not necessarily *intervening* in any consequential sense. Indeed, says McQuillan, today, 'the endless articles on Foucault and football are not "doing" cultural studies anymore' (49). No matter how 'political' they may sound, such works have become something of a 'conservative force' nowadays (49). They are straightforwardly *disciplinary* work. Rather than intervention, this is precisely what Stuart Hall means by 'a mere repetition, a sort of mimicry or deconstructive ventriloquism which sometimes passes as a serious intellectual exercise' (1992: 287): not a disruption, interruption, or irruption of anything; but rather, the reiterative consolidation of a new disciplinary order, in which making 'politicized' critiques is the order of the day.[3] In short, it is the end of the intervention.

Retheorizing political critique

Is 'politicized critique' then to be rejected, because it is now just 'ventriloquism', sound and fury, signifying nothing, an empty gesture? McQuillan's response to the problem is instructive: as opposed to such 'conservative' critiques, he calls for 'transformative critique'. Of course! But what could such a thing possibly be, given that politicized critique has ceased to be transformative, precisely because what it fundamentally 'connected with' ('cognate fields') *has* altered? Does the problem lie in the contemporary political value or efficacy of 'critique' *per se*? Or is it something to do with the mode, manner, orientation, location or execution of the critiques that are being done?

To borrow a witticism from Slavoj Žižek, perhaps the search for a 'transformative critique' is a bit like the proverbial man searching for a lost key in the pool of light cast by a lamp post: he sees no sense in looking outside the pool of light because he won't be able to find his key in the surrounding darkness (Žižek 2001a: 208). Thus, although it may seem pointless or self-contradictory to look for our own lost political effectiveness anywhere other than in 'critique' – *because that's what intellectuals 'do'; that's what intellectual work 'is'* – perhaps we may merely be 'flogging a dead horse'. Perhaps 'critique' is a political relic. Yet, on the other hand, rejecting 'critique' *tout court* would seem to be tantamount to 'throwing the baby out with the bathwater' – i.e., a regression from the post-Gramscian insights of the institutional and fundamentally contingent (articulated, reticulated and discursive) basis of culture and society, and the crucial role that 'knowledge' surely plays within it.

Of course, some have argued that the problem is that the terrain within which (and the way in which) the arts, humanities and social sciences *can* intervene is in a strong sense now 'irrelevant'. For Bill Readings (1996), culture becomes contestable precisely when power has moved on. For, Hardt and Negri (2000), today 'power itself' chants along with all supposed radicals, 'Long live difference! Down with essentialist binaries!' (139) Or, as Lyotard crushingly puts it: 'radical' politicized critique 'is not thrust aside today because it is dangerous or upsetting, but simply because it is a waste of time. It is "good for nothing", it is not good for gaining time. For success is gaining time' (1988: xv). With this, Lyotard brilliantly makes the argument that today 'we' are simply not where the 'action' is. What *matters*, what *determines*, what *dominates*, is what Lyotard calls 'techno-science', what Heidegger called the 'modern technicalization and industrialization of every continent' (1971: 3), or what Deleuze called 'the 3 Ms' which rule 'the New

International order': 'Money, Media and Military' (quoted in Peters 2001: 107).

There are many ways to characterize this hegemony. And (notwithstanding Jameson's caveat that macro-perspectives tend to instil a crushing sense of our own insignificance and impotence) in *any* representation of the contemporary dominant hegemony, it clearly doesn't really matter what 'we' say, precisely because *our voices are not the voices that matter*. The voices that do matter are those that produce, legitimate and institute techno-scientific knowledge, knowledge that is performative and articulated with, as or at centres of power: governmental, military, media, corporate, educational, policy-making, and so on.

However, as academic contexts that 'matter' in a macro-political sense include the disciplines that inform, supplement, confirm and legitimate various forms of policy, I am not going to reiterate the proposal that 'therefore' cultural studies should become 'cultural policy studies' (Bennett 1996). For such a step remains ensnared in what I think of as the *old* alterdisciplinary logic of 'critique from afar'. Indeed, my point is that whether carried out in the pages of cultural studies journals or in broadsheets or on high-brow talk shows, such critique does not remove those involved from the status of simply being busybodies – *other* busy-bodies, *elsewhere*: busy-bodies that don't matter. Indeed my whole argument is this: it is precisely the compulsion to repeat the gesture of critiquing the other (*as other*) that 'we' now need to overcome – and in the name of reinventing critique as effective intervention. Hence, there is an irony to the fact that so much dispute within cultural studies takes the form of arguing about *what* should be argued about. There is little consideration of *how* what is being argued about might come to make a difference. (Žižekian polemics about 'capitalism' are an exemplary case here.) Yet, in the quest to establish the alchemy of intervention, the Philosophers' Stone to be discovered is the answer to this very question.

Altering alterdisciplinarity

The question is how to reinvent alterdisciplinarity as a strategy of intervention. The answer relates to *contingency* and to *disciplinarity*. For, in a sea of contingency, there is no necessary reason why the 'cognate fields' of cultural studies should remain those of the arts and humanities. And besides, these are now quite tied up in the process of altering in light of having their 'collusion with an elitist white-male politics of exclusion' firmly impressed upon them (Bal 2003: 30). So, what of the other, more 'otherwise-influential' disciplines? In the 'political' field, one might mention economics, econometrics, management, IT, informatics, international relations, education, law, government policy, among others, as being fields that have academic centres which are firmly articulated (indeed *reticulated*) with determinant centres of power. Are they immune to intervention? Surely not. So, what are the conditions of possibility for intervention in them? The answer is in the question: intervention must be *'in'* them, and not just *'about'* them.

In the face of perceived problems with the *other* discourse, the point is not to critique it 'here', but rather to intervene *in* that other discourse, 'there'. This intervention is not to be polemical denunciation, and it is not to be located either 'here' (in our own disciplinary academic contexts) or in the so-called 'public realm' or media. The aim, rather, is to intervene *directly* 'there' – namely, within the very academic contexts wherein 'that' knowledge is produced and legitimated. In short, the objective remains alterdisciplinary, but the context and languages must be transformed. For, today, the problematic object of attention is no longer simply, solely, or necessarily the hegemony of white male patriarchy in culture. Hence, the subjects, languages and contexts of critique are no longer those of the arts and humanities disciplines. So, if one's object of concern is with, say, the deleterious effects of managerialism or economic policy, then one's preliminary task is to ascertain the disciplinary and institutional sites of the production and legitimation of the 'knowledge' or 'rationales' to which reference or appeal is made in the organization of micro- or macro- policy implementation.

Now, this will never be easy. This is because the contemporary academic 'condition' is one of heterogeneous language games in a (dislocated) web of disciplinary differences and intensified *disciplinary enclaving*. The unavoidable proliferation of disciplinarily specific technical languages (what Lyotard called 'paralogies') equals *mutual unintelligibility* and the *disarticulation* of different subjects and disciplinary realms. This is precisely why 'critique' 'from our perspective' will either be *unintelligible* to the other(s) or *dismissible* according to the *others' criteria*. The linguistic and conceptual abyss can be bridged only through mastery of the others' criteria, the others' language, the others' logic, in the others' 'context'. Thus, the point is precisely to intervene in and to alter *other* disciplinary discourses and their productions (knowledges) not by 'critiquing' them but by intervening in the disciplinary spaces of their production and legitimation – that is: getting *inside knowledge*, *undoing methodologies*, and arguing (in the others' language) for *other conclusions*.

Altering conclusions

Žižek suggests that to intervene, to act, one must change the 'co-ordinates' of a situation. As Marchart has pointed out, this ultimately refers to a kind of suicide (2007: 109). In Žižek's argument, an act requires 'striking at one's self' (Žižek 2000: 122–3). Translated into alterdisciplinary practice, this means, first and foremost, acknowledging what Derrida called the 'monolingualism of the other' (Derrida 1998a). Thus, it means necessarily using the *others'* language, in the *others'* context. It does *not* mean shouting about how terrible capitalism or managerialism or bureaucracy or militarism or nanotechnology or genetics or legislation or government policy is solely in our own disciplinary sites and scenes, books, journals and conferences. It means, rather, engaging with the others in *their* journals too. For, frankly, which scientists or policy-makers have even *heard of* never mind *read* cultural studies or arts and humanities journals, or, even if so, given the slightest bit of attention to what is said about genetics or 'geopolitics' therein?

My point here is not to disparage disciplinary work. (Nor is it to forget the value of the deconstructive 'perhaps'. Rather, my point is: perhaps blind faith in 'the perhaps' is a particular kind of refusal to think, a particular kind of irresponsibility.) It is simply to suggest that talking about something 'here' is not to make any difference to it, 'there'. To call for change is not to make a change. To publish within one's own well-institutionalized field is not to have 'intervened' in anything other than that field. Of course, if that is what you want to alter or contribute to, then fine. But all faux radical pseudo-political tub-thumping and soap-box pontificating should be recognized for what it is. Rather than this, what is required is to move with the others' moves; to analyse, read, 'connect' with and deconstruct their connections, in *their* language, in order to make critiques that 'make sense' *there*, where making new sense might reorient *that*.

In a very practical sense, this will be to strike at oneself – to relinquish one's comfortable disciplinary identity, to stop 'being disciplined'. Rather than disciplined repetition, alterdisciplinary intervention requires yielding to the other discourse, the other protocols, the other language, the other scene, through a renewed emphasis on listening *to*, engaging *with*, connecting *with* the other, on other terms, in order to 'deconstruct' it where that deconstruction could count. I am not suggesting 'doing a Sokal' (Sokal and Bricmont 1998) by sneaking Trojan Horses into other disciplines in order to discredit them (although you could). Rather, I am proposing taking the notion of interdisciplinary dialogue *seriously*, rather than relying either on the enclave comfort of 'our spaces' or the easy alternative of holding onto some rather nebulous faith in the 'general' power of critique and journalistic 'public debate'. For the point is to change it; and without changing the co-ordinates by striking at oneself in this way and fully accepting the other's terms (in what Žižek calls a strategy of 'overidentification' (2000c)), we remain in the face-off characterized by Wittgenstein, in which: 'Where two principles really do meet which cannot be reconciled with one another, then each man declares the other a fool and a heretic' (1979: 611–12). For there will always be the problem of the 'differend' or the 'disagreement' between knowledges, between institutions, between disciplines.

Indeed, not just 'between' disciplines. For, although we talk of disciplines as 'fields', it is not the case that disciplines are actually homogeneous terrains (like actual fields), demarcated by fences, hedges, or walls. Nor are they even straightforwardly Kantian or Lyotardian paralogical islands, or hermetic enclaves, or internally transparent communicative rationalities. The disciplinary field '*itself*' is not a unity. This discipline is not one. That field is not one. The conflict of the faculties does not *just* consist in the differends *between* putatively distinct disciplines like these. It is also internal to and constitutive of disciplinary fields as such. As Derrida argues:

> ... a field is ... a field of battle because there is no metalanguage, no locus of truth outside the field, ... ; and this ... makes the field necessarily subject to multiplicity and heterogeneity. As a result, those who are inscribed in this field are necessarily inscribed in a *polemos*, even if they have no special taste for war. (Derrida 2003: 12)

Derrida concludes: 'all this is not an opposition between the legitimate and the illegitimate, but rather a very complicated distribution of the demands of legitimacy' (2003: 18). (This is related to Lyotard's account of the 'legitimation crisis in knowledge'. But for Derrida, it is *constitutive*.) In a sense, what we want is to make the other *understand*. We want to make the other understand that although we may *appear* to be heretics, we are not fools; and that if only they would listen and try to understand, they would see that our so-called heresy is not foolish but justified, while their refusal to take the step and follow our path is (in Lacan's formulation) *knavish* (see Žižek 2000: 324–5; Bowman 2003, 2007).

Of course, Rancière adds, the urge to make the other *understand* is equally the urge to make them *obey* (1999: 45). To understand is to 'stand under', to be led, to fall in line, behind a *hegemon*; to be *hegemonized*, colonized. Thus, to want the other to take *our* solution, to stand under our understanding, is – says Derrida – 'to say no to the other'; to say instead: 'choose my solution, prefer my solution, take my solution, love my solution; you will be in the truth if you do not resist my solution' (1998b: 9–10). This is Foucauldian power/knowledge, of course. But without an Archimedean point, an agreed metalanguage. Hence Lyotard's differend, Rancière's disagreement, Laclau and Mouffe's antagonism, Derrida's 'abyss'.

For Lyotard, 'differend' names conflict which cannot be 'resolved' *as such*; a wrong which cannot be righted for both parties; and upon which no internal or external agency can adjudicate with legitimacy. But, Rancière adds: 'each party's difference from itself as well as of the differend [is] the very structure of community' (1999: 18). The differend is always only an 'ontic',[4] legalistic, or in his terms, 'police' problem. The basic political concept, for Rancière, is *disagreement*; which is

> a determined kind of speech situation: one in which one of the interlocutors at once understands and does not understand what the other is saying. Disagreement is not the conflict between one who says white and another who says black. It is the conflict between one who says white and another who also says white but does not understand the same thing by it or does not understand that the other is saying the same thing in the name of whiteness. (Rancière 1999: x)

Thus, comments Benjamin Arditi, 'a disagreement is less a confrontation between two established positions – as in the case of a debating society – than an engagement between "parties" that do not antedate their confrontation. A disagreement constructs the object of argumentation and the field of argumentation itself' (2007: 115). For Rancière, the political relation is born with the inkling that there is an other who is addressing us and trying to make sense (or vice versa), an *equal* in command of *logos*, and not a grunting animal. Then the problem becomes that of establishing *topos* and *ethos*: how to make sense, to the other; how to be audible or intelligible; how to be able to *make* the difference. Rather than heretics trying to persuade fools of the legitimacy of their transgression, the problem is trying to persuade the other that 'we' are not a grunting, lowing, herd of cattle, but equals in possession of sense – and, specifically, in possession (indeed, mastery) of *their* sense. As the Sokal / *Social Text* Affair – in which physicist Alan Sokal managed to get a spoof 'postmodern physics' article published in a cultural studies journal – made clear (in different ways, to different parties), it is perfectly possible for impostors to ventriloquize the noises and make the signs of different *topoi* and *tropoi* without actually having or making sense.

This is the problem of alterdisciplinarity. Different discursive language games produce different institutions. 'Institution' does not mean the four walls surrounding us, but rather the very structure of our interpretation (Derrida 1992b: 22–3). There is an indissoluble link between institution and interpretation. There is no transcendent metalanguage to order difference, only antagonism at the sites of the limits of this or that objectivity.[5] Alterdisciplinarity names the aim of intervening in the other – the effort to alter the other – in awareness of the rivalrous structure of disciplinarity and the disciplinary structure of micro- and macro- hegemonies.

So, any theory and proposed practice or strategy of intervention must confront disciplinarity. I have been discussing the project of cultural studies, as formulated by Hall. But we can broaden the terms and add that this argument implies that we hesitate before accepting liberal 'faith and hope' arguments about the possibility of 'transparent communication' (Habermas) or the efficacity of 'public debate'. This is the same as to say, in other words, that *if* academics want to intervene, then offering journalistic or media 'comment' or even intellectual 'critique' is not the best model of intervention available. Faith in the power of 'critique' as cultural or political intervention is precisely that – an article of *faith* rather than thought or analysis. Instead of faith, we need to rethink intervention.

To conclude, let us recall that cultural theory of almost all stripes agrees that politics is a matter of *articulation*. I agree. But I do not take the word 'articulation' (or indeed 'discourse') to mean 'speech' or 'conversation'. Rather, I take it to mean *relationality*, institutional reticulation, connection, hinging. And I think that there is a problematic *disarticulation* of the realms of 'public debate' and 'academic critique' from, so to speak, the forces and the contexts that could be said to *count*. These contexts are those of the institutional production of the knowledges that underpin and that *legitimate* practices. Hence, I think that the primary academic or intellectual intervention needs to be *in* other academic and intellectual scenes – particularly but not exclusively those which are most closely connected to power. But the question is *how*: *how* to do this; *how* to intervene in such contexts. My suggested strategy is not to *critique* the others from afar (in our own disciplinary sites and scenes); but to engage *with* the others 'there' (in *their* disciplinary sites and scenes). Obviously, engagement in the others' field must necessarily take place in *their* language, according to *their* protocols and proprieties; otherwise our efforts will *obviously* look like those of 'a fool and a heretic'. And fools and heretics are laughed at and burned.

In other words, just because we cannot agree on what rationality, logic, or rigour should look and act like, in Derrida's words, the point is to make interventions which will not seem 'eccentric or strange, incomprehensible or exotic (which would allow [others] to dispose of [them] easily)', but to produce work that others should – *according to their own declared standards, values and protocols* – find 'competent, rigorously argued, and carrying conviction'. This can work towards a 're-examination of the fundamental norms and premises of . . . dominant discourses, the principles underlying many of their evaluations, the structures of [their] academic institutions, and the research that goes on within them'. As we have seen, Derrida concludes: 'What this kind of questioning [seeks to do] is to modify the rules of the dominant discourse, it tries to politicize and democratize the university scene' (1995: 409–10).

Afterword: (An Incomplete) Glossary of (Impossible) Terms

> I will speak, therefore, of a letter.
>
> Of the first letter, if the alphabet, and most of the speculations which have ventured into it, are to be believed.
>
> I will speak, therefore, of the letter a, this initial letter which it apparently has been necessary to insinuate, here and there, into the writing of the word difference; and to do so in the course of a writing on writing, and also of a writing within writing whose different trajectories thereby find themselves, at certain very determined points, intersecting with a kind of gross spelling mistake, a lapse in the discipline and law which regulate writing and keep it seemly.
>
> Jacques Derrida, 'Différance' (1982: 3)

A – but not the – much-remarked problem with deconstruction (and, indeed, with the term popular culture) is its sheer slipperiness. According to people who like it or have read a lot of it or have time for it, it is always said to be not quite this and not quite that, but sort of both at the same time (différance). According to people who do not have time for it, it is written off or dismissed as either too much or not enough – too excessive in one way or another or too little in one way or another. You could say the same about the slippery term 'popular culture'. Both terms seem to have an element of the impossible to them – but at the same time as they are also familiar and everyday. Where does popular culture begin or end? What is deconstruction? You might feel the need to look them up, to seek out a definitive or authoritative answer. So you might reach out for the first reference resource that comes to hand; something so convenient that it is hard to avoid, like Wikipedia, perhaps. Or you might prefer a more 'trusted' (re)source. But this is where the plot thickens.

187

According to the online encyclopaedia Wikipedia, Wikipedia itself was set up in 2001. It was designed to be an 'open-access' resource, available to all, writable, rewritable and editable by any. And indeed it is. Many of the 'facts' in this very book were also looked up or checked on Wikipedia. Of course, the much-remarked problem of referring to Wikipedia, or with regarding it as a reliable reference source, is precisely that because it is open-access and can be edited by anyone, the information it provides cannot therefore simply be trusted in quite the same way as can a 'legitimate' resource like, say, *The Encyclopaedia Britannica*. But what the democratic character of Wikipedia thereby does is reveal the way that knowledge, its perceived reliability, and indeed legitimacy itself, is always established through a tacit trust, or a silent 'according to'. And you should notice by now that this trust is always trust in an institution. That is, because Wikipedia is quite (but not completely) democratic, it is as such chaotic, polyvocal, dissensual, provisional, ongoing, and therefore not really to be trusted. It has never spoken the final word on a subject, or made the definitive pronouncement. Indeed, it has never quite done the very thing that one would expect from an encyclopaedia, in fact. In other words, when relaying information garnered from Wikipedia, you soon realise that you really ought to take the precaution of saying something like 'according to Wikipedia' (on such-and-such a date). On the other hand, you don't *seem* to have to do this sort of thing with apparently 'reliable', 'trustworthy', 'legitimate' resources like *The Encyclopaedia Britannica*. But if you look closely, you can see here an aporia.

Aporia is used in deconstruction to refer to an impasse, abyss, logical 'black hole', or a kind of impossible situation. The aporia that Wikipedia reveals is that knowledge, certainty, or legitimacy – these apparent opposites of blind faith – cannot be divorced or disentangled from trust, or, that is, an ultimately blind faith. The basic form this takes is a faith or belief in the legitimacy of this or that institution – in this case, the example being faith in the reliability of an institution like *The Encyclopaedia Britannica*. (But the examples could be multiplied.) Wikipedia draws this out into the open. Who or what does one believe or trust or have faith in at any given time, and for what reason? That is the question. Wikipedia is criticized because it sometimes leads people to take on trust that this or that assertion made on one of its many virtual pages is a 'fact' when 'in actual fact' it may either be contentious, debatable, or just plain wrong. But is this not *always* the fact of the matter? Name *one* source whose words or claims one *should* take on trust. Why? Authority and legitimacy demand belief. The desire for and the belief in the final or at least the definitive word on this or that matter is arguably, then, something of a desire to relinquish our critical faculties, to abdicate from active engagement, or to retreat from what Derrida used to refer to as the vigilance of always 'putting in question'. This is what deconstruction is about. It is not about declaring 'the final word'. Period . . . . But what about this Appendix, then? Is it not a bit problematic to have a supposedly definitive glossary here?

Appendix means addendum, addition, postscript, supplement. Like this glossary, it refers to something extra, coming afterwards, added on, supposed to finish off or complete a text. As appendices are extra additions, this suggests that what came before was not quite enough. Reciprocally, of course, on their own, appendices would not be enough. However, such additions also modify or even subvert the identity of the text to which they are added. They certainly change it from what it was or would have been. The addition of something extra to what has gone before always modifies it. (Derrida also calls this différance.) So, in deconstruction, a glossary to a text, to be used either as a source or resource for a quick interpretive fix ('what does it mean, really, finally, properly?') or for cross-referencing ('better check that'), is something that is deeply problematic. For, a glossary – *like this* – attached to the end of a book – *like that?* – is this inside or outside of that text? – is this a proper part of the book or another sort of thing altogether? – is a deeply problematic or indeed even 'dangerous' supplement. For, first of all, if it is really going to provide definitive, authoritative and concise explanations of all of the key preceding terms, then doesn't it mean that the preceding book was in a sense unnecessary? Why would you read all of *that* if you could just turn to *this* appendix and 'get the correct meaning' of it all? Secondly, there is the problematic sense in which a glossary, in appearing to be definitive, is utterly anathema to deconstructive questioning, interrogation, and performative interpretation. A glossary is in a sense disciplinary. For although on the one hand, one needs to establish meaning; on the other hand, meaning is never final, fixed, permanent, no matter how much we may want it to be so or how much we may believe it to be so. So trying to state definitively what it supposedly 'is' is to try to fix something in place – to try to *police*, to *manage*, or to discipline things. (This is another, less reassuring aspect of the meaning of words like 'authoritative': *authoritarian*.) Meaning, and indeed action, is a process of articulation, and change comes about through processes of rearticulation.

Articulation is what determines what something is or does. Articulation should be understood as having both the sense of being spoken, written or expressed, and the sense of connecting, linking, relating. It is ongoing, often a real effort, never final or complete, despite what any particular or putative authority (such as a glossary or encyclopaedia, educator, institution or indeed political party) may wish to suggest.

Authority is in fact what deconstruction always seeks to begin questioning. This is not just for the sake of it, but for ethical and political reasons. Now, this is not simply to suggest that glossaries are necessarily 'bad', for instance, while open-ended or 'open-access' texts are necessarily 'good', or that *The Encyclopaedia Britannica* is somehow necessarily 'bad' while Wikipedia is somehow necessarily 'good'. Far from it. Rather, it is to embrace the necessity of ongoing critical vigilance rather than retreating into trusting authority. In actual fact, this is precisely what deconstruction aims at when, throughout various works, thinkers like Derrida and Barthes isolated such ideas as 'authorial intention' or the notion that 'the author' is the first and last authority on his or her own words, meanings, or texts. Now, this is not to claim that texts aren't written or constructed by people (although, given the technological basis of the world, this is increasingly less necessary or inevitable). It is rather to point out that the decision about what something 'really means' or 'really is' is always a decision, imposed by someone claiming (to be an) authority (such as an 'expert' who claims to know what an author 'really meant', and who also thereby claims the ability to declare things like 'this text could not possibly mean that, even if to the uninformed it may seem like it could'). So, deconstructing the notion of authorial intention (in other words, acknowledging that a text can and will come to mean a lot more and other than an author could possibly have imagined), and deconstructing the notion of the author *per se* (by showing, as we saw in Chapter 2, that 'the inside is outside' – that an author is not really the sole 'genius' responsible for a work with a single 'proper' meaning) is also to challenge the authority of any authority which wants to claim for itself the authority to decide what's right and wrong, good and bad, proper and improper, allowed and forbidden, in and out.

Be that as it may, you may say, but *what difference does all of this make?* One answer is that it makes *all the difference in the world.* 'To be' is always to be some thing, in some place, within some relationship (or articulation): attributed a value, allocated a worth, placed in a category. 'Being' itself is always relational. There is no 'essence' to a 'being' outside of a relationship. What something is able to be is always going to have particular conditions of possibility.

Conditions of possibility are those relationships that enable something to be what it is, where it is, how it is, and why it is. There would, for instance, be no glossary without the (incompleteness of the) text that seemed to call for it. There would be no Wikipedia without the

World Wide Web. There would arguably have been no book entitled *Deconstructing Popular Culture* had there not been certain hospitable discursive conditions of possibility that enabled its emergence: a history, a discourse, a perceived lack or gap in the market that could be supplemented. However, in deconstructive terms, conditions of possibility are also, at the same time, and by the same token, 'conditions of impossibility'. The democratically 'open' character of Wikipedia subverts the possibility of it being anything like the traditional notion of an encyclopaedia that is apparently unquestionably reliable, trustable, etcetera. There should really be no need for a glossary for this book – or indeed, for this very book – for those who have been able to read this book. This supplement, which seems necessary to *complete* the book, is *also* strangely *excessive* . . . and even more strangely, it is *also* strangely *preliminary*: for, if you really do need it in order to read it, then why did it not come first? And, by the same token, if you have been able to read this far, why do you need it now? It is also strangely *improper*. It is also, of course, something entirely different, too. Again, another way of approaching this is through the notion of the supplement – something added, something that seems necessary to complete something, but that is also an extra, something other, something completely different. A glossary for this book was always going to be both inside and outside, both the same and different, both called for but unnecessary. The decision to include one, then, demands some questioning.

Decision – if it is a decision – is never *necessary*, one way or another, never *certain* in advance, and never, in fact, *decidable*. That is, it is *undecidable*. Undecidability is not the same as being on the horns of a dilemma, in which you can't choose between two equally undesirable alternatives. Rather, undecidability refers, for instance, to the way that any apparent decision can also be shown to have been not completely free or spontaneous, and therefore not *really* or not *necessarily* a decision at all. This is because, after you've made a decision (or thought you have), it is always going to be possible to look back and wonder whether you were entirely free in making that decision, or whether there were external forces guiding your thought or your actions. Did you, for instance, *really* decide to go to university? Or was it perhaps the force of family hopes or expectations, or because all your friends were going, or some other kind of pressure – or even indecisiveness – that led you to go down a certain path? In such a case, it would not have been an entirely *free* decision; not, therefore, entirely a decision; perhaps not even a decision at all, but rather, as Derrida liked to put it, the implementation of a predetermined programme, or the elaboration of a predetermined pattern or set of rules. This would seem to make us a bit like a twig or a leaf floating down a river, carried along entirely by external factors, but imagining ourselves to have made all of our own decisions (I decided to fall off the branch. I decided to fall downwards. I decided to float in this direction . . .). In other words, every apparent decision can also be shown to have been the outcome of a determined programme or system – a reflection of certain values, and therefore something like 'the other's decision in me' or not really my decision at all. In other words, in deconstruction, everything hangs on decision. Is it possible? If so, which decision is to be made? Deconstruction really twists the screws by going on to point out that if such a thing as decision is possible, the knotty matter of what to decide will always remain undecidable – because you can't know the outcome of a decision in advance and hence can't really know how to decide, and if you do know in advance what a decision will cause to happen then it isn't really a decision but the implementation of a predecided programme. Etcetera.

Deconstruction reveals such aporias. It arises there, resides there, operates there. But where is this 'there' and what is this 'it' – this 'place' that deconstruction 'is' or might perhaps happen or be happening? That is the question! Deconstruction is not simply all about 'meaning'. It is not simply an eccentric or excessive form of semiotic analysis. Rather, deconstruction *happens* or threatens to happen in 'places' or relations or conjunctures or conclusions or articulations or institutions that are unclear, contradictory, complex, disjointed, undecidable – like in every addition of a supplement to try to complete something, or in every opening or chance for the democratization of an institution which could radically transform or subvert it – not unlike what Wikipedia is always threatening to do to the traditional or former notion of the encyclopaedia. So deconstruction is not a thing or a place. It is something that happens – might happen, could happen, might already have started happening, is already happening – wherever something might come to seem to be incomplete or limited or biased or, indeed, impossible.

Différance, perhaps. Derrida's combination of 'to differ' and 'to defer'. Final meanings are always deferred. Perfect situations are always in the post. There is always more to be said, more to be done. One has never finished reading. A reading is always a kind of rewriting. You may read these words once and take away a certain sense. The next time you read them, your relation to the text will have altered, and so you will get more and other and different things from the text. Or, at least, you might, perhaps. But readings are often *disciplined* – orientated in a certain limited way, closed or blind to certain possibilities. We don't just learn *to* read. We learn *how* to read. We don't just learn to study or analyse. We learn *how* to study and analyse. This is the work of discipline.

Discipline disciplines. Disciplines discipline. Disciplines are institutions which try to discipline *what* is to be read and *how* it is to be read and what is to be looked for and found. Disciplines and other institutions have traditionally tried to discipline or institute the proper or final meanings that are to be 'found' in texts. Thus, discipline is at once a condition of possibility for learning or doing or thinking (it is *a way* of doing, one that you have to learn) and therefore a condition of impossibility (because it is just one *partial, limited, partisan* way, therefore it is not *The* (only, definitely correct, or best) *Way*. In addition to this, discipline is always going to be based on some kind of founding exclusion. And as we now know, deconstruction looks for 'the constitutive force of exclusion, erasure, violent foreclosure, abjection, and its disruptive return within the very terms of discursive legitimacy' in every 'construction' (Butler 1993: 8).

Etcetera. And so on. (As is perhaps inevitable, given that 'finality' is effectively impossible, even though institutions and authorities regularly try to exclude otherness, etcetera.)

Exclusion is what deconstruction looks for, perhaps above all else. It asks: What does this discipline/institution/text/interpretation *exclude*? Why? With what consequences?

Final meanings, final signifieds are permanently deferred. However (much) institutions keep trying to institute them, to establish them. They fail. However, what they succeed in doing is establishing *'proper' meanings*. Institutions inherit, reiterate and establish interpretations and actions that they deem to be legitimate, and that they actively and often aggressively police all of the time. Meanings and interpretations, values and investments that have been instituted successfully as the norm or the law or as 'just the way we do things around here' or – even better – 'just the way it is' or – better still – 'the way it has to be', can be said to have become *hegemonic*.

Glossaries, then, do not merely or innocently denote natural meanings: they are part and parcel of a work of instituting, imposing or even policing meanings. Of course, this need not be taken to mean that all institutions or groups that share the same terms and values and that could therefore make use of glossaries are *conspiracies* which seek to dominate the world by trying to make everyone see things like they do (with themselves clearly identified as the highest authority). Of course, such a desire may well be there – the desire to dominate, to control. People sometimes accuse institutions of behaving in precisely this manner. But, if anything is suggested by our earlier reflections on the trust and faith that we tend to place in authorities and institutions, it may rather be that the desire is not to dominate but to be dominated, to be controlled, to be looked after, and that this may take the form of placing faith in an institution that promises to look after us by promising to tell us the truth. But why would we do that? Arguably because this is how we attain any subjectivity or identity at all. Louis Althusser called it interpellation: the way in which our subjectivity and our value are conferred on us by the social relationships into which we are thrown and 'find ourselves' in or 'recognize ourselves' in (by *being told* who we are).

Hegemony arguably works like this. Hegemony means dominance. It comes from Greek (*hegemon*) and means prince, leader, or guide: namely, that which is to be imitated, emulated, obeyed, followed, repeated, or indeed, reacted to or revolted against. (But often revolutions against whatever is hegemonic are themselves actually another version – or reiteration – of the same sort of thing.) Hegemony is often considered to be the way in which a power or agency imposes itself as dominant, or comes to attain dominance in this or that, or these or those, or more or less, contexts. But this shouldn't necessarily be taken to imply that a hegemony actually has a prince or leader at the controls who is self-consciously machinating to achieve hegemony. Rather, hegemony can work through interpellation. And interpellation works through institutions.

Identity is (therefore) impossible.

Impossible doesn't (therefore) mean simply 'not possible'. Rather, the impossible is always a part of the process (see Gödel on undecidability, below) – the process of identity 'formation', for instance, or decision, or the establishment of meaning, or any process of institution at all, for that matter. For, if the conditions of possibility for identity are a process of identification (and 'disidentification'), this means that identity is not *one*, not possible in such (metaphysical) terms. Similarly, if to be is to be in a relationship, then to be is not to be *one*, and is impossible when thought of in those terms. Conditions of possibility are also conditions of impossibility. *Being* is rather more a process of *becoming* (it is permanently deferred, in différance), which also means *un-becoming* or being in deconstruction. Institutions (*have to try to*) institute. Identifications (try to) identify. Etcetera. Hence, it is only because unity or completeness or identity or being is impossible that *change* is both possible and inevitable, and hence that there is the (political) chance to try to make a difference – to try to *make* an intervention. This book has tried to reiterate the argument that political intervention is always intervention in an institution.

Institution is both a noun and a verb. An institution is a thing. It is also a process: the process of instituting something – something which involves practices, procedures, systems, hierarchies, values, and of course, exclusion, prohibitions and transgressions. Institutions are contingent and consequential and hence political. Perhaps they are at their most consequential and political in the way that they are intimately involved in interpellation – transforming individuals into subjects.

Interpellation refers to the way in which we are 'called into', placed, identified, allocated a position, a value, a role, in a relationship. As I often say to my students, I interpellate them *as students* simply by addressing them as such, and they prove me right by recognizing themselves in my address (as in: 'Oh no! he's talking to me and he's my teacher, so I have to behave accordingly *because I am* what he's taking me for'). So, an interpellation is a call. If I ask someone in a lecture hall or seminar room, 'What is interpellation?', they will most probably try to formulate an answer, even if it's 'I don't know'. If I ask people on the street in a city centre 'What is interpellation?', they will most probably ignore me, or nervously shake their head, or move away from me, or become confused. They may not even have heard me but still say, 'No thanks' or 'No, sorry'. This is because they do not recognize me as an authority or someone who demands a response. Which means that it is not 'me' or something essential to my being which commands (or urges) students sitting in a lecture to respond in some way to my questions (whether that response be an audible answer or, as is more usual, pretending to be writing something down so that they 'haven't seen me asking them', so that they don't catch my eye and hence don't come under more pressure to speak). It is not my 'essential character' which confers identity or authority on me. It is rather the classroom itself, or rather, the institution which interpellates *me*.

Intervention is (therefore) the important thing to establish. How is one to intervene? Into what? In whose or what name? Deconstruction answers: in the name of justice.

Justice is undecidable. Justice is permanently deferred. We cannot know what justice is. Has justice ever been done? Has justice ever even been started? Surely, things could always be *more* just. Justice cannot be deemed to have arrived, definitely, decisively. Moreover, an institution that believes itself to be perfectly just will stop listening to others, will stop trying to make itself more just, will feel able to act with impunity and absolute authority. This will lead to a surely unjust violence.

Knowledge is therefore intimately bound up in this complex web, too. What I teach my students must be knowledge, right? But what if – as is often the case – it disagrees with what the professor in the next class is teaching? We all know that that depends on whether the professor in the next class is 'one of us' or 'one of them'. Other disciplines are, of course, foreign countries. 'They' do things differently there. 'They' have different values and questions and perspectives to 'us'. 'We' are meant to broadly agree on most things. That is to say, 'we' are meant to be part of a discipline or a shared space. What we 'share' are a set of questions, or rather a set of recognizable approaches to questions. These are *disciplined* approaches. Disciplines are institutions. They interpellate us, too. We feel, or we have been taught through reiterated exposure, that *our* approaches are the *correct* and *proper* approaches. It is through their familiarity, their reiteration, that they come to seem proper, stable, reliable, correct – legitimate.

Legitimacy or legitimation arguably proceeds through reiteration, through making reference to established authority, authorities or approaches that have come to seem authoritative. Different institutions have different ways of establishing legitimacy – different archives, approaches, methodologies, systems of reference and verification. Hence, the field of knowledge is actually a field of dissensus and disagreement. (As one narrative goes, this became so much so, and apparently grew much more palpable from about the 1980s, that people increasingly started to refer to the 'legitimation crisis' in knowledge – the crisis around how one establishes something as knowledge, as reliable, as acceptable to all.) Deconstruction seeks out the arguments and rhetorical manoeuvres by which legitimacy is claimed, and sets to work examining and questioning these procedures and manoeuvres. Significantly, time and again, Derrida discerns family resemblances among many canonical – and hence hugely influential – Western thinkers. According to Derrida, they share what he calls an investment in the metaphysics of presence.

Metaphysics of presence is Derrida's term for the widespread presumption or belief that the foundation of everything is an individual's self-conscious and fully self-present consciousness and identity in the present – the 'I am here now'. Masses and masses has been written about this, but basically it boils down to a *faith* (metaphysics) in the common-sense notion that the start of everything is an 'I am conscious', like Descartes' 'I (am) think(ing) therefore I am'. Deconstruction problematizes this, in lots of different ways, such as through the deconstruction of the notion of the unity (or reliable self-presence) of identity, as we have seen.

Multiplicity is one popular word used for characterizing this complexity. This is OK as far as it goes, but the idea of 'multiplicity' may still imply a 'one, and another one, and another one', and hence may rely on a belief in unity or identity or the possibility of 'the one' – which is the very thing that deconstruction deconstructs. I tend to prefer to think of all of this through the notion of différance, which emphasizes complex incompletion, relationality and articulation as central to the ongoing production or transformation of any so-called identity. Either way, just because something has a name, this does not mean that it is either *natural* or *singular*.

Names, any act of naming, tends to suggest that what is being named is 'one'. But in the case of supposed entities like, say, 'the West' or 'the East', or 'America', 'India', 'China', or even 'me' or 'you', for instance, what has been reduced to 'one' is rather more of a complex and heterogeneous multiplicity. So, naming does not simply denote or point to a single already-existing thing. Rather, it *invents* an entity, *introduces* it into discourse. The entity is a discursive construction. It condenses many differences into one, and *produces* that supposed identity. Naming, designating, categorizing, differentiating, defining, and so on are all performative inventions. They too are therefore contingent, consequential and political. When George W. Bush, the then-president of the USA, gave a speech after the September 11th 2001 attacks on the World Trade Center, he named what he called the 'Axis of Evil'. He said, henceforth, you are either with us or against us. If you are 'with us', this means you are 'against' 'terrorism'. Terrorism is what we define it as. Hence, Bush invented an image of the world in terms of a simple divide: us/them. He invented a supposed entity called the 'Axis of Evil'. All of this instituted a significant new worldview, which took immediate hold on politics and policies and people's attitudes, opinions and pre-occupations. This act of naming was therefore not neutral or natural or descriptive. It was prescriptive, inventive and consequential. It was in fact ontological.

Ontological, at least according to Wikipedia, is a 'study of the conceptions of reality and the nature of being'. We already knew this, right? And we already had an inkling that in deconstruction ontology is *ontopolitical* – or, in other words, that our conceptions of reality and the nature of being are contingent. (What we may not know – and we wouldn't necessarily find out if we jumped straight to the 'Ontology' page of Wikipedia, is that Wikipedia also currently makes the following claim about glossaries: 'a glossary contains explanations of concepts relevant to a certain field of study or action. In this sense, the term is contemporaneously related to ontology'. Interesting, eh?) And, as we have learned by now, things that are contingent are also therefore political.

Perhaps. Maybe. You never can tell, in advance. And things aren't finished yet, so we can't yet know the outcome, the final significance (as if there could be such a thing), so how can we decide for sure?, well we can't, so we shouldn't write anything off before we've undertaken a thorough analysis of it and about it, and of its articulation and its relations and its potential effects.

Political studies may not agree with the proposition that *all* contingencies are – perhaps – political. But deconstruction insists that because culture and society and politics are fundamentally *instituted*, then all institutions, all acts of institution, and all decisions and orientations taken or instituted within them, potentially have effects which have ethical ramifications and political consequences. To indicate this political character, deconstruction tends to look for whatever has been *excluded* from institutions and interpretations, whatever has been rejected, overlooked or downplayed.

Popular culture is, of course, also contingent. Is it therefore political? Perhaps. It depends on what we take it to be. Most approaches to popular culture try to construct it as a 'field', or else they use metaphors like 'sphere' or 'realm'. But these are enormously problematic metaphors. Indeed, terms or names like 'popular culture' are designations, categorizations, differentiations, definitions, and so on, which are all therefore performative inventions for something or some things that could conceivably have gone by other names, definitions and metaphors. Under such different conditions, 'it' would therefore substantially be something else. Indeed, in John Mowitt's terminology, the very notion of 'popular culture' is what he calls a *disciplinary object*. That is, a notion invented by a discipline. For, despite how comfortable and familiar the term is, there is not really a 'field' or a 'place' out there with a sign above the gate saying 'popular culture', which you enter in order to see all of the fun stuff, as if you were entering a fairground. No. Popular culture is a disciplinary invention, a notion circulating in a particular set of disciplinary discourses. It is not *one* thing. It is not even *a* thing. It is a *disciplinary object*. This is why the book you are holding now has turned increasingly from looking at 'cultural things that are or have been popular' to looking at the discipline that has most taken popular culture to be its object of attention: cultural studies.

Questioning is (therefore) extremely important in deconstruction. We should not just blindly or passively accept an inheritance – like terms or names that seem familiar to us, like, say, popular culture – and use it without interrogating it. What is demanded is critical vigilance. In what way is this *legitimate*? What does this *institute*? On what grounds should this authority be trusted? Deconstruction is arguably the radicalization of questioning – a radical form of questioning.

Radical tends to suggest dramatic or drastic. Questioning may not seem to be particularly radical. However, if we combine this with the political character of institution and of academic discipline, then deconstruction suggests that there is always a chance to intervene, to change things. One may want to change things 'over there' – stop the war, stop the injustice, etc. But what it is important to realise is that what one wants to change in any political effort is the relationship of the 'we here' to 'that or those there'. Thus, even when an issue seems to be really far away 'over there', what one must try to change is 'our' relationship to it or involvement with it or intervention in it. This is a reiteration of a familiar cultural studies argument, in which a suggestion is that the way to combat, say, racism 'on the street' is to change the way race and ethnicity are engaged or addressed (or not) in dominant institutions – the university, first of all, not to mention the police force. In terms of the street-fetishism of some notions of political action, this does not appear to be very radical at all. But the reiteration of the argument about the importance of the (contingent) institutional dimension of politics and of culture is crucial.

Reiteration 'itself' is a key aspect of popular culture and of deconstruction. In terms of culture and politics, discourse theory has it that it is the reiteration of this or that thing (belief, action, practice, performance, etc.) in more and more contexts which makes it become hegemonic – i.e., the norm, something which feels natural, normal, proper, necessary, and so on. In deconstruction, reiteration is sharply distinguished from 'repetition'. This is because, according to Derrida, there can be no such thing as a simple repetition. This is because the act of 'repeating' – or rather, of reiterating – is always a modification. Think about the repetition of a sound, like a beat. You hear one thud. It could just be something falling over. You hear two thuds. Is that somebody at the door? The second thud adds something that modifies the first. You hear two thuds, which are repeated. Is this the start of a rhythm? The repetitions *alter* each other. Every earlier 'iteration' is transformed by its reiteration. The same goes for all things. You read a sentence. Its meaning may be unclear. You read it again. You get an understanding of it. At different times, different thoughts and experiences supplement your understanding of it and transform it. Etcetera. It does not s(t)ay the same thing twice. It is not repeated. It is reiterated. Foucault talked about the 'regularity in dispersion' of the reiteration of statements. Laclau and Mouffe picked up this notion and used it to argue that this is the way hegemony is established. People like Judith Butler have developed this notion to argue that it is a strong part of the way in which identity is established: we are all reiterating materials, gestures, positions, etc. that have in some sense gone before. But in reiterating them we are also modifying them, altering them. Again, this is an aspect of what Derrida called différance.

Street-fetishism has no time for the argument about the political dimension of the institutional character of culture and society, or about the political character of reiteration. 'Street-fetishism' is my favourite term for a fixation on the idea that proper political action involves 'direct' action, normally 'on the street'. It can only regard thinking and theorizing (and anything it regards as non-direct action) as a supplement to whatever it regards as the *proper* direct form of action. As we saw in the 'Street-fetishism' chapter (Chapter 4), this kind of thinking is subject to the metaphysics of presence.

Subject, in the sense of 'subjected *to*' or 'subject *of*', always refers (us) to one or another form of (power of) institution, authority or hegemony – those elements from 'outside' that supplement the 'inside'.

Supplement is another one of those words, like institution and discipline, etcetera, which is both noun and verb, but even more so – and less so – because 'supplement' names an element that is not one, not complete, not quite an identity. It is also something of a process, something of a (part of a) thing. Derrida wrote a chapter called 'That Dangerous Supplement', which deals with the way supplements are regularly treated by the dominant mode of thinking characteristic of Western institutions (which Derrida called the metaphysics of presence). Namely, supplements are grudgingly regarded as necessary, but are also regarded with suspicion, as insufficient. As argued in the 'Street-fetishism' chapter, in particular, you could argue that 'political action' is always defined by some kind of *theory* of what sorts of actions might have political effects. Hence, theory plays a fundamental role in the decision about what is valid or real 'action', but metaphysical thought rigorously distinguishes and tries to separate theory *from* action. Thus, theory is sometimes grudgingly acknowledged as necessary, but it is also regarded as insufficient. It is also eyed with suspicion, because *too much* theory (or too much of any supplement) is also regarded as not enough of *the proper thing* – in this case 'action'. In other words, the supplement is regarded as dangerous because if you 'give it an inch it will take a mile', as the expression goes. In this case, if you think too much or theorize about what political action is, you may stop doing whatever you have earlier decided proper action is or should be. Heaven forbid you turn into a theorist! Street-fetishists are people who refuse to think *too much* about political action because they have already decided that they know what political action is. Etcetera. (Derrida himself provides some wonderful analyses of influential thinkers' relationships to different sorts of supplements – perhaps the most amusing being his analysis of Rousseau's reflections on masturbation, which Rousseau regarded as a 'dangerous supplement' to 'proper' procreative heterosexuality.) When one starts to think things through in terms of the supplement, stable definitions, concepts and distinctions (like inside versus outside, human versus machine, the living versus zombies, conscious versus unconscious, us versus them, etc.) start to collapse or start to appear a lot more complex. Perhaps the most radical version of this comes in the form of Derrida's declaration: 'There is nothing outside the text'.

Text is most usually taken to refer to words, such as words in books, or indeed text (words) in texts (books). More recently it has come to refer to sending text messages using mobile phones, or indeed to the style of writing used in texts that irritates old-fashioned people like me, who like 'proper' punctuation and 'proper' spelling. (Or, that is: th stl v wrtng tht irit8z ppl lk me.) In many respects, text can still carry these meanings in deconstruction. But in deconstructive thinking, there is nothing outside the text because we basically have to relate to everything in more or less the same sort of way that we relate to a written text. That is, just as the words you are reading now are textual, so is everything else. Doctors try to *read* symptoms. You try to *read* a situation. Etcetera. There is nothing outside the text. This does not mean that nothing is real or that there is no reality. Rather, it means that our relationship to reality and indeed to ourselves is textual. Words like *context* demonstrate the textuality of reality: what something is or means or does is *contextual*. What this means is that making sense always requires an active work of *reading* and *interpretation*. And here comes the twist: how do we know when a reading, an interpretation, an understanding is finished or final? How do we know when we have fully understood and can finish reading? Because of the nature of textuality, of the re-experience or reiteration of the 'same' thing in different contexts, any text, any context, will always remain to be (re-)read. The end-point is undecidable. And deconstruction is interested in undecidability.

The 'the' is undecidable because it is always a decision. *The* end-point, '*the*' meaning, '*the*' definition, etcetera: all of these are contingent institutional decisions. Deconstruction looks at the ways decisions are taken or instituted or imposed, and starts questioning the implications that congregate around making interpretations, designations, classifications, judgements, and interpretations. As with names, deconstruction reveals acts of definition and designation to be deeply partisan and often 'violent' reductions of a far greater complexity and undecidability.

Undecidability refers us to aporia. But in a different way. Derrida takes the word from its use by the scientist Kurt Gödel, who argued for the existence of 'undecidable propositions' within complex systems; as Derrida puts it, propositions that are 'neither an analytical nor deductive consequence of those axioms, nor in contradiction with them, neither true nor false with respect to those axioms. *Tertium Datur*, without synthesis' (Derrida 1997a: 219). But the example from science that most people prefer (perhaps because it is more immediately graspable), comes from Heisenberg's Uncertainty Principle, which demonstrates 'the impossibility of establishing simultaneously the position and velocity of an electron' (Weber 1987: xi). This is significant because it reveals the way that 'the instrument of measure, the photon, alters the object in the very process of measurement, and similarly has its own frequency modified in the encounter' (xi). According to Sam Weber, this principle 'strikes at the founding premise not only of traditional science, but also of the intuitive thinking that it sought to systematize (and to legitimize)' (xi). Translated, by analogy, into the problem of trying to work out what is 'in' a text, and what is 'put there' by the act of reading it or the interpretive decision, the similarities are striking. However, Derrida preferred to use the term 'undecidability' rather than 'uncertainty' because this is connected directly with the idea of decision. In other words, Derrida's suggestion is that there are aporias and undecidabilities all the time, but we make decisions so that we can stop agonizing about which interpretations (or decisions) to reach. In other words, when faced with a plurality of possible interpretations, we do not 'arrive at' a decision. Instead, we *make* a decision. A decision is a forceful and consequential act. Derrida in fact takes this much further, and insists that the decision itself is undecidable, because if I don't know why I make it, then it must be someone or something else 'in me' that makes 'my' decision. This idea is perhaps very difficult to take on board first time around. But, in brief, it boils down to the fact that every time you *think* you have made a decision, it is equally possible to look back at it and conclude that it wasn't a decision at all, but rather the *predetermined* result of a 'system' or a 'programme'. For instance, you may think you have decided to go to university. It may have felt like it was you who made the decision. But when you look back you could also think, well, you know, it was *expected* of me, all my friends were going, etcetera. So, really, was it a *free* decision? Was it entirely *your* decision? This may be undecidable. Who decides?

Vigilance, my friends: what is demanded is responsible vigilance. As Derrida saw it: 'The best liberation from violence is a certain putting into question, which makes the search for an *archia* tremble . . . *an-archy* . . . .' (Derrida 1978: 141).

Violence is to be regarded as *irreducible* – that is, inevitable, attending all acts of institution. Deconstruction shows that this violence takes the form of exclusions, and the effects of exclusion on the excluded. And there are exclusions all the time. For instance, arguably we exclude others, even when we say 'we'.

We tend to say 'we' very easily. But who are 'we' – in any context, at any time? Questioning who we think we are points us back to the importance of being aware of the productive, inventive and consequential aspect of names. So, who are we? How many are we? And where are we? What is required to be 'one of us'? Who is excluded from this group? What is the cost of membership? Who decides? Are we part of popular culture? Is (it) this or that? Are we able to make our own decisions? Or are we rather more like zombies? Do we make decisions about our own culture? If not, then who decides?

X marks the spot. It is the place of the decision. Deconstruction demands that when we are called, we respond, responsibly; that we say 'Yes?' – in other words, that we are prepared to affirm (Yes!) and prepared to respond openly ('Yes?') and prepared to question ('?').

Yes, deconstruction is affirmative, interrogative, transformative, engaged, engaging, urgent, committed, responsible. However, people have worried that deconstruction seems to say 'No': people have suggested that deconstruction denies 'reality', that it is not political, that it is not interested in anything but this or that text, etcetera. However, such worries and such criticisms have often simply missed the point of deconstructive questioning. For deconstructive questioning does not seek to destroy. It seeks to identify the ethical and political problems of bias, exclusion, hierarchy, hegemony, etcetera, in the name of seeking out, for instance, injustice, or the times when we think we've taken a decision but when we have perhaps been operating not unlike zombies.

Zombies are, of course, undead: neither properly alive nor properly dead. Others conjure them up, play with them, make them obey. Zombies cannot be said to have their own consciousness, or their own conscience. Zombies are the performance in them of the other's decision. Deconstruction is the identification of the risk that zombies may not just be undecidable and non-existent creatures of myth, legend and popular culture, but that the main risk we face is that – more often than we may be aware – we may be passive agents of institutions and authorities that we could and should be actively questioning in the name of a vigilant search for justice.

Notes

2 Can I Help You? Deconstructing(,) Words & Music

1. There are other ways in which musical texts such as this song might be thought of as 'institutional'. Although musical 'institutions' are not necessarily literally incarnated in 'buildings, their publications, their uniformed officials', popular music is clearly institutional in the sense that *what* gets made and heard relies on the recording contract with a record company, a distribution network, airplay on the radio, and so on. But this whole network itself is also 'institutional' in the sense of 'contextual' and 'contingent' – as the growth of non-contracted yet successful internet-driven popular music and cultural productions testifies. The point here is not that the former is institutional while the latter is not. It is rather that institutions (contexts) change.
2. The allusion is to Jean-François Lyotard's *The Postmodern Condition: A Report on Knowledge* (Lyotard 1984), but should conjure up the massive array of work that has focused on the increasing *experience* of life *as* uncertainty, anxiety, confusion, alienation from power, etc. See, for instance, Zygmunt Bauman, *Intimations of Postmodernity* (1991), especially the chapter 'Towards a Sociological Theory of Postmodernity'; and Guy Debord's *Comments on the Society of the Spectacle* (1990).
3. See Judith Butler's reflections on this issue in *Contingency, Hegemony, Universality: Contemporary Dialogues on the Left* (Butler 2000: 263–79); Wendy Brown, *Politics Out Of History* (2001: 91–120); Michael A. Peters, *Poststructuralism, Marxism and Neoliberalism* (2001); and Ernesto Laclau, 'Preface', and Chapter 1, 'Beyond Emancipation', *Emancipation(s)* (1996b).
4. See Wlad Godzich's excellent account of de Man's idea of *Blindness and Insight* in his Afterword to Samuel Weber's *Institution and Interpretation* (Godzich 1987: 155).

3 Ghost Dog: The Deconstruction of Identity

1. The video for 'JCB Song' is available on YouTube at: www.youtube.com/watch?v=k3WhQB7Hq0Q

2. Of course, this Althusserian notion has a rather a bad name; first, because it apparently remains bound to an unfashionable Marxism (although, according to Mowitt, the 'Marxist' dimension of interpellation is not at all certain. For interpellation 'has also played a constitutive role in the emergence of what is now, somewhat reluctantly, referred to as post-Marxism. To this extent, interpellation participates in a "properly" dialectical elaboration of the very theoretical tradition which it might otherwise be said to have sublated' (Mowitt 2002: 43)). But mainly because it apparently simplistically implies that *what* interpellates individuals as subjects must always be determinate 'Ideological State Apparatuses' (Althusser 1971). The problem here would be that subjects must be 'entirely the effects of the state apparatus' (Mowitt 2002: 49), and this would suggest that agency, let alone 'resistance . . . is all but foreclosed' (49). However, as Mowitt has argued, given the plurality and complexity of addresses, hails, commands, suggestions, sources of identification, and the contingency of response, interpretation and performance, a 'conflict of interpellations' easily and often arises (49). So the subject is not merely a passive reflection of structure. Rather, subjectivity is an ongoing performative process amidst conflicting interpellations. In the postmodern, polyvocal and media-saturated world, the interpellations which tend to prevail are, one might say, *those calls that answer a call*.

3. Gary Krug (2001) offers a history of the American 'appropriation' of the oriental martial art of karate. This history involves three stages: 'discovery and mythologization', 'demystification', and 'appropriation'. He places Bruce Lee films on the cusp of the first and second stages. However, Krug deals only with Bruce Lee's cinematic kung fu. Considered together with his 'real' jeet kune do practice, it is arguably the case that we see each of these 'historical' stages played out in the case of Bruce Lee. Thus, in Lee's films we see discovery and mythologization; in his writings and certain interviews and TV roles we see demystification; and in his hybridization or 'bricolage' construction of jeet kune do, we see deterritorialization and appropriation. Freud proposed that phylogeny recapitulates ontogeny. Arguably, we see this here.

4. Gilbert and Pearson (1999) enquire into the nature of music's effects and note that the 'non-verbal aspect of music's effectivity which has given rise to its strange status in western thought' (39). The dangerous, hedonistic bodily effects of music led Socrates to want only simple, functional, militaristic music (in Plato's *Republic*); many others still try to tie music down to 'meanings' (40); Kant hated *'Tafelmusik'* – table music, music that is not designed for *contemplation* (41), etc. They argue: 'this tradition tends to demand of music that it – as far as possible – be *meaningful*, that even where it does not have words, it should offer itself up as an object of intellectual contemplation' (42). However, music is felt by the body. They propose: 'music – like all sound – is registered on a fundamentally different level to language

or modes of visual communication' (44); and 'music can be said, as Robert Walser suggests, to "hail the body directly"' (46). I am simply saying, so does Bruce Lee.

5. The magnificent 'Rex Kwon Do' scene from *Napoleon Dynamite* can be seen on YouTube at www.youtube.com/watch?v=5nfr4–J3fio

7 McDeconstruction, the Popular: Deconstructing 'Deconstructing'

1. Gary Hall (2002) would seem to disagree with me, in that he criticizes any demand to justify *in advance* what a work will turn out to have achieved. But he does so as an argument against what I would here call the impulse towards 'McPoliticization' in cultural studies. Namely, his argument is against those who would have cultural studies 'return' to politics 'directly'. So he argues: 'to move away from theory because it is apparently *not political enough* is to subordinate everything to political ends. It is to imply that things are only worth doing if it can be established *in advance* that they will have a practical, political outcome; an outcome which is itself decided *in advance*' (5). His first and last point is that 'it is the theoretical analysis . . . which is likely to prove the more "politically" effective, at least to the extent that it will be more self-consciously aware of the politico-institutional factors which affect its operation and development, and therefore less prone to being blindly shaped and controlled by them' (5). This is similar to McQuillan's position, of course. But I think that, given Hall's championing of cultural studies *vis-à-vis* McQuillan's championing of deconstruction, an examination of the differences of emphasis and the theoretical and practical ramifications that these differences suggest or precipitate could be valuable.

2. Here 'producing good readers' seems to imply that 'good' obviously means 'deconstructive', and that this is somehow therefore free from the denudations of unfortunate forms of institutionalization (lack of self-reflexivity, nerdiness, conservativeness, etc.). As I argue, this is not something 'from which everything else flows, including all the political and institutional claims made for cultural studies' (McQuillan 2003b: 54). Of course, auto-critique may be good form. Good reading may be good academic work. But it does not necessarily make any difference. Moreover, it does not even necessarily guarantee ethical or political vigilance. I have heard other deconstructionists (notably Hillis Miller) make the same claim – i.e., that the way to preserve the radical ethical and political work of university English departments is by representing themselves to the institutional powers that be as being merely innocuous producers of 'good readers'. The implication is that this is a loophole by which to avoid being smitten from existence for being too partisan or politicized whilst instituting the necessity of radical reading

as the norm. I am not convinced by this argument. Or rather, not yet. It is incomplete. This is because there is no good reading, only contingently motivated forms of reading. So, my argument is that McQuillan's suggested legitimating gesture does not 'play and erase' important ethico-political problematics as constitutive. Rather, it threatens to *erase* the problematic of cultural studies to which he and his own work are indebted.

3. Moreover, this view relies on a very problematic, traditional (albeit quite ego-gratifying) notion of education: namely, 'we teach' the 'others' who 'do'. Again, this undeconstructed theory/practice binary overlooks the *heterogeneity* of micro- and macro-stabilizations of hegemonies and discourses, the *paralogical* micro- and macro-stabilizations of *institutions*. It also reduces politics to a numbers game, a recruitment drive: convert as many disciples as possible – and those who will *listen to you will 'do'*. This is extremely problematic. Both Chapter 4 and the following, final chapter (Chapter 8) engage with its problems.

8 Alterdisciplinarity: Deconstructing Popular Cultural Studies

1. As Protevi argues:

> That the basic problem of deconstruction, even in Derrida's technically detailed readings of phenomenology, is thus basically political is clear: the names of philosophers as signatories are indices of texts which are indices of real history. The role of presence in the West is the target; philosophy texts are only paths to this target. The long-debated relation of philosophy and politics, the difference between the history of the West and the history of metaphysics, is thought by Derrida under the rubric of 'force'. (Protevi 2001: 20)

2. When he makes this point, Mowitt is discussing cultural studies as interdisciplinary intervention. However, it is equally valid in this sense. Mowitt writes:

> Cultural studies . . . thus comes to embody the institutional space where disciplines have projected their own particular interdisciplinary fantasies. Needless to say, like all fantasies, this space is to some degree impossible. On the one hand, the very existence of cultural studies testifies to an institutional affirmation of an interdisciplinary project within and between the humanities and the social sciences. On the other hand, due precisely to the kernel of disciplinarity at work within this affirmation, cultural studies can only succeed by failing, that is, it exists

as the space where the disciplines investing in it (both intellectually and economically) come face to face with the profound inadequacy of interdisciplinarity. In effect, cultural studies is institutionally impossible because – at the end of the day – no one, especially those authorized to do so, can really do interdisciplinary work the way we think it *ought* to be done. (Mowitt 2003: 184)

3. This is what Robert Young refers to when he calls 'political truth' the new 'architectonic' of knowledge. For, Young argues that today 'political truth' has replaced other forms of truth as the most important rubric for academic work to organize itself under, and the ultimate yardstick of evaluation. Organizing a study under the aegis of looking for 'the political' is the exemplary orientation. This has led to what might be called the 'hegemony of hegemony' (Valentine 2001) or what Slavoj Žižek characterizes as the new dominant fashion for organizing academic intellectual work in terms of looking for 'different discursive formations [to be] evaluated not with regard to their inherent truth-value [whatever 'inherent truth value' is supposed to mean – and it might mean any number of things], but with regard to their sociopolitical status and impact' (2001a: 219). Žižek's argument is that this 'discursive' approach entails what he calls a 'cognitive suspension' of 'refusing' to ask 'direct ontological questions'. Ironically, then, because Žižek thinks that such so-called 'politicized approaches' are now apparently 'hegemonic' – because everybody's doing it – therefore he is deeply suspicious. This is because, for Žižek, 'hegemonic' means 'ideological' and ideology is something that happens 'within' and 'for' capitalism. Thus, Žižek rejects this putatively 'politicized' approach because its very dominance and currency suggests that it is an ideological symptom that hence cannot properly be an effective or consequential intervention at all – if it ever was. The crux of Žižek's argument is that if such politicized approaches ever were politically effective, that moment has passed. As evidence of this, he simply gestures to the international proliferation of cultural studies, and particularly its success in the US. In this Žižek is not alone. For none other than Stuart Hall also suggested that such easy proliferation ushered in the danger of depoliticization and as such constituted a serious risk. Thus, perhaps surprisingly, Stuart Hall and Slavoj Žižek share the same concerns about cultural studies becoming nothing more than 'ersatz engagement' or empty 'radical chic'.

4. As Chantal Mouffe explains, in Continental-based forms of political theory, a distinction is normally drawn between 'politics' and 'the political':

If we wanted to express such a distinction in a philosophical way, we could, borrowing the vocabulary of Heidegger, say that politics refers to the 'ontic' level while 'the political' has to do with the 'ontological' one. This means that the ontic has to do with the manifold practices of conventional politics, while the ontological concerns the very way in which society is instituted. (Mouffe 2005: 8–9)

However, as discussed in Chapter 4 of this book, Rancière effectively dismisses this distinction, and argues instead that the most relevant distinction to be made is that *politics is rare*, while *what is common is police* (Rancière 1999: 17, 139). By 'police', what Rancière refers to is work and actions which protect the status quo. What is normally thought of as *politics* is in Rancière's terms most often *policing*. Ironically, the best example of this police work is the administrative tinkering of politicians' 'political' actions. So, what for Rancière is politics? On the one hand, 'Politics, in its specificity, is rare. It is always local and occasional' (1999: 139). But on the other and at the same time, it always reflects a social convulsion, a social conflict around a wider dispute.

5. As Laclau explains in *Emancipation(s)* (1996b): 'Between two incompatible discourses, each of them constituting the pole of an antagonism between them, there is no common measure, and the strict moment of the clash between them cannot be explained in objective terms' (3–4).

References

Althusser, L. (1971), *Lenin and Philosophy*, New York: Monthly Review Press.

Arditi, Benjamin (2007), *Politics on the Edges of Liberalism: Difference, Populism, Revolution, Agitation*, Edinburgh: Edinburgh University Press.

Arditi, Benjamin and Jeremy Valentine (1999), *Polemicization: The Contingency of the Commonplace*, Edinburgh: Edinburgh University Press.

Autry, James A. and Stephen Mitchell (1998), *Real Power: Business Lessons from the Tao Te Ching*, London: Nicholas Brealey.

Baggini, Julian (2004), quoted in Stephen Moss, 'Deconstructing Jacques', *Guardian, G2*, 12 October, p. 14.

Bahti, Timothy (1992), 'The Injured University', in Richard Rand (ed.), *Logomachia: The Conflict of the Faculties*, Lincoln, NE and London: University of Nebraska Press.

Bal, Mieke (2003), 'From Cultural Studies to Cultural Analysis: "a controlled reflection on the formation of method" ', in Paul Bowman (ed.), *Interrogating Cultural Studies: Theory, Politics and Practice*, London: Pluto.

Barthes, Roland (1990), *A Lover's Discourse*, London: Penguin.

Bauman, Zygmunt (1991), *Intimations of Postmodernity*, London and New York: Routledge.

Behr, E. Thomas and Lao Tzu (1997), *The Tao of Sales: The Easy Way to Sell in Tough Times*, Shaftesbury: Element.

Belsey, Catherine (2003), 'From Cultural Studies to Cultural Criticism?', in Paul Bowman (ed.), *Interrogating Cultural Studies: Theory, Politics and Practice*, London: Pluto.

Bennett, Tony (1996), 'Putting Policy into Cultural Studies', in J. Storey (ed.), *What is Cultural Studies?: A Reader*, London: Arnold.

Bennington, Geoffrey (1994) *Legislations: The Politics of Deconstruction*, London: Verso.

Bennington, Geoffrey (1998), 'Inter', in M. McQuillan, G. MacDonald, R. Purves and S. Thompson (eds), *Post-Theory: New Directions in Criticism*, Edinburgh: Edinburgh University Press.

Blate, Michael (1978), *The Tao of Health: The Way of Total Well-being*, Davie, FLA: Falkynor.

Bolen, Jean Shinoda (1982), *The Tao of Psychology: Synchronicity and the Self*, San Francisco: Harper & Row.

Bourdieu, Pierre (1990), *The Logic of Practice*, trans. Richard Nice, Stanford, CA: Stanford University Press.

Bourdieu, Pierre (1998), *Acts of Resistance: Against the New Myths of Our Time*, trans. Richard Nice, Cambridge: Polity.

Bowman, Paul (2001a), 'Between Responsibility and Irresponsibility: Cultural Studies and the Price of Fish', *Strategies: Journal of Theory, Culture & Politics*, 2, November, 277–93.

Bowman, Paul (2001b), 'Proper Impropriety: The Proper-Ties of Cultural Studies (Some More Aphorisms, Apriorisms, and Aporias)', *Parallax*, 2, April, 50–65.

Bowman, Paul (2002), 'Ernesto Laclau, Chantal Mouffe and Post-Marxism', in Julian Wolfreys (ed.), *The Edinburgh Encyclopaedia of Modern Criticism and Theory*, Edinburgh: Edinburgh University Press.

Bowman, Paul (2003), 'Promiscuous Fidelity to Revolution, or, Revaluing 'Revolutionary' Left Intellectualism', *Contemporary Politics: New Agendas and Global Debates*, 9:1 (March), 33–44.

Bowman, Paul (2004), 'The Task of the Transgressor', *Culture Machine*, 6, 2004.

Bowman, Paul (2007), *Post-Marxism versus Cultural Studies: Theory, Politics and Intervention*, Edinburgh: Edinburgh University Press.

Braidotti, Rosi (2002), *Metamorphoses: Towards a Materialist Theory of Becoming*, Cambridge: Polity.

Brown, Terry (1997), *English Martial Arts*, Frithgarth: Anglo-Saxon.

Brown, Wendy (2001), *Politics Out of History*, Princeton, NJ and Oxford: Princeton University Press.

Butler, Judith (1993), *Bodies That Matter: On the Discursive Limits of 'Sex'*, London and New York: Routledge.

Butler, Judith and William Connolly (2000), 'Politics, Power and Ethics: A Discussion Between Judith Butler and William Connolly, *Theory & Event* 4:2, http://muse.jhu.edu/journals/theory_and_event/v004/4.2butler.html

Butler, Judith, Ernesto Laclau and Slavoj Žižek (2000), *Contingency, Hegemony, Universality: Contemporary Dialogues on the Left*, London: Verso. (This title is referred to in the text as Butler 2000.)

Byrne, Eleanor and Martin McQuillan (1999), *Deconstructing Disney*, London: Pluto.

Capra, Fritjof (1975), *The Tao of Physics: An Exploration of the Parallels between Modern Physics and Eastern Mysticism*, Boston, MA: Shambhala.

Chan, Stephen (2000), 'The Construction and Export of Culture as Artefact: The Case of Japanese Martial Arts', *Body & Society*, 1.

Clarke, J. J. (1997), *Oriental Enlightenment: The Encounter Between Asian and Western Thought*, London and New York: Routledge.

Clarke, J. J. (2000), *The Tao of the West: Western Transformations of Taoist Thought*, London and New York: Routledge.

Connor, Steven (2003), 'What Can Cultural Studies Do?', in Paul Bowman (ed.), *Interrogating Cultural Studies: Theory, Politics and Practice*, London: Pluto.

Critchley, Simon (2003), 'Why I Love Cultural Studies', in Paul Bowman (ed.), *Interrogating Cultural Studies: Theory, Politics and Practice*, London: Pluto.

Debord, Guy (1990), *Comments on the Society of the Spectacle*, London: Verso.

De Man, Paul (1978), 'The Epistemology of Metaphor', in S. Sacks (ed.), *On Metaphor*, Chicago and London: University of Chicago Press.

Derrida, Jacques (1974), *Of Grammatology*, Baltimore, MD: Johns Hopkins University Press.

Derrida, Jacques (1978), *Writing and Difference*, London: Routledge & Kegan Paul.

Derrida, Jacques (1982), *Margins of Philosophy*, Brighton: Harvester.

Derrida, Jacques (1987), *The Post Card: From Socrates to Freud and Beyond*, Chicago and London: University of Chicago Press.

Derrida, Jacques (1992a), 'Canons and Metonymies: An Interview with Jacques Derrida', in Richard Rand (ed.), *Logomachia: The Conflict of the Faculties*, Lincoln, NE and London: University of Nebraska Press.

Derrida, Jacques (1992b), 'Mochlos; or, The Conflict of The Faculties', in Richard Rand (ed.), *Logomachia: The Conflict of The Faculties*, Lincoln, NE and London: University of Nebraska Press.

Derrida, Jacques (1994), *Specters of Marx: The State of the Debt, the Work of Mourning, and the New International*, London and New York: Routledge.

Derrida, Jacques (1995), *Points . . . : Interviews, 1974–1994*, Stanford, CA: Stanford University Press.

Derrida, Jacques (1996), 'Remarks on Deconstruction and Pragmatism', in Chantal Mouffe (ed.), *Deconstruction and Pragmatism*, London and New York: Routledge.

Derrida, Jacques (1997a), *Dissemination*, trans. B. Johnson, London: Athlone.

Derrida, Jacques (1997b), *Politics of Friendship*, London: Verso.

Derrida, Jacques (1998a), *Monolingualism of the Other; or, The Prosthesis of Origin*, Stanford, CA: Stanford University Press.

Derrida, Jacques (1998b), *Resistances of Psychoanalysis*, Stanford, CA: Stanford University Press.

Derrida, Jacques (2001), 'The Future of the Profession or the University without Condition (Thanks to the "Humanities", What Could Take Place Tomorrow)', in T. Cohen (ed.), *Jacques Derrida and the Humanities: A Critical Reader*, Cambridge: Cambridge University Press.

Derrida, Jacques (2002), *Who's Afraid of Philosophy?: Right to Philosophy 1*, Stanford, CA: Stanford University Press.

Derrida, Jacques (2003), 'I Have a Taste for the Secret', in Jacques Derrida and Maurizio Ferraris, *A Taste for the Secret*, Cambridge: Polity.

Docherty, Thomas (1993), *Postmodernism: A Reader*, London: Harvester Wheatsheaf.

Downey, Greg (2002), 'Domesticating an Urban Menace: Reforming Capoeira as a Brazilian National Sport', *International Journal of the History of Sport*, 4, December, 1–32.

Downey, G. (2006), ' "Practice without Theory": The Imitation Bottleneck and the Nature of Embodied Knowledge', unpublished manuscript.

Eagleton, Terry (2004), 'Don't Deride Derrida: Academics Are Wrong to Rubbish the Philosopher', *Guardian*, 15 October.

Ferraris, Maurizio (2001), 'What Is There?', in Jacques Derrida and Maurizio Ferraris, *A Taste for the Secret*, Cambridge: Polity.

Foucault, Michel (1978), *The History of Sexuality, Vol. 1*, London: Penguin.

Freud, Sigmund (1899), 'Screen Memories', in *The Standard Edition of the Complete Psychological Works of Sigmund Freud, Vol. III (1893–1899): Early Psycho-Analytic Publications*, ed. and trans. J. Strachey, London: Hogarth.

Freud, Sigmund (1976), *Jokes and Their Relation to the Unconscious*, London: Penguin.

Fukuyama, Francis (1992), *The End of History and The Last Man*, New York: Free Press.

Gilbert, Jeremy (2001a), 'A Question of Sport? Butler contra Laclau contra Žižek: Review of Butler, Laclau and Žižek,*Contingency, Hegemony, Universality*', *New Formations*, Autumn, 151–6.

Gilbert, Jeremy (2001b), 'Against the Empire: Thinking the Social and (Dis)Locating Agency "before, across and beyond any national determination" ', *Parallax*, 3, July–September, 96–113.

Gilbert, Jeremy (2003) 'Friends and Enemies: Which Side Is Cultural Studies On?', in Paul Bowman (ed.), *Interrogating Cultural Studies: Theory, Practice and Politics*, London: Pluto.

Gilbert, Jeremy and Ewart Pearson (1999), *Discographies: Dance Music, Culture and the Politics of Sound*, London and New York: Routledge.

Giroux, Henry A. (2000), *Impure Acts: The Practical Politics of Cultural Studies*, London and New York: Routledge.

Godzich, Wlad (1987), 'Afterword: Religion, the State and Post(al) Modernism', in Samuel Weber, *Institution and Interpretation*, Minneapolis, MN: University of Minnesota Press.

Gramsci, Antonio (1971), *Selections from the Prison Notebooks*, London: Lawrence & Wishart.

Gramsci, Antonio (1988), *A Gramsci Reader*, London: Lawrence & Wishart.

Grossberg, Lawrence (1997), *Bringing It All Back Home: Essays on Cultural Studies*, Durham, NC and London: Duke University Press.

Hall, Gary (2002), *Culture in Bits: The Monstrous Future of Theory*, London: Continuum.

Hall, Stuart (1981), 'Notes on Deconstructing "the Popular"', in R. Samuel (ed.), *People's History and Socialist Theory*, London: Routledge & Kegan Paul.

Hall, Stuart (1992), 'Cultural Studies and Its Theoretical Legacies', in Lawrence Grossberg, Cary Nelson and Paula Treichler (eds), *Cultural Studies*, London and New York: Routledge.

Hall, Stuart, David Morley and Kuan-Hsing Chen (1996), *Stuart Hall: Critical Dialogues in Cultural Studies*, London and New York: Routledge.

Hardt, Michael and Antonio Negri (2000), *Empire*, Cambridge, MA and London: Harvard University Press.

Heath, Joseph and Andrew Potter (2005), *The Rebel Sell: How the Counterculture Became Consumer Culture*, Chichester: Capstone.

Hegel, G. W. F. (1977), *Phenomenology of Spirit*, trans. A. V. Miller, Oxford: Oxford University Press.

Heidegger, Martin (1971), 'A Dialogue on Language: Between a Japanese and an Inquirer', trans. Peter D. Hertz, in Heidegger, *On The Way To Language*, New York: Harper & Row.

Hicks, Bill (2005), *Bill Hicks: Love All The People*, London: Constable.

Hobson, Marion (1998), *Jacques Derrida: Opening Lines*, London and New York: Routledge.

Hoff, Benjamin (1982), *The Tao of Pooh*, New York: E. P. Dutton.

Hunter, Lynette (1999), *Critiques of Knowing: Situated Textualities in Science, Computing and the Arts*, London and New York: Routledge.

Inosanto, D. (1980), *Jeet Kune Do: The Art and Philosophy of Bruce Lee*, Los Angeles: Know How.

Johnson, Spencer (1998), *Who Moved My Cheese?: An Amazing Way to Deal with Change in Your Work and in Your Life*, New York: G. P. Putnam's Sons.

Kennedy, Brian and Elizabeth Guo (2005), *Chinese Martial Arts Training Manuals: A Historical Survey*, Berkeley, CA: North Atlantic.

Kingsnorth, Paul (2003), *One No, Many Yeses: A Journey to the Heart of the Global Resistance Movement*, London: Free Press.

Krug, Gary J. (2001), 'At the Feet of the Master: Three Stages in the Appropriation of Okinawan Karate Into Anglo-American Culture', *Cultural Studies: Critical Methodologies*, 1:4, 395–410.

Laclau, Ernesto (1996a), 'Deconstruction, Pragmatism, Hegemony', in Chantal Mouffe (ed.), *Deconstruction and Pragmatism*, London and New York: Routledge.

Laclau, Ernesto (1996b), *Emancipation(s)*, London: Verso.

Laclau, Ernesto (2000), *Contingency, Hegemony, Universality: Contemporary Dialogues on the Left*, Judith Butler, Ernesto Laclau and Slavoj Žižek, London: Verso.

Laclau, Ernesto (2004), 'Glimpsing the Future', in Simon Critchley and Oliver Marchart (eds), *Laclau: A Critical Reader*, London and New York: Routledge.

Laclau, Ernesto (2005), *On Populist Reason*, London: Verso.

Laclau, Ernesto and Chantal Mouffe (1985), *Hegemony and Socialist Strategy: Towards a Radical Democratic Politics*, London: Verso.

Landsberg, Max (1996), *The Tao of Coaching: Boost Your Effectiveness at Work by Inspiring and Developing Those Around You*, London and New York: HarperCollins.

Landsberg, Max (2000), *The Tao of Motivation: Inspire Yourself and Others*, London and New York: HarperCollins.

Laplanche, Jean and Jean-Bertrand Pontalis (1988), *The Language of Psychoanalysis*, London: Karnac.

Lee, Bruce (1975), *The Tao of Jeet Kune Do*, Santa Clarita, CA: Ohara.

Lee, Bruce and John R. Little (1997), *The Tao of Gung Fu: A Study in the Way of the Chinese Martial Art*, Boston, MA: Charles E. Tuttle.

Liu, E. (2005), *The Travels of Lao Ts'an*, trans. Harold Shadick, Nanjing: Yi Lin Chu Ban She.

Lyotard, Jean-François (1984), *The Postmodern Condition: A Report on Knowledge*, Manchester: Manchester University Press.

Lyotard, Jean-François (1988), *The Differend: Phrases in Dispute*, Minneapolis, MN: University of Minnesota Press.

Macheray, Pierre (1978), *A Theory of Literary Production*, London: Routledge & Kegan Paul.

Maley, Willy (2001), 'The Collapse of the New International', *Parallax*, 7, 73–82.

Marchart, Oliver (2007), 'Acting and the Act: On Slavoj Žižek's Political Ontology', in Paul Bowman and Richard Stamp (eds), *The Truth of Žižek*, London: Continuum.

Marx, Karl and Friedrich Engels (1967), *The Communist Manifesto*, Harmondsworth: Penguin.

May, Reinhard (1996), *Heidegger's Hidden Sources: East-Asian Influences on His Work*, London and New York: Routledge.

McQuillan, Martin (2001), 'Spectres of Poujade: Naomi Klein and the New International', *Parallax*, 3, July–September, 114–30.

McQuillan, Martin (2003a), 'Deconstruction', in *The Year's Work in Critical and Cultural Theory 2003*, Oxford: Oxford University Press.

McQuillan, Martin (2003b), 'The Projection of Cultural Studies', in Paul Bowman (ed.), *Interrogating Cultural Studies: Theory, Politics and Practice*, London: Pluto.

Messing, Bob (1989), *The Tao of Management*, Aldershot: Wildwood House.

Metz, Pamela and Jacqueline Tobin (1996), *The Tao of Women*, Shaftesbury: Element.

Miller, Davis (1997), *The Tao of Muhammad Ali*, London: Vintage.

Miller, Davis (2000), *The Tao of Bruce Lee*, London: Vintage.

Mouffe, Chantal (2005), *On the Political*, London and New York: Routledge.

Mowitt, John (1992), *Text: The Genealogy of an Antidisciplinary Object*, Durham, NC and London: Duke University Press.

Mowitt, John (2000), ' "– perhaps even violently, via the jolts of fashion – "': An Interview by Paul Bowman', *Parallax*, 15, April–July, 'in violence', 9–27.

Mowitt, John (2002), *Percussion: Drumming, Beating, Striking*, Durham, NC and London: Duke University Press.

Mowitt, John (2003), 'Cultural Studies, in Theory', in Paul Bowman (ed.), *Interrogating Cultural Studies: Theory, Politics and Practice*, London: Pluto.

Murata, Sachiko (1992), *The Tao of Islam: A Sourcebook on Gender Relationships in Islamic Thought*, Albany, NY: State University of New York Press.

Myers, Tony (2003), *Slavoj Žižek*, London and New York: Routledge.

Nagl, Ludwig and Chantal Mouffe (eds) (2001), *The Legacy of Wittgenstein: Pragmatism or Deconstruction*, Oxford: Peter Lang.

Negri, Antonio and Danilo Zolo (2003), 'Empire and Multitude: A Dialogue on the New Order of Globalization', *Radical Philosophy*, 120, July/August, 23–37.

Nietzsche, Friedrich (1999), Section 13 of ' "Good and Evil", "Good and Bad" ', trans. Douglas Smith, in Nietzsche, *On the Genealogy of Morals: A Polemic*, Oxford: Oxford University Press.

Owen, David (2001), 'Democracy, Perfectionism and "Undetermined Messianic Hope": Cavell, Derrida and the Ethos of Democracy to Come', in Ludwig Nagl and Chantal Mouffe (eds), *The Legacy of Wittgenstein: Pragmatism or Deconstruction*, Oxford: Peter Lang.

Peters, Michael A. (2001) *Poststructuralism, Marxism and Neoliberalism: Between Theory and Politics*, Lanham, MD and Oxford: Rowman and Littlefield.

Protevi, John (2001), *Political Physics: Deleuze, Derrida and the Body Politic*, London: Athlone.

Pulver, David and John Python (2000), *Ghost Dog: The Way of the Samurai*, Guelph, Ontario: Guardians of Order.

Rancière, Jacques (1999), *Dis-agreement: Politics and Philosophy*, Minneapolis, MN: University of Minnesota Press.

Rand, Richard (ed.) (1992), *Logomachia: The Conflict of the Faculties*, Lincoln, NE and London: University of Nebraska Press.

Readings, Bill (1996), *The University in Ruins*, Cambridge, MA and London: Harvard University Press.

Rojek, Chris (2003), *Stuart Hall*, London: Polity.

Rorty, Richard (1996), 'Remarks on Deconstruction and Pragmatism' and 'Response to Ernesto Laclau', in Chantal Mouffe (ed.), *Deconstruction and Pragmatism*, London and New York: Routledge.

Rutherford, Jonathan (2005), 'Cultural Studies in the Corporate University', *Cultural Studies*, 3, May, 297–317.

Salih, Sara (2002), *Judith Butler*, London and New York: Routledge.

Sandford, Stella (2003), 'Going Back: Heidegger, East Asia and "the West" ', *Radical Philosophy*, 120, July/August, 11–20.

Siu, Ralph G. H. (1957), *The Tao of Science: An Essay on Western Knowledge and Eastern Wisdom*, Cambridge, MA: MIT Press.

Smith, Huston and Philip Novak (2003), *Buddhism*, London and New York: HarperCollins.

Smith, Robert W. (1999), *Martial Musings: A Portrayal of Martial Arts in the 20th Century*, Erie, PA: Via Media.

Sokal, Alan, and Jean Bricmont (1998), *Intellectual Impostures: Postmodern Philosophers' Abuse of Science*, London: Profile.

Spivak, Gayatri (1974), 'Translator's Preface', in Jacques Derrida, *Of Grammatology*, Baltimore, MD and London: Johns Hopkins University Press.

Spivak, Gayatri (1993), 'Questions of Multiculturalism', in Simon During (ed.), *The Cultural Studies Reader*, London and New York: Routledge.

Spivak, Gayatri (1999), *A Critique of Postcolonial Reason: Toward a History of the Vanishing Present*, Cambridge, MA and London: Harvard University Press.

Thomas, Bruce (2002), *Bruce Lee: Fighting Spirit*, Basingstoke and Oxford: Sidgwick & Jackson.

Unknown (1971), *Secrets of Shaolin Boxing*, Taipei: Zhonghuawushu.

Valentine, Jeremy (2001), 'The Hegemony of Hegemony', *History of the Human Sciences*, 14:1, 88–104.

Walsh, Michael (2002), 'Slavoj Žižek (1949–)', in Julian Wolfreys (ed.), *The Edinburgh Encyclopaedia of Modern Criticism and Theory*, Edinburgh: Edinburgh University Press.

Watts, Alan (1957), *The Way of Zen*, London: Penguin.

Watts, Alan (1995), *The Tao of Philosophy: The Edited Transcripts*, Boston, MA: Charles E. Tuttle.

Weber, Sam (1987), *Institution and Interpretation*, Minneapolis, MN: University of Minnesota Press.

Wheen, Francis (2004), *How Mumbo-Jumbo Conquered the World: A Short History of Modern Delusions*, London: Fourth Estate.

Wile, Douglas (1996), *Lost T'ai-chi Classics from the Late Ch'ing Dynasty*, Albany, NY: State University of New York Press.

Wittgenstein, Ludwig (1979), *On Certainty*, trans. Denis Paul and G. E. M. Anscombe, Oxford: Basil Blackwell.

Wolfreys, Julian (2003), '... as if such a thing existed ...', in Paul Bowman (ed.), *Interrogating Cultural Studies: Theory, Politics and Practice*, London: Pluto.

Xu, Jian (1999), 'Body, Discourse, and the Cultural Politics of Contemporary Chinese Qigong', *Journal of Asian Studies*, 58:4, 961–91.

Yamamoto, Tsunetomo (1979), *Hagakure: The Book of the Samurai*, trans. William Scott Wilson, Tokyo: Kodansha.

Young, Lola (1999), 'Why Cultural Studies?', *Parallax*, 11, April–June, 3–16.

Young, Robert (1992), 'The Idea of a Chrestomathic University', in Richard Rand (ed.), *Logomachia: The Conflict of The Faculties*, Lincoln, NE and London: University of Nebraska Press.

Zhang, Longxi (1992), *The Tao and the Logos: Literary Hermeneutics, East and West*, Durham, NC and London: Duke University Press.

Žižek, Slavoj (1989), *The Sublime Object of Ideology*, London: Verso.
Žižek, Slavoj (1998), 'A Leftist Plea for "Eurocentrism" ', *Critical Enquiry*, 2, 988–1009.
Žižek, Slavoj (2000), *Contingency, Hegemony, Universality: Contemporary Dialogues on the Left*, Judith Butler, Ernesto Laclau and Slavoj Žižek, London: Verso.
Žižek, Slavoj (2001a), *Did Somebody Say Totalitarianism?: Five Interventions in the (Mis)use of a Notion*, London: Verso.
Žižek, Slavoj (2001b), *On Belief*, London and New York: Routledge.
Žižek, Slavoj (2001c), *Repeating Lenin*, Zagreb: Arkzin.
Žižek, Slavoj (2002), *Revolution at the Gates: Selected Writings of Lenin from February to October 1917*, London: Verso.
Žižek, Slavoj (2005), *Interrogating the Real*, London and New York: Continuum.
Zylinska, Joanna (2001), 'An Ethical Manifesto for Cultural Studies . . . Perhaps', *Strategies: Journal of Theory, Culture & Politics*, 14:2, 175–88.

Discography

Black Eyed Peas (2003), 'Let's Get Retarded', *Elephunk*, © A&M.
Nizlopi (2005), 'JCB Song', Nizlopi, © FDM Records.
Oasis (1995), 'Wonderwall', *What's The Story (Morning Glory)?*, © Creation Records.
Sunz of Man f / 12 O'Clock, Blue Raspberry Lyrics (1999) 'Strange Eyes', *Ghost Dog: The Way of the Samurai Soundtrack*, © Razor Sharp Records.
Travis (1999), 'Writing To Reach You', on *The Man Who*, © Independiente Ltd.

Filmography

Enter the Dragon (1973), Robert Clouse, HK/US.
Ghost Dog: The Way of the Samurai (1999), Jim Jarmusch, US.
Napoleon Dynamite (2004), Jared Hess, US.
Rashomon (1950), Akira Kurosawa, JAP.
Strictly Ballroom (1992), Baz Luhrmann, Australia.

Index